TIM CHESTER
EXODUS
FOR YOU

thegoodbook
COMPANY

Exodus For You
© Tim Chester/The Good Book Company, 2016

Published by:
The Good Book Company

Tel (UK): 0333 123 0880
Tel (US): 866 244 2165
Email (UK): info@thegoodbook.co.uk
Email (US): info@thegoodbook.com

Websites:
UK: www.thegoodbook.co.uk
North America: www.thegoodbook.com
Australia: www.thegoodbook.com.au
New Zealand: www.thegoodbook.co.nz

(Hardcover) ISBN: 9781784980245
(Paperback) ISBN: 9781784980238

Design by André Parker

CONTENTS

SERIES PREFACE

Each volume of the *God's Word For You* series takes you to the heart of a book of the Bible, and applies its truths to your heart.

The central aim of each title is to be:

- Bible centred
- Christ glorifying
- Relevantly applied
- Easily readable

You can use *Exodus For You:*

To read. You can simply read from cover to cover, as a book that explains and explores the themes, encouragements and challenges of this part of Scripture.

To feed. You can work through this book as part of your own personal regular devotions, or use it alongside a sermon or Bible-study series at your church. Each chapter is divided into two (or occasionally three) shorter sections, with questions for reflection at the end of each.

To lead. You can use this as a resource to help you teach God's word to others, both in small-group and whole-church settings. You'll find tricky verses or concepts explained using ordinary language, and helpful themes and illustrations along with suggested applications.

These books are not commentaries. They assume no understanding of the original Bible languages, nor a high level of biblical knowledge. Verse references are marked in **bold** so that you can refer to them easily. Any words that are used rarely or differently in everyday language outside the church are marked in grey when they first appear, and are explained in a glossary towards the back. There, you'll also find details of resources you can use alongside this one, in both personal and church life.

Our prayer is that as you read, you'll be struck not by the contents of this book, but by the book it's helping you open up; and that you'll praise not the author of this book, but the One he is pointing you to.

Carl Laferton, Series Editor

Bible translations used:

- NIV: New International Version, 2011 translation (this is the version being quoted unless otherwise stated)

- ESV: English Standard Version

- KJV: King James Version

- AV: Authorised Version

INTRODUCTION TO EXODUS

A princess goes to bathe in the river and has her heart won by the cries of an abandoned baby.

A bush on fire never burns up, and from it speaks a voice that will change history.

An unarmed shepherd walks out of the wilderness to do battle with the most powerful man on earth.

The people of Egypt turn back their sheets to find frogs in their beds.

The lone cry of a bereaved mother is joined by another and then another and then another until a loud wailing echoes across the land.

A whole nation walks through a sea, with walls of water on either side.

God is put on trial and, when the verdict is announced, God receives the judgment of the court.

Amid thunder, lightening, thick cloud and an earthquake, the voice of God booms across the plain.

In the wilderness, a man argues with God about the future of a people, and God relents.

The glory of God so fills a tent that everyone must evacuate.

There is no shortage of dramatic moments in the book of Exodus. It is a story that has repeatedly captured the public imagination and which has been a favourite of film-makers. Its story of deliverance from oppression has inspired liberation movements from the Pilgrim Fathers and the English revolutionaries of the seventeenth century to the anti-slavery campaigns of the nineteenth century to the civil rights movements in the twentieth century. Its cry of, "Let my people go" has echoed down across the centuries (5:1; 7:16; 8:1, 20; 9:1, 13; 10:3).

But in truth, its message is more dramatic than these dramatic moments and more revolutionary than these revolutionary movements. Exodus is a book about…

Liberation

The book of Exodus is a story of liberation. The Israelites are rescued from slavery in Egypt through a series of extraordinary encounters and spectacular miracles. But it's a liberation that points to a greater liberation: the liberation of God's people from slavery to sin.

Sacrifice

Exodus points to this spiritual liberation because at the key moment, the Passover night, the Israelites are threatened by death just as much as the Egyptians. Like everyone else, God's people are guilty and deserve the judgment of death. But they are saved by daubing the blood of sacrifice on the lintels of their homes. Redemption through sacrifice is then built into the rhythms of Israel's life.

God's presence

The book of Exodus does not end with the escape through the Red Sea in chapter 14. God's people are not only liberated *from* slavery; they are also liberated *for* God's presence. The law and the tabernacle create a framework in which God's people can enjoy God's glory.

Servitude and worship

The word used to describe Israel's "slavery" is the same word which is used to describe her "worship". The movement in the book of Exodus is not so much from slavery to freedom as from slavery to slavery. But serving God is completely different from serving Pharaoh. Indeed, God's service is true freedom.

Mission

At key moments in the story, God reveals his name to Moses. In the book of Exodus, God gets intimate and personal—and, at the same time, God also reveals his name to the whole world. The exodus takes place, God tells Pharaoh, so that "my name might be proclaimed in all the earth" (9:16). And God's people are called to bear his name in a worthy manner (20:7). Shaped by God's law, they are to be a royal priesthood and holy nation, displaying God's character to the world (19:4-6).

All creation

Again and again in the book of Exodus, God un-creates in judgment and recreates in salvation. The law begins the reordering of a broken world, and the tabernacle-tent is full of echoes of Eden because it is a blueprint of God's new creation. Our future—and creation's future—are woven into its fabric.

Our story

The book of Exodus is not simply an inspiring tale from the past. It is our story. The Old Testament prophets promised a new exodus: a repeat of the exodus that would be more dramatic and more revolutionary. The exodus sets God's story on a trajectory that comes to a climax with the life, death and resurrection of Jesus.

Jesus sets us free from slavery to sin. He is our Passover Lamb, whose sacrifice rescues us from judgment and death. He is God's presence on earth, God "tabernacling" among us. We have seen God's glory in the face of Jesus Christ. And his resurrection is the beginning of a new creation. So the book of Exodus is key to understanding the person and work of Jesus. It graphically reveals the means of our salvation (redemption through sacrifice) and the content of our salvation (enjoying God's presence in a world made new).

Exodus is an exciting story. It is a historical story. And, as it points us to and inspires us to worship Christ, it is our story.

1. A PEOPLE AND A LAND

We live at a time in the West when the church is under increasing pressure. It is not just that Christian truth has move from the mainstream to the margins—on many issues what we believe is now seen as immoral and offensive. Many, both inside and outside the church, wonder whether Christianity has a future.

How can we live well, optimistically and positively in the face of hostility? This is the question faced by God's people in Exodus 1 – 2, and that we need to grapple with today.

A missing "and"

The book of Exodus begins with the word "And". It's missed out in most English translations, but it's there in the original Hebrew, in which Exodus was first written. And you may have been taught not to start sentences with the word "And" (a rule I have just broken). Yet here is a whole book that starts with "And". It immediately alerts us to the fact that this story is part of a bigger story. The end of the previous book, Genesis, has already hinted at a sequel (Genesis 50:24-25), and the first nine words of Exodus are an exact repetition of Genesis 46:8: "These are the names of the sons of Israel". The book of Exodus is in many ways chapter two of the Pentateuch, the first five books of the Old Testament. And so the whole book needs to be read in the light of what has gone before.

In Genesis 12, 15 and 17 God made a promise to Abraham, the man he called out of idolatry to know, obey and follow him, and he sealed that promise in a **covenant**†. There were two key components to God's promise:

1. The promise of a people—Abraham would become a great nation.

2. The promise of a land—Abraham's family would inherit the land of Canaan.

Above all, God promised a "**seed**" from Abraham: a Saviour who would defeat Satan, who would "crush [his] head", just as he had promised even further back in history (Genesis 3:15). So God promises to bless all nations, by fulfilling all his purposes, through Abraham's family.

The people threatened

Four hundred years before the events of Exodus 1, that promise had been under threat. It looked as if famine would wipe out the family of Abraham. But in his **providence**, God arranged things so that Joseph, one of Abraham's great-grandsons, became "prime minister" in Egypt. Joseph gathered grain during years of good harvest so that Egypt could survive the years of famine. And Joseph extended this relief to his father's family. They moved to live in Egypt and enjoy Egypt's provision. The future of the promise was secured, for now at least. God's people had blessed the nations through Joseph and the people of God had been preserved.

And four centuries later, at the beginning of the book of Exodus, the promise of a nation is being fulfilled. Exodus **1:1-5*** lists the sons of Israel who came to Egypt. The total number of those who made that original journey 400 years previously was just 70 (**v 5**). But now, those 70 people have become a great nation. They have "multiplied greatly", so they fill the land (**v 6-7**).

This is a story of economic migrants. Initially they are welcomed. But as they prosper, they are resented and feared. Oppressive

---

† Words in **grey** are defined in the Glossary (page 267).

* All Exodus verse references being looked at in each chapter are in **bold**.

measures are imposed. The fear is they will outnumber the local people and change their way of life:

"Then a new king, to whom Joseph meant nothing, came to power in Egypt. 'Look,' he said to his people, 'the Israelites have become far too numerous for us. Come, we must deal shrewdly with them or they will become even more numerous and, if war breaks out, will join our enemies, fight against us and leave the country.'" (**v 8-10**)

It is a situation replicated across our world today.

So once again the promise is under threat. At first, Pharaoh enslaves the Israelites (**v 11-14**). He works them ruthlessly. He gives them no time or energy to plot rebellion. W. Ross Blackburn translates **verses 13-14** more literally as:

"And the Egyptians forced the sons of Israel to serve with violence. And they caused their lives to be bitter with hard service, with mortar and with brick and with all kinds of service in the field. In all their service with which they served in violence."

(The God who Makes Himself Known: The Missionary Heart of the Book of Exodus, page 32)

Each reference to "service" is like another crack of the whip. But this ploy doesn't work, as Philip Ryken clarifies:

"In verse 10 Pharaoh says *pen-yirbe*, which means 'lest they multiply'; but in verse 12 God says—'the more they shall multiply.' The Bible uses this Hebrew pun to show that the joke was on Pharaoh." *(Exodus: Saved for God's Glory,* pages 35-36)

And so, his initial plan having been thwarted, Pharaoh tells the Hebrew midwives to kill every newborn baby boy (**v 15-16**). But the midwives "feared God"—they are willing to defy the authority of Pharaoh. They let the boys live (**v 17**), and when challenged, they claim the Hebrew (that is, Israelite) women give birth before their midwives arrive (**v 18-19**).

Foiled again, Pharaoh tries a third time to eradicate the threat posed by the Hebrews. This time, he turns to genocide. He orders a general execution of all infant boys (**v 22**). They must all be thrown into the River Nile.

Plans thwarted

But again, Pharaoh's plans are thwarted. One particular Hebrew family hide their newborn son (**2:1-2**). Three months on, it's getting harder to keep him hidden, so they place him in a basket on the River Nile (**v 3-4**). The river that is supposed to bring death to the boys brings life to this boy—he is found by Pharaoh's daughter, who has pity on him (**v 5-6**). The boy's sister intervenes, offering his mother as a nurse (**v 7-9**), and so this boy is raised by his mother and then becomes a member of the Egyptian royal court (**v 10**).

Only at the end of this episode are we told his name—Moses. And you don't need to know much of Israel's history to know Moses will be its great liberator. The first readers would certainly have heard this name many times before. In this child, there is hope for God's people.

In **1:10**, Pharaoh says the Egyptians must be shrewd. Here, as so often, evil is dressed up as wisdom. But in fact Pharaoh is outwitted by five women—the two Hebrew midwives (Shiphrah and Puah), the mother and the sister of Moses, and his own daughter.

But behind all of this, we are meant to see the providential hand of God. It is a remarkable sequence of events: the coincidences of Pharaoh's daughter coming, the pitiful cries of the baby, the provision of a **wet-nurse**. And it leads to a remarkable scenario: Moses being cared for by his mother and her being paid to do so. This means that Moses is raised a Hebrew with the privileges of Egypt. In Acts 7:22, the early Christian (and first **martyr**) Stephen says that Moses "was educated in all the wisdom of the Egyptians and was powerful in speech and action". Moses is saved from Pharaoh to live in his court, and one day he will defeat him, rescuing God's people.

All this happens with God hardly being mentioned. Yet the writer invites us to see his hand—and perhaps to seek to detect his hand in our own lives when we trust God's covenant promises. After all, Moses is kept safe in the place of violence and death. Here is sin at its most cruel and insane—and yet right here, the hand of God is at work. Even sin is a context in which God is at work, for he incorporates acts of sin into his purposes. That is what he is doing here; it's what he did when two other rulers opposed not his people but his own Son (Acts 4:27-28); and it's what he does in and around us still today as he works for our good in *all* things (Romans 8:28).

Fear the Promise-Keeper

The three statements of blessings and multiplication here (Exodus **1:7, 12, 20**) give the chapter its structure. Despite being in Egypt (**v 1-7**), despite being oppressed (**v 8-14**) and despite being threatened (**v 15-22**), God's people prosper because of his promise.

Again and again, throughout their history, the future of Israel would look fragile as successive foreign armies threatened to wipe them out. Throughout those times God's people could return to this story and find hope—find confidence that, however bleak the setting, God would be at work to keep his promises. And that matters, because what is at stake each time is not just the future of a people, but the future of God's promise and the future of our salvation.

Hundreds of years later, another king ordered the slaughter of innocent children. King Herod ordered every boy under the age of two in Bethlehem to be killed (Matthew 2:16-18). Again, what was at stake was the life of God's Saviour and the future of God's promise. Again, the king was thwarted when the baby's adoptive father, Joseph, was warned in a dream to flee and, somewhat ironically, escaped with Jesus to Egypt (Matthew 2:13-15).

This repeated threat to the people of God—and therefore to the promise of God—is part of Satan's on-going rebellion against God. Satan is trying to destroy God's people in order that he might defeat God's promise. And the whole Old Testament is dominated by the promise of God that the One who will crush Satan will come from

Abraham's family (see Genesis 3:15; 22:18). So if Satan can destroy Abraham's family, then he can prevent the Saviour being born and prevent his own defeat.

That Saviour was born, and Satan is defeated—yet still today, he tries to wipe out the church. And what is at stake is the promise of that Saviour, who said, "I will build my church, and the gates of **Hades** will not overcome it" (Matthew 16:18). Under Soviet communism, under Mao in China, and today in the Middle East, Satan has tried to destroy the church and prevent the preaching of the gospel. But each time God has demonstrated his **sovereign** power. Adapting Exodus **1:7**, Christians have been "fruitful and multiplied greatly and become exceedingly numerous, so that the [earth is] filled with them."

In the 1970s, President Mengistu in Ethiopia implemented what was called the Red Terror. 1.5 million people died and church buildings were closed down. When Mengistu fell, no one was sure what would remain of the church. But Christians had been meeting secretly in homes, and the church had not only survived but grown. God has purposed to keep his promises, and he will not allow anyone—not Pharaoh, not Satan—to thwart them.

> Confidence in the purposes of God enables us to be courageous in obeying God.

This confidence in the purposes of God enables us to be courageous in obeying God. This confidence is what enabled the Hebrew midwives to act in the way they did: "The midwives, however, feared God and did not do what the king of Egypt had told them to do … because the midwives feared God, he gave them families of their own" (**v 17, 21**).

As we read their story, we are confronted with the choice they faced: to fear man or to fear God. Don't underestimate the pressure they were under or the risks involved in what they did. Why did they act as they did? Because they feared God—they held him in higher awe than the ruler of the superpower of their day, and they so trusted him to keep to his plans that they were prepared to defy those of Pharaoh. The seventeenth-century **Puritan** William Gurnall put it well when he wrote, "We fear men so much because we fear God so little". These midwives are an example of how we can act with courage when we trust in the promise of God, which Paul describes in Galatians 3:8 as the gospel announced in advance. The midwives are rewarded with children, a sign of having a share in Israel's future. Indeed this blessing is itself a confirmation that God will keep his promises, for these children are born at a time when newborn children are supposed to be killed (Exodus **1:21**).

How can the church today survive in the face of increasing hostility? How can you survive in your workplace or your home? How can you be fruitful in the service of Christ when your colleagues and friends despise your faith? How can your church multiply in the face of hostility?

Because God has promised to fill the earth with the glory of Christ. Christ has promised to build his church. God is still on the throne. And he is the One we should fear. No one else.

Questions for reflection

1. How does the failure of Pharaoh's plans to extinguish Israel encourage you as you look at what is happening in the world today?

2. Who or what do you find it easy to live in greater awe of than God? Why?

3. In what ways are you being called to act in courageous obedience by trusting the promises of God?

PART TWO

The promise of a land

The promise of a people was only half the promise. The other half was a land of blessing, a place of rest.

In Exodus 1, the promise of a land is literally far away. Israel are foreigners in a foreign land. And they are certainly not a people who enjoy rest. Slavery is the very opposite of the fulfilment of the promise, for it is work without rest. But all that is about to begin to change, for by **2:11** the baby in the basket has become a man.

When the time comes, Moses chooses to be a foreigner. "One day, after Moses had grown up, he went out to where his own people were and watched them at their hard labour" (**v 11**). He chooses to be a Hebrew, to go out to his own people. Acts 7:25 suggests Moses knew even at this point that "God was using him to rescue them".

But at this point, Moses lacks the maturity to lead his people. He takes matters into his own hands as he attacks "an Egyptian [who is] beating a Hebrew" (Exodus **2:11**). "Beating" (**v 11**), "killed" (**v 12**, literally "beaten down"), "hitting" (**v 13**) and to "kill" (**v 14**) are all the same word in the Hebrew. Moses responds to the unjust aggression of Egypt with unjust aggression of his own—and so he becomes a murderer and has to flee to **Midian** (**v 15**). Not only is Moses threatened by Pharaoh, but he has lost the respect of his own people. "Who made you ruler and judge over us?" one asks when Moses challenges him for striking a fellow Hebrew. "Are you thinking of killing me as you killed the Egyptian?" (**v 14**).

We know Moses will liberate God's people from Egyptian slavery. But here he behaves like an Egyptian slave master. He needs to unlearn the ways of the Egyptian court. It is a reminder that we cannot do God's work in worldly ways. But perhaps the real point is that it's not Moses who will liberate Israel through human politics. It's God who will liberate his people through divine power.

When Moses escapes from Egypt, he immediately finds a welcome and a home in Midian (**v 16-20**). Is this a coincidence? No, because Midian is home. The Midianites were nomads, but they wandered around the Sinai Peninsula and the land of Canaan—all areas that were part of the land promised to Abraham. And here, in contrast to Egypt, the LORD is worshipped freely (the reference to a "priest" in **verse 16** raises this possibility; 18:9-12 confirms it). In leaving the only home he has ever known, Moses has come home.

Moses settles down, he gets married and he starts a family (**2:21-22**). He rescues a group of women in distress at a well before marrying one of them (**v 16-19**). It is a story full of echoes of the patriarchal narratives (Genesis 24:15-17; 29:1-14). Again, we are seeing that Moses has come home.

But this scene of domestic bliss for Moses cannot be the end of the story. In Exodus 1, we saw the promise to Abraham fulfilled in a people—Israel had become a nation. In chapter 2, Moses finds the fulfilment of the second part—he finds a home in the promised land. But the rest of the people are hundreds of miles distant and further away from experiencing rest. We have a people without a land; and we have Moses in the land without a people.

And so, in the final verses of chapter 2, we return to the promise to Abraham:

"During that long period, the king of Egypt died. The Israelites groaned in their slavery and cried out, and their cry for help because of their slavery went up to God. God heard their groaning and he remembered his covenant with Abraham, with **Isaac** and with **Jacob**. So God looked on the Israelites and was concerned about them." (**v 23-25**)

God "remembered his covenant with Abraham". What is going to drive this story is the promise to Abraham. "Remembering" is a covenantal term. It means deciding to act in order to fulfil a covenant. It's not that the promise to Abraham had somehow slipped God's mind. It's not that he got distracted by other things. "Remembering" means

God is about to take the next step in the fulfilment of his promises. **Verse 25** is literally, "God saw the people of Israel and he knew"—he knew their suffering and he knew his promises.

This story is not just the story of how God liberates one particular oppressed people. It is the story of how God fulfils his promise to bring salvation to all people. What's at stake is not just the liberation of one nation. This story will set the pattern for the liberation of all nations from bondage to Satan. The Bible is the story of God leading us back home.

The question of identity

Moses grew up as both a Hebrew and an Egyptian. The name "Moses" itself could be both Egyptian and Hebrew. A number of Egyptian names have a *ms* syllable like "Rameses", which means "born of Ra" (Ra was the Egyptian sun god). So "Moses" could mean "born of the Nile". But "Moses" also sounds like the Hebrew word "drawing out".

This raises the question: What is Moses' true identity? When he must choose, Moses identifies with the Hebrews, even though Egyptian princes were taught to despise manual labour. He opts for the oppressed people of promise over the glamour of Egypt (**v 11**). His identity is defined by the promise of God. And so should ours be.

Even his new profession loosens the grip of Egypt on his heart. Genesis 46:34 says, "All shepherds are detestable to the Egyptians". So Moses becomes something that would have been unthinkable to his old Egyptian friends.

Perhaps a similar process was happening to the Israelites back in Egypt. Left to themselves, the Israelites might well have integrated with the Egyptians, have been absorbed, and have disappeared from history. But their ethnically-defined persecution meant their identity was maintained and clarified. Again, left to themselves, the Israelites might well have settled down to life as a marginalised people in Egypt.

Even with their sufferings, it was hard to get them to leave and they quickly wanted to return (see, for instance, Exodus 16:3). One of the ways in which God works good from suffering is that he uses it to make us cling to him in faith, to clarify our identity as his children and to increase our longing for the new creation.

For Moses, his time in the wilderness as a shepherd prepares him for leadership. The writer of Psalm 77 recalled how God "led [his] people like a flock by the hand of Moses and Aaron [Moses' brother]" (Psalm 77:20). The prophet Isaiah spoke of how God's people "recalled the days of old, the days of Moses and his people—where is he who brought them through the sea, with the shepherd of his flock?" (Isaiah 63:11). One day, Moses will lead Israel like a shepherd leading sheep. So he is prepared for this great task by being a literal shepherd, leading literal sheep. From the moment Moses comes home to Midian, in fact,

> God uses suffering to make us cling to him, clarify our identity and increase our longing.

he is changing into a man who can lead God's people. In contrast to the violence of his actions in Egypt, Moses rescues the Midianite women without violence and then serves them in a way that surprises them because he is a man serving women: "He even drew water for us and watered the flock" (Exodus **2:19**).

Moses calls his first son "Gershom". The tense of the verb in Moses' explanation of this name is ambiguous. The NIV translates it, "I have become a foreigner in a foreign land" (**v 22**). But the ESV fits the context better: "I have been a **sojourner** in a foreign land". The point is not that Moses is away from home, but that Moses has come home. Moses is enjoying rest and peace in the promised land. Despite Egypt being the place of his birth and upbringing, Moses now sees it as a foreign country.

The best commentary on this story is Hebrews 11:24-27:

"By faith Moses, when he had grown up, refused to be known as the son of Pharaoh's daughter. He chose to be ill-treated along with the people of God rather than to enjoy the fleeting pleasures of sin. He regarded disgrace for the sake of Christ as of greater value than the treasures of Egypt, because he was looking ahead to his reward. By faith he left Egypt, not fearing the king's anger; he persevered because he saw him who is invisible."

We face the same choice as Moses. Every Christian is in the same situation. After our **conversion**, the land of our birth and our upbringing becomes a foreign land to us. Now we are **pilgrims** heading for the promised land, the home that is kept for us in heaven.

We have to choose. Which home will set our priorities? Which home will shape our behaviour? Which home will define our standard of living? Will we choose the "pleasures of sin" and "the treasures of Egypt"? Or will we choose "to be ill-treated along with the people of God"? Will we choose "disgrace for the sake of Christ"? There is the stark choice: will you live for pleasure and treasure, or will you live in disgrace?

Moses chose the disgrace. Why? Because he "was looking ahead to his reward … By faith he left Egypt, not fearing the king's anger.". Notice again how his faith meant he did not fear the king—just lie the Hebrew midwives.

How do we live in the face of hostility? By looking to the home that God has promised. And by fearing God rather than men. The story of Exodus is part of the bigger story of God's promise to Abraham—a story of which we are a part. But that's not all.

The story of creation and re-creation

We have seen that "the Israelites were exceedingly fruitful; they multiplied greatly, increased in numbers and became so numerous that the land was filled with them" (Exodus **1:7**); and that, in response to their risky obedience, "God was kind to the midwives and the people increased and became even more numerous" (**v 20**).

We have heard this kind of language before in the Bible story—back in Genesis 1:28: "God blessed them and said to them, 'Be fruitful and increase in number; fill the earth and subdue it.'" This command is reiterated after Noah comes out of the ark: "God blessed Noah and his sons, saying to them, 'Be fruitful and increase in number and fill the earth'." (Genesis 9:1). So notice the links:

- God tells humanity to "be fruitful". Israel is "exceedingly fruitful".

- God tells humanity to "increase in number". Israel has "increased in number".

- God tells humanity to "fill the earth". Israel has filled the land.

Exodus **1:7** uses seven different words to describe the fruitfulness of the Israelites. "They multiplied greatly" is literally "they swarmed", the same word that is used in Genesis 1:21 to describe the waters "teeming" with life. What is happening in Exodus 1 is not just the fulfilment of the covenant with Abraham, but the fulfilment of the covenant with the first human, Adam. God's people are fulfilling the command which humanity has neglected.

And the links with God's creation continue. In Exodus **2:2** we are told that the mother of Moses "saw that he was a fine child"; literally, "she saw that he was good". It is the same language as in Genesis 1:31: "God saw all that he had made, and it was very good". Here in Egypt the world is being recreated.

And all might be well—"very good"—were it not for the fact that Pharaoh becomes a kind of anti-creator. Pharaoh tries to restrain this explosion of creative power. In place of life, he ordains death. The newborn boys—the fruit of this creative energy—are to be thrown into the Nile. In Genesis 1, humanity was told to subdue the earth. In Exodus 1, humanity in the person of Pharaoh is subduing… humanity.

And what happens? God's liberator is placed in the Nile. He is placed in the place of death—and he lives. As we've noted, the name

"Moses" sounds like the Hebrew words "to draw out". Moses is drawn out of the waters of death, just as Israel will be in chapter 14.

The word basket in Exodus **2:3** is literally "ark" (*tebha*). The baby Moses is placed in an "ark". The only other time this word is used in the Bible is to describe Noah's ark. Both Noah and Moses escape a watery judgment in a bitumen-coated ark.

In the midst of the waters of judgment, the people of God are safe. Both Noah in Genesis 6 – 9, and Moses here, experience an act of re-creation, or resurrection. They enter the waters of death and pass through to a new life (1 Peter 3:20-22). We'll return to this idea when we get to Exodus 14, but it is exciting to see it here!

Pharaoh is trying to impede this creative fruitfulness—and so he has set himself on a collision course with God. Both Pharaoh and God lay claim to Israel, though the nature of their respective rules is very different. One rule is oppressive and deadly; the other is liberating and life-giving. Pharaoh's hostility is the latest manifestation of the ancient hostility which was written into history after the **fall** of Adam, when God told the snake, "I will put enmity between you and the woman, and between your offspring and hers" (Genesis 3:15). Egypt will be the site of the latest battle between those who belong to the snake, and those who belong to the promise. Pharaoh will try to undo God's re-creation—God will unleash the forces of creation on him. And as he does so, he will save his people. And the world will know that he is God.

The church continues to experience that enmity—and the story of the exodus stands as a reminder that, no matter how bitter the fight, there is only ever going to be one winner. The church will experience the battle—we will also experience God's salvation and enjoy his liberating, life-giving rule.

Questions for reflection

1. Looking back at the beginning and the ongoing experience of your Christian life, how have you found yourself identifying as a "sojourner in a foreign land"?

2. "Will you live for pleasure and treasure, or will you live in disgrace?" As you look at your own life, how are you able to answer this question in ways that encourage you? In which areas of your life does this question challenge you?

3. How does knowing the end of the story—God's victory and re-creation—enable you to live positively and excitedly as you experience the battle of the Christian life now?

2. WHAT'S IN A NAME?

"Ignorance of God—ignorance both of his ways and of the practice of communion with him—lies at the root of much of the church's weakness today … The modern way with God is to set him at a distance, if not to deny him altogether; and the irony is that modern Christians, preoccupied with maintaining religious practices in an irreligious world, have themselves allowed God to become remote … Churchmen who look at God, so to speak, through the wrong end of the telescope, so reducing him to pigmy proportions, cannot hope to end up as more than pigmy Christians."

So wrote Jim Packer in the Introduction of his classic work, *Knowing God*. What might be included in Packer's phrase, "preoccupied with maintaining religious practices"? Books, articles, conferences on corporate worship, evangelism strategies, relevant preaching, discipleship models, contextualised ministry, outreach programmes—all these are worthy pursuits, and necessary topics of conversation. But if they become our primary focus then God can be strangely absent from our lives. We become experts in all sorts of areas, but at the same time remain pigmy Christians. We want "practical topics", but nothing is less practical than God-lite Christianity.

Packer's warning of pigmy Christians who have reduced God would have been relevant to the Israelites in Egypt, as we'll see again and again. Chapters 1 – 2 have set the scene. The Israelites have multiplied but become enslaved. But these chapters barely mention God's name, which is especially notable once we see the frequent references to it from chapter 3 onwards. In 2:23, the cry of the Israelites reaches

God, but we're not told that they addressed their cry to him. But in response to the cry going up, now God says, "I have come down" (**3:8**). Israel may have forgotten God, but God is about to give them a big reminder. He is about to reveal his name.

Today, people like to define God for themselves. Think about people who say, "I'm not religious, but I am spiritual" or, "I think God is like…" What they're saying is, "I don't want anyone to tell me what to think about God. I'll decide for myself what God is like. I'll imagine him or her or it in whatever way I choose."

Christians are not immune to this. Of some aspect of God's character or Christian truth we might say, "I don't like the sound of that … I just don't think God is like that." It might be his judgment, or his sovereignty, or his sexual standards. We make a god in our image and he becomes a fluffy god—a god who suits our desires but cannot help us when we are in need. We think of God in the way we want to think of him.

> A god made in our image suits our desires but cannot help us when we are in need.

But to do this is to detach yourself from reality. You might as well say, "I like to think of elephants as two-legged animals". What you want to think about elephants is irrelevant! It won't change the fact that they have four legs. And what you or I or anyone wants to think about God doesn't change who God actually is. God is not a concept that we can shape as we choose. God *is*. God is a reality—the ultimate reality. So in this passage God says, "I AM WHO I AM" (**v 14**). God is self-defining. It is God who determines and announces who he will be and what he will be like—not our imagination. When confronted with the real God, we discover that God is more terrifying and more loving than we could ever have imagined and than any god we could dream up.

So what is God like? Who is God?

Above us

Moses is looking after his father-in-law's flock and ends up in the wilderness near Horeb (**v 1**). And there, he sees a bush on fire (**v 2**). We often call it the "burning bush", but the one thing we know about it is that it wasn't burning! "Though the bush was on fire it did not burn up." A fire often draws you towards it, and this fire draws Moses (**v 3**). But equally, we also instinctively keep our distance from fire. We know that if we go too close, it will harm us. Perhaps God appears in this way to highlight this need for distance. That's going to be a key theme in the book of Exodus (e.g. 19:10-13, 20-24).

The non-burning nature of this bush is not the biggest surprise, though. Next, God calls to Moses from the bush: "Moses! Moses! ... Do not come any closer" (**3:4, 5**). Moses has to take off his sandals. It's not clear why, except that it was a sign of "holy ground", because it was ground where God was (**v 5**). The word "holy" means "different" or "distinctive". God is not like us. He is holy, glorious and majestic.

God then reveals himself as God. Up until now Moses has encountered a talking bush, but now he is told that "I am ... God" (**v 6**). And Moses' immediate instinct is to hide his face, "because he was afraid to look at God". This response is spot on, for in 33:20 God will tell Moses, "You cannot see my face, for no one may see me and live".

There's more to be said about God, as we shall see. But what we will see of his love and **grace** does not take anything away from his holiness and glory. God is awful and terrible in the old meaning of those words—he evokes awe and terror. You don't treat him lightly. God is not your "mate". Indeed, if you were to meet God, your instinct would be to hide your face. Even the sinless, glorious seraphim cover their faces in the presence of God (Isaiah 6:2). God is above us. The **theological** term for this is "transcendence".

Among us

Yet look at what God says to Moses in this encounter: "I have indeed seen … I have heard … I am concerned" (Exodus **3:7**). God is above us. But he is also among us. We will only appreciate his "among-ness" if we first are awed by his "above-ness". God is present among his people even though his people don't sense his presence. God is close enough to see and hear and be concerned.

Most of us know what it is like to feel forgotten by God or when God seems far away—perhaps you feel that way right now. You cry out because of your suffering, just as the Israelites did (**v 7, 9**). And you feel, as perhaps they felt, that God doesn't hear or is uninterested. But God says, "I have seen … I have heard … I am concerned".

More than that, God then says, "I have come down" (**v 8**). God is not absent. He has, as it were, rolled up his sleeves to get stuck into his people's story. He is going to rescue his people, so that he can "bring them … into a good and spacious land", as he promised (**v 8**). God is present among us. The theological term for this is "immanence".

When people define God for themselves, they typically think of God as either wholly transcendent or wholly immanent. The gods of Islam and of **deism** are all transcendence. Many in the West are **functional** deists—they believe in God, but he doesn't affect their lives. As far as they're concerned, God doesn't see, doesn't hear, doesn't care, hasn't come down. In contrast, the gods of **mysticism**, **Sufism** and Eastern religions are all immanence. These beliefs teach that God is within us or everything is in some way divine (perhaps this is why Eastern religions are often attractive to Westerners who have been brought up as functional deists). But the God who is, the God who revealed himself to Moses, is both above us and among us.

One question is worth dealing with quickly. **Verse 2** says that "the angel of the Lord appeared to" Moses, but from then on it is God who is said to speak (**v 4, 5, 6, 7**). Sometimes in the Old Testament, as here, the angel of the Lord appears to be synonymous with God himself. Yet at other times, he is distinguished from God (e.g. 2 Samuel 24:16).

Theologians have often understood this "angel of the LORD" to be a reference to Jesus who, in the words of John 1:1, both "was with God" and "was God" from the beginning. And in Jesus, God has "come down" to be "Immanuel"—God with us (Matthew 1:23).

The sting in the tail for Moses is Exodus **3:10**: "So now, go. I am sending you to Pharaoh to bring my people the Israelites out of Egypt". I wonder if you see a problem and you long to hear God say, "I have seen … I have heard … I am concerned". But you don't hear him, because he's also saying, "I am sending you". In other words, often he intends you to be the solution to the problem. Are you ready to hear that?

Who am I?

Moses then enters into an extended dialogue with God which is built around three questions that Moses asks of God.

1. Who am I? (**v 11-12**)

2. Who are you? (**v 13-22**)

3. What if they don't believe? (**4:1-17**)

"But Moses said to God, 'Who am I that I should go to Pharaoh and bring the Israelites out of Egypt?'" (**3:11**). Moses feels inadequate because of his weakness ("Who am I?"), Pharaoh's power ("that I should go to Pharaoh") and the scale of the task ("and bring the Israelites out of Egypt?"). It is a very understandable question to ask!

"Who am I?" Our modern culture invites us to ask this all the time. Identity has become fluid or malleable. A century ago, who you were was determined by where you had grown up and who your parents were. You were likely to do the job your mother or father did and live in the same area. But now we can invent and reinvent ourselves almost on a daily basis. We switch careers. We move around. We join sub-cultures. We have online identities. It's a world of opportunity—but it also creates angst and anxiety. Moreover, there is nothing bigger than us to form our identity. The breakdown of families, national identities and belief in God all mean we ourselves have become the measure of our lives. In the past, you might have had a humble job, but you were proud to be part of the company, and proud to be part of your nation. But those corporate identities don't matter so much now. Now identity is down to me. Identity has become something you achieve rather than something you receive.

For Moses, the questioning of his identity was prompted by a task he felt unable to complete. It's the same today. We enjoy creating our own identity, until we find ourselves unable to deliver. For many people the pressure to achieve and sustain our self-built identities becomes too much. Rates of depression are higher than ever before, and part of that is caused by the brittleness of our sense of who we are, which means we are constantly evaluating and re-evaluating our identity, striving to confirm it and dealing with failures to live up to it.

So the question is: Who am I? God's answer? "I will be with you" (**v 12**). Is that an answer?! How does it help you know who you are to know that someone else is with you? I think it is an answer—in fact, *the* answer. God is saying to Moses that his identity is tied to God's identity. Moses says, "Who am I that I should go to Pharaoh?" We might have said, "Moses, you're the ideal person. You were brought up in the Egyptian court. You have seen your people's suffering. And you have been protecting and providing for your flock for years. You can do it." But God says, "I will be with you". God is the One who will make the difference. Moses does not need to have higher self-esteem; he needs a greater sense of God's presence.

You can be a self-made person. And for a while, you may enjoy your **autonomy**. But it's hard work. Whether you're trying to fit in at school or prove yourself in your career or keep up with the latest fashions, eventually the cracks will appear. Always the question remains: Will my self-made identity withstand the pressures of this life, and then the test of divine appraisal beyond this life?

And God says to you, "I will be with you". *You can walk through life with me. You can base your sense of self on your knowledge of* me—*find your confidence and worth in knowing that I am there for you, and here with you. You can know that I am with you, and your achievements and your failures will not affect that status.* "I will be with you."

Imagine trying to visit the Queen at Buckingham Palace. You're going to be asked, "Who are you?" In other words, "What gives you the right to be here?" Most of us are not going to get past the front gate. But what about Kate Middleton? When she was 15 years old, she would have got no further than us. Now, she can say, "I'm with him. I married the prince." Who is she? She is Her Royal Highness The Duchess of

> God says, *I am with you, and your achievements and failures will not affect that.*

Cambridge. She gets that identity from her husband. In the same way, we get our identity from Jesus our Husband. "I'm with him." United to Christ, we are children of God the Father.

Moses here is a picture of Israel. This encounter with God takes place at "Horeb, the mountain of God" (**v 1**). Horeb is another name for Mount Sinai. God tells Moses that the "sign"—the proof that he is with Moses—is that "when you have brought the people out of Egypt, you will worship God on this mountain" (**v 12**). This is what happens when Israel comes to Mount Sinai in Exodus 19. Israel will repeat the experience of Moses. They will encounter the holy God, tread on holy ground, and hear his voice. Israel as a whole will receive their identity from God, becoming his "treasured possession … a kingdom of priests and a holy nation" (19:5-6).

In **4:22**, we'll hear God say that "Israel is my firstborn son". In the New Testament, we hear God say that to those who received him when he came among us in the person of his Son, the Lord Jesus: "To those who believed in his name, he gave the right to become children of God" (John 1:12). Who am I? One of the children of God. We are the people who are defined by our God. Yesterday you may have been a great employee or you may have had a terrible day at work. You may have been a great parent or child, or a selfish one. You may have been praised, or mocked, or ignored. You may have been mainly obedient or horribly sinful. But if you have received Christ as your Lord and Saviour, then you are a child of God—and nothing can change that. That means that today you can go out with confidence—not in what you can do, but in who is with you. Who am I? I am a child of God. "I am with you", God says to you.

Questions for reflection

1. Which aspect of God's nature as "I AM WHO I AM" most thrills you today? Does your view of who he is need to change in any way?

2. Is there any problem you're facing in which the solution to the problem might be you? How might God be "sending" you today?

3. To what extent do you allow your identity—what gives you confidence, and how you feel about yourself—to be founded on the truth that God says, "I am with you"? When is believing this truth hardest for you? How might remembering God's "I am with you" help you in those times or circumstances?

PART TWO

Who is God?

"Who am I?" says Moses. "I will be with you," says God. Which raises the question; Who is God? Who is the "I" who will be with him? And this is precisely what Moses asks in Exodus **3:13**: "Suppose I go to the Israelites and say to them, 'The God of your fathers has sent me to you,' and they ask me, 'What is his name?' Then what shall I tell them?"

So God reveals his name to Moses. "I AM WHO I AM. This is what you are to say to the Israelites: 'I AM has sent me to you'" (**v 14**).

This is a statement deliberately designed to burst our definitions. We normally say, "I am *something*". I am a father. I am a teacher. I am lonely. I am tall. But this statement circles back on itself. God is not defined by anything outside of himself. Moreover, the Hebrew verb used here indicates an action with no particular instance in view. It's literally "I be who I be". It can refer to habitual action in the past ("His mother *used to make* for him a little robe", 1 Samuel 2:19, ESV). It can refer to action which is generally true in the present ("The heart of man *plans* his way, but [Yahweh] *establishes* his step", Proverbs 16:9, ESV). It can refer to future actions ("I *will lay waste* mountains and hills", Isaiah 42:15). All these verbs have the same form as the verb "I am" in Exodus **3:14**. And so this leaves God's statement there intentionally ambiguous. It could be translated:

- "I have always been who I have always been." The God of Abraham, of Isaac and of Jacob (**v 6**) will act in a way which is consistent with his track record.

- "I am who I am." God is self-defining rather than shaped by others or by his relationship with others.

- "I will be who I will be." God will determine the future and/or God will be what matters in the future.

We cannot automatically assume a word in a given context means all that a word can mean. (There are not many contexts, for example, in which the word "fast" can mean both "not eating food" and "quick" at the same time.) But here, there are good reasons for thinking all these three senses are in view. The context includes the idea that the God of the **patriarchs** (in the past) is going to liberate his people (in the present) to give them the promised land (in the future).

In **verse 15**, the "I AM WHO I AM" reveals his name: "The LORD". It is the word "Yahweh" or "Jehovah". This is God's personal name. Just as I am a man called Tim, so God is a God called Yahweh. Later, the Jews refused to speak this personal name of God for fear that they might do so in a **blasphemous** way. Instead, they would use the word "Lord" or "Master" (ădōnāy). The Hebrew Bible was originally written in consonants alone. In the sixth century, vowels were added for those unfamiliar with biblical pronunciation. But to avoid reading Yahweh by mistake, the vowels from ădōnāy were superimposed on the consonants of Yahweh. In the sixteenth century, Christian scholars mistook this combination and transliterated it as "Jehovah". But the correct form is YHWH. We cannot be sure what the vowels should be (as these were never written), but it is usually written and pronounced as "Yahweh" (with a hard first "h"). In most contemporary English translations, this is translated as "LORD", using capitals letters to distinguish it from "Lord" (ădōnāy).

So "the LORD" appears to be the short version of I AM WHO I AM, since the word for "LORD" sounds like "I AM" in **verse 14**. If "Yahweh" (the LORD) were listed in a book that gave definitions of names, the definition would be "I AM WHO I AM".

But what does all of this add up to?! When we say God is Yahweh, what are we saying?

Above us as our sovereign LORD

My identity is shaped by other people. I'm an Englishman living in the twenty-first century. So I deflect compliments, I'm understated in my enthusiasm, I'm slow to praise others—all because deep down I regard these things as unseemly. I try to be effusive in my encouragement, but it doesn't come naturally. Who I am is profoundly shaped by my culture. Moreover, my identity is radically constrained. I would like to have been an England international cricketer. But it was never going to happen. My lack of ability limits who I can be. I would like to have been a perfect husband and father. But I couldn't be.

But God's identity is unconstrained. He will be who he decides to be. He will do what he decides to do. God is radically free—free to be and do whatever he chooses.

> God has the power to keep the promises he has made.

Or, to be more precise, God is unconstrained by external factors. Nothing and no one can force him to be or do anything against his will. But God is constrained by his own character and promises. He will always act in a way that is consistent with his holiness and with his word. This is our great hope, proved through his actions in history.

- Because God is not constrained by others, we can be sure he can deliver.

- Because God is constrained by himself, we can be sure he will deliver.

This means God has the power to keep the promises he has made. This is what he says in **verses 16-22**. Moses is to ask Pharaoh to liberate God's people (**v 18**). Pharaoh, however, will refuse. So God, the sovereign LORD, will force him (**v 19-20**). Indeed, God will make the Egyptians want Israel to leave (**v 21-22**). "Plunder" in **verse 22** is the language of victory in battle. God and Pharaoh are on a collision course. It will be a battle of will and power. But there can only be one winner because God is "I AM WHO I AM".

So God is dependable. He's not just "I WAS". For the Israelites, that meant the God of their ancestor Abraham was still God in their own day. For us, it means the God of the exodus is still God today. The God who sent the plagues, parted the Red Sea and came down at Sinai is the God to whom you pray.

Further, God is not "I MAY BE". He is "I AM" and "I WILL BE". I put "ifs" near many of my commitments, because I can't be sure that I can deliver. "I'll help if I can," I say. "I'll come if I'm free." "I'll do it if there's time." But you can be sure God will deliver all that he has promised because he is "I WILL BE WHAT I WILL BE".

Among us as our covenant LORD

Verse 17 says, "And I have promised to bring you up out of your misery in Egypt into the land of the Canaanites, Hittites, Amorites, Perizzites, Hivites and Jebusites—a land flowing with milk and honey". God is a covenant-making God. He enters into covenants with his people. And "the LORD" is God's covenant name.

At the heart of any covenant is a promise. And this is true of God's covenants. God promises Noah that he will never again destroy creation through a flood. He promises Abraham a nation and a land enjoying his blessing. And he is about to promise Moses that these people will be his people and he will be their God (6:7).

But a covenant is more than a promise. It is also a contract. It is a legally agreed promise. We make covenants or contracts because human beings are unreliable—we don't always do what we say. So we need legal contracts to bind us to our promises. In this sense, a covenant is redundant for God because God always does what he says. But he makes covenants for our benefit so we can be doubly sure. Hebrews 6 says God promises he will save us and then he swears on oath that he will save us (Hebrews 6:13-18). One would be enough, but God gives us two reasons to trust him. As a result, "we have this hope as an anchor for the soul, firm and secure" (v 19). We have it in writing.

Or rather, we have it in blood. In Exodus 24:8, once the people had been rescued by God and had come to worship at Horeb, just as he had promised Moses in Exodus 3, "Moses then took the blood, sprinkled it on the people and said, 'This is the blood of the covenant that the LORD has made with you in accordance with all these words.'" The blood is like God's signature on the contract (Hebrews 9:11-15). God's promise is written in blood, and kept in blood. On the night before he died, Jesus "took the cup, saying, 'This cup is the new covenant in my blood, which is poured out for you'" (Luke 22:20). Every time we take the wine in communion, we are reminded that God has signed the covenant with the blood of his own Son. That is how committed he is to keeping his promise.

But a covenant is also more than a contract. Twenty-five years ago, I promised a young woman that I would love her for the rest of my life. But I did something more significant than that. I covenanted with her, and as a result she became my wife and I became her husband. Our relationship changed in a profound way. Our covenant-making changed the nature of our relationship. In other words, covenants bind people together in a relationship.

And so it is with God's covenants. They change our identity. We become God's people. This is why some of God's covenants can appear unconditional and conditional at the same time. They are unconditional because God does not require conditions for his promises. But they are conditional in the sense that the covenant creates a new relationship, and that new relationship has implications.

An everlasting name

"This is my name for ever," God tells Moses, "the name you shall call me from generation to generation" (Exodus **3:15**). This matters for us, living over three millennia after these events.

"The LORD" is not just God's personal name—it's also his covenant name, the name that signifies his commitment. So God has given this name "from generation to generation" as a sign of his covenant commitment to his people. In a sense, "Mrs Chester" is my wife's covenant name, because it's a sign that she's committed to me. If she started calling herself by her maiden, unmarried name of "Miss Freeman", I'd be worried. And God does not change his name "from generation to generation"; it is, and will remain, Yahweh. He was, remains, and always will remain committed to the people he has revealed himself to personally and covenanted with. So every time you hear the name "the LORD" or "Lord Jesus", it's a reminder that God has committed himself to a relationship with you—and that that will never, ever change.

Maybe your suffering makes you wonder whether God is no longer for you. Maybe your sin makes you wonder whether God might give up on you. God says, "I AM WHO I AM": *I am "the LORD, the God of your fathers" (v 15). I can save you because I'm your sovereign LORD. I will save you because I'm your covenant LORD.* And nothing can change that.

Questions for reflection

1. Which aspect of God's nature most excited you or comforted you as you read this section?

2. What causes you to doubt God's promises? How does his name help you to counter those doubts?

3. Imagine you had three sentences in which to explain who God is to someone. Basing your answer on Exodus 3, what would you say?

PART THREE

Defined by action

Some friends of our recently had a son and a group of us were discussing possible names. Someone suggested Oliver. A teacher in the
group immediately objected. "Oh no," she said, "you can't call him
Oliver. All the Olivers I've known have been horrible!" (Apologies if
your name is Oliver—I'm sure you're the exception!) Whether it is
rational or not, our understanding of a name is shaped by the people
we've known with that name—what they were like and what they did
for us (or to us).

The real definition of God's name is going to be the exodus itself:
"And this will be the sign to you that it is I who have sent you: when
you have brought the people out of Egypt, you will worship God on
this mountain" (**v 12**). This sounds strange—it looks as though God is
saying, *The proof I'll redeem my people is that I'll redeem my people*!
But perhaps God is saying, *The sign that I am God is that I will save
my people.* God then says, "I AM WHO I AM"—or "I WILL BE WHAT I WILL
BE"—before describing in **verses 16-22** what he's about to do. *This is
what I WILL BE to you*, he's saying.

Moses will discover who God is through God's saving acts. God is
self-defining, and he is about to provide a definition of his name—and
that definition is the exodus. In the exodus we will see the holiness of
God in his judgment on Egypt. We will see the power of God in his
triumph over Pharaoh and the gods of Egypt. We will see the grace
of God in the **redemption** of Israel. We will see the rule of God in his
words on Mount Sinai.

Moses' questions in **verse 13** (and Pharaoh's in 5:2) may indicate
that God was little known among the Israelites. Chapters 3 – 15 then
remedy this with a strong focus on God making himself known: the
phrase "I am the LORD" is repeated throughout these chapters (6:2,
6, 7, 8, 29; 7:5, 17; 10:2; 12:12; 14:4, 18; 15:26 plus 20:2; 29:46;
31:13). The scholar and theologian Walter Brueggemann says:

"the entire Exodus narrative is an exposition of the name of Exodus 3:14, requiring all its powerful verbs for an adequate expression."　　　　　(Cited in W. Ross Blackburn, *The God who Makes Himself Known*, page 34)

So God's name is going to have meaning for his children because of what he will do. In the years that followed, if you had asked an Israelite, "Who is God?" they would have told you a story—the story of the exodus.

Now fast-forward more than a millennium to an Israelite man who says, "Before Abraham was born, I am!" (John 8:58). Jesus was claiming to be I AM WHO I AM; and his actions would prove his claim and define his identity. Time and again in the New Testament, he is not simply named "Jesus" but "the Lord Jesus". Echoing the summary of Israelite faith in Deuteronomy 6:4-5, Paul says, "There is but one Lord, Jesus Christ" (1 Corinthians 8:6). Jesus is Yahweh.

> If you had asked an Israelite, "Who is God?" they would have told you a story— the exodus.

In Jesus, God has come down, just as he said he would in Exodus 3:8. God has rolled up his sleeves, put on human flesh and entered our world to rescue his people. The God who is above us has walked among us: "No one has ever seen God, but the one and only Son … has made him known" (John 1:18).

God is self-defining and his ultimate definition is the life, death and resurrection of Jesus. At the cross and the empty tomb we see the holiness of God in his judgment on Jesus; we see the power of God in his defeat of Satan and his raising of his Son; and we see the grace of God because Jesus was judged in our place and rose to give us life. God defines himself... and his definition is Jesus. When you find God's ways mysterious—when you find God's character inscrutable,

or his conduct confusing, or his presence distant—look to Jesus. John
Newton wrote:

How sweet the name of Jesus sounds
in a believer's ear!
It soothes his sorrows, heals his wounds
and drives away his fear.

It makes the wounded spirit whole
and calms the troubled breast;
it satisfies the hungry soul
and gives the weary rest.

Dear name, the rock on which we build,
our shield and hiding place,
our never-failing treasury, filled
with boundless stores of grace!

Proverbs 18:10 says, "The name of the Lord is a fortified tower; the
righteous run to it and are safe". Whatever troubles you face, you can
run to the name of Jesus and find refuge.

What if they don't believe?

In his encounter with God, Moses asks three questions. God's response
to Moses' second question ends with the words, "You will plunder the
Egyptians" (Exodus **3:22**; see 12:35-36). The confrontation that will
begin with a request for a three-day worship festival (**3:18**) will end
with the defeat of the Egyptian empire and the victory of the slaves.
It does seem unlikely—so Moses' third question is not entirely surprising: "What if they do not believe me or listen to me and say, 'The Lord
did not appear to you'?" (**4:1**).

   In response, God offers Moses three signs, two of which he per-
forms for him on the spot: a staff that turns into a snake (**v 2-5**), a
hand that turns leprous (**v 6-7**), and water that turns to blood (**v 8-9**).
These are signs for the Israelites—but they will also be the first signs
performed for the Egyptians (7:8-24). The third of these signs is the

first plague to fall on Egypt. **4:8-9** suggests that the third sign is to be held in reserve in case Israel do not believe the first two signs. There is perhaps a sense in which Israel will taste the judgment of God if they are unbelieving.

These signs are not mere tricks that Moses can perform at will to grab a crowd. They are God's salvation and judgment in miniature. The real sign will be the exodus itself, plagues included. This will be the sign for future generations of the identity of God, and this will be the event that shapes the identity of his people.

So it is for us. God does not give us signs like magic tricks to wow a crowd. The signs we have are the cross and resurrection—the reality pictured by the exodus. When people asked Jesus for a sign, he said that it is "a wicked and adulterous generation [that] asks for a sign" and informed them that the only sign they would be given would be the sign of Jonah—a man going to the place of the dead for three days and nights, and then emerging alive (Matthew 12:38-40). In Jonah's case that was the belly of a fish; in Jesus' it would be a tomb. Paul put it this way: "Jews demand signs and Greeks look for wisdom, but we preach Christ crucified … the power of God and the wisdom of God" (1 Corinthians 1:22-24).

God kindly gave the people three signs to establish his chosen leader's credibility—but a year, a decade and a century later, those were not the signs Israel reflected on or rejoiced in. They recounted the rescue of the Passover and the passage through the Red Sea, the place of the dead. We have been given still greater signs than those, and those are all we (or anyone else) need to show us the power and the wisdom of God.

I will help you

In Exodus **4:10**, Moses seems to interrupt God's response with an objection. In **verse 1**, his concern is: *they might not listen well.* In **verse 10**, his concern is: *I might not speak well.* In **verses 11-12**, God addresses both concerns:

"The LORD said to him, 'Who gave human beings their mouths?
Who makes them deaf or mute? Who gives them sight or makes
them blind? Is it not I, the LORD? Now go; I will help you speak
and will teach you what to say."

God speaks both of those who are deaf (who can't listen well) and
those who are mute (who can't speak well). And then, for good measure, he speaks of those who can't see—a picture of those who lack
insight into the identity and purposes of God. In other words, he addresses both of Moses' fears—his fear that people will not listen well
and his fear that he will not speak well.

God's response is, *I give words. I give hearing. I give insight.* It's true
that Moses can't speak well and it's true that the people don't listen
well. But God gives words and God gives hearing. God opens blind
eyes to see the truth.

Moses makes one more attempt to avoid the task; this time, he
provokes God's anger (**v 14**), by asking God to send someone else
(**v 13**). *No*, says God. *You must go.* But God graciously allows Moses
to take his brother as his spokesperson (**v 14-17**). God sends Aaron to
meet him as he returns to Egypt (**v 27-28**), and it is Aaron who relates
God's words to the people of Israel (**v 29-31**).

Verse 16 contains a striking phrase: "It will be as if he were your
mouth and as if you were God to him". We find a similar expression in
7:1. The words of Moses via Aaron will be the words of God. It will be
as if God himself is speaking. The sixteenth-century **Reformer** John
Calvin wrote:

"Christ acts by [his ministers] in such a manner that he wishes
their mouth to be reckoned as his mouth, and their lips as his
lips; that is, when they speak from his mouth, and faithfully declare his word." (*Commentary on Isaiah 11:4*)

We often feel we can't speak well about God. Opportunities arise
to tell people about Jesus, and we miss them. People ask questions
which we can't answer. We share the gospel and then afterwards
think of all the things we should have said. We feel we cannot speak

well; and we feel that people don't listen well. Indeed they are adept at deflecting or derailing our attempts to have a conversation about spiritual things. It's so easy to give up, to hope that someone else will go—but not us. But God says:

> "Who gave human beings their mouths? Who makes them deaf or mute? Who gives them sight or makes them blind? Is it not I, the LORD? Now go; I will help you speak and will teach you what to say." (Exodus **4:11-12**)

We are to hear that challenge, and then let the promise of God echo in our ears as we open our mouths: "I will help you speak".

My firstborn son

Moses gets permission from his father-in-law to return to Egypt and sets off with his family (**v 18-20**). In **verses 21-23** we have a summary of God's words to Moses in Midian. In **3:19** we are told that the king of Egypt will not let Israel go so God will have to compel him, and **4:21** adds that this is because God will harden his heart. We'll return to this theme in chapters 7 – 11.

But next, we get a statement that has significance for the whole Bible story: "Then say to Pharaoh, 'This is what the LORD says: Israel is my firstborn son, and I told you, "Let my son go, so that he may worship me." But you refused to let him go; so I will kill your firstborn son'" (**4:22-23**). This is the first time God's people are described as God's son—but it will not be the last, and it is fundamental to our appreciation of who God is and our understanding of who we are.

We get a glimpse of God's fatherly affection—what it is that he is saying in **verses 22-23**—in Hosea 11:1-4:

> "When Israel was a child, I loved him,
>   and out of Egypt I called my son …
> I led them with cords of human kindness,
>   with ties of love.
> To them I was like one who lifts

a little child to the cheek,

and I bent down to feed them."

Israel is God's "firstborn" because they were the first nation to be God's people. Today, they are joined by the **Gentiles**, a reality anticipated in Exodus 12:38. It is a theme that will unfold through the Bible story, both in terms of **rebirth** and **adoption**, until John says: "See what great love the Father has lavished on us, that we should be called children of God! And that is what we are!" (1 John 3:1).

Exodus **4:22-23** predicts what will happen in the next chapters. God will demand that Pharaoh let Israel, his firstborn, go free. But Pharaoh will refuse, and so the firstborn of Egypt will die. The judgment will match the crime: Pharaoh abuses God's firstborn so Pharaoh's firstborn will die. It is only grace that breaks this principle. Humanity abuses God's firstborn, so humanity's firstborn should die. But at the cross, God's firstborn—the **incarnate** Son of God—dies in our place.

Bridegroom of blood

There now follows a strange episode, which raise questions which we can't readily answer 3,000 years on. There is much we do not know about what is happening in **verses 24-26**:

- *We don't know whom God attacked.* **Verse 24** simply refers to "him": "the Lord met him and was about to kill him". It's not clear whether the Lord is about to kill Moses or Gershom. But Gershom is not introduced until **verse 25**—so the most likely answer is that the "him" is Moses.

- *We don't know how God was about to kill him.* Was he having a seizure or struck by an illness or attacked by an angel?

- *We don't know why God was about to kill him.* It seems to be related to **circumcision**. It could be that Moses was uncircumcised, and Gershom is circumcised on his behalf. "Feet" (**v 25**) could be a **euphemism** for genitals. But Moses' parents had hidden him for three months before his discovery by Pharaoh's daughter, so there was plenty of time for them to circumcise him (although they may have delayed in order to avoid detection). So it's more likely that the problem here is that Gershom was uncircumcised.

■ *We don't know how Zipporah knew what to do.* Perhaps there was an element of **divine revelation**, but there is another possibility that relates to the next question.

■ *We don't know why Gershom was uncircumcised.* The Midianites probably only circumcised men as they became adults—so perhaps Moses had conformed to Midianite culture. Maybe Zipporah had persuaded him not to circumcise Gershom as a child because it was distasteful to her. This would explain how, in **verse 25**, she knows what to do. Another possibility is that circumcision had become distasteful to Moses as a result of his upbringing in the Egyptian court.

■ *We don't know whether Zipporah's words were said in love or anger.* In **verse 25**, she may be speaking in love: *First, you became a bridegroom to me through marriage. Now I've received you again back from death as a bridegroom, this time through blood.* But it's also possible that she's speaking in anger: *I've been forced against my will to circumcise my child so blood has stained our marriage.* The word "touched" could be translated "threw", suggesting an act of anger (though it could also be because speed was of the essence). 18:2 says Moses sent Zipporah away—so this event may have caused a rift in their marriage. The image of a "bridegroom" suggests circumcision mirrors a wedding—like a wedding, circumcision (and baptism in the new covenant) is a sign of covenant love and commitment.

There is a lot we don't know! So, let's focus on what we *do* know.

God has just drawn a line between the firstborn of God and the firstborn of Egypt. Not only that, we are heading towards a point where the firstborn of Egypt will die because of Egypt's refusal to liberate the firstborn of God. So the line that God has drawn is stark. On one side are grace and life. On the other side are judgment and death. There is no middle ground or third option.

Or think of it like this. Circumcision was a sign of God's covenant with his people. Within the covenant there is grace and life. Outside of the covenant are judgment and death. But Moses' own son is on the uncircumcised side of the line. Moses has, it would seem, treated his firstborn son as an Egyptian or a Midianite, rather than as part of the firstborn of God. So Moses himself is acting like an Egyptian or a Midianite, rather than a member of God's covenant people. God's attack on Moses (or Gershom) anticipates his attack on Egypt. The only hope is to cross the line—which is what Zipporah does when she circumcises Gershom (or Moses).

That line runs all the way through human history. And it leads to the day of judgment. On that day, this line will matter more than anything else. On one side will be eternal grace and life. On the other side will be eternal judgment and death. What matters is whether you are part of the covenant people of God. Membership of that covenant is by faith (as it always was), though the sign of covenant membership has changed from circumcision (as it once was) to baptism (as it is now). Baptism has replaced circumcision because the picture of cleansing through shed blood has been fulfilled in the cleansing blood of Jesus. So Paul writes in Colossians 2:11-12:

> "In him you were also circumcised with a circumcision not performed by human hands. Your whole self ruled by the flesh was put off when you were circumcised by Christ, having been buried with him in baptism, in which you were also raised with him…"

Now baptism is the sign that you have crossed the line. Safety is found in Christ, the fulfilment of all God's promises, through blood—just as it was for Moses and his family on their way from Midian to

The line between death and life is stark. Baptism is the sign that you have crossed the line.

Egypt, to announce the nature and promise of God to the people whom he had promised to rescue and bless.

Questions for reflection

1. The signs God has given us of his reality and character are the cross and the empty tomb. How should this shape the way we share our faith with those who don't believe in him?

2. God gives us our mouths and helps us to speak. How will this change the way you think about sharing your faith, and the regularity with which you actually do it?

3. Do you need to be baptised? And if you are baptised, how does reflecting on Gershom's circumcision cause you to appreciate what your baptism signifies?

3. WHEN LIFE GETS HARDER, NOT BETTER

Imagine I'm in bed when, through the haze of sleep, I become aware that someone is banging on my front door. I hear them shouting, "It's John Smith. Let me in." What am I going to do? I'm probably going to shout, in a not particularly friendly tone, "Who are you and why should I let you in?"

But now imagine the banging is accompanied by the shout, "It's Hannah. Let me in." I'm going to race down stairs and open the door straight away—because Hannah is my daughter. I know that name, and that changes everything.

Or imagine that the shout comes, "Open up in the name of the law". Again, I'm going to open that front door quickly—because I recognise an authority that I need to obey.

A name can make all the difference. That's certainly true in the Bible, where names often carry a lot of weight. That's because, first, a name can be a summary of a person's character. We have something similar when we give people nicknames. We talk, for example, about William the Conqueror, Charlemagne (which means "Charles the Great"), and Ivan the Terrible.

Edward I, the thirteenth-century English King, was named Edward by his father after the pious Anglo-Saxon king, Edward the Confessor. His father clearly hoped he would become a godly ruler. He became known as Edward "Longshanks" because he was exceptionally tall ("longshanks" means "long-limbed"). Then he acquired the nickname "Hammer of the Scots", because of his brutal campaigns against the Scots. A name can be a summary of someone's nature, power or character.

Second, a name can be a shorthand for the whole person. Sometimes people say, "Just mention my name". Imagine ringing a restaurant to make a booking, only to be told they're full, and being able to say, "I'm making the reservation in the name of Angelina Jolie". I predict space would suddenly be found. Conversely, if you were making that reservation in the name of "Tim Chester", the extra table would not be found. A name represents a person—and some names (though not others!) can open virtually any door.

The significance of a name

We see the same sort of thing in Exodus 5 – 6. Moses and Aaron arrive in Pharaoh's presence, and tell him, "This is what the Lord, the God of Israel, says: 'Let my people go, so that they may hold a festival to me in the wilderness'" (**5:1**). And Pharaoh responds:

> "Who is the Lord, that I should obey him and let Israel go? I do not
> know the Lord and I will not let Israel go." (**v 2**)

"Lord" is Yahweh or Jehovah—God's personal name, which he revealed to Moses in chapter 3. Pharaoh is saying, *Who is this Yahweh? I've never heard of him. Why should I obey him?* After all, he is Pharaoh, the supreme ruler over a vast empire with almost unprecedented power and wealth. He is not in the habit of letting other people tell him what to do. His is not a question of definition like Moses' in 3:13—this is a declaration of defiance.

Pharaoh's question sets the agenda for the story of the exodus in chapters 5 – 14. Pharaoh asks, "Who is the Lord?" The plagues and the exodus are God's response. This is God showing who he is. *Who is this Yahweh?* asks Pharaoh. And God sends ten plagues, takes the life of every firstborn Egyptian, and parts the Red Sea, in order to declare,

This is who I am. This is what I can do. I am the LORD. I am the Lord over Egypt—even over you, Pharaoh.

The phrase "I am the LORD" doesn't occur in Exodus before Pharaoh's question here. But then it is repeated a dozen or so times throughout the story (**6:2, 6, 7, 8, 29**; 7:5, 17; 10:2; 12:12; 14:4, 18; 15:26; 20:2; 29:46; 31:13). "Who is the LORD, that I should obey him?" Emphatically, God answers again and again, "I am the LORD". After the exodus from Egypt is complete, Israel responds in song and that song begins, "The LORD is a warrior; the LORD is his name" (15:3). "I am the LORD" is a declaration of God's control over people, nature, history and other "gods"—and a declaration that defiance is folly.

A revelation to God's people

7:5 says that the exodus will be a revelation to Egypt: "And the Egyptians will know that I am the LORD when I stretch out my hand against Egypt and bring the Israelites out of it". 9:15-16 goes further. God says to Pharaoh (via Moses), "For by now I could have stretched out my hand and struck you and your people with a plague that would have wiped you off the earth". In other words, *I could have made this much easier for me and much quicker for my people.* "But," he goes on, "I have raised you up for this very purpose, that I might show you my power and that my name might be proclaimed in all the earth". The exodus is a revelation to all the nations.

But it is not just Egypt and the nations who need to know the name of the LORD. The point of chapters 5 – 6 is to set up the exodus as a revelation of God's name to Moses and to Israel—to God's own people. God's people need to know who the LORD is.

As we've seen, in chapter 3 Moses said to God, "Suppose I go to the Israelites and say to them, 'The God of your fathers has sent me to you,' and they ask me, 'What is his name?' Then what shall I tell them?" (3:13). Because in the Bible someone's name represents them, "What is his name?" is a way of asking, *Who is this God, that we can trust him?* After 400 years the kings of Egypt had forgotten

Joseph—he "meant nothing" to them (1:8). But it seems that those same 400 years have caused the people of Israel to have forgotten God. To them, God means nothing.

Now, as Moses again questions God in **5:22-23**, God responds: "Now you will see what I will do to Pharaoh" (**6:1**). *You will see.* This is an act of revelation to Moses and God's people. God's people need to know who the Lord is. And that's why things get harder before they get better. That's why the events of chapter 5 unfold as they do.

Harder, not better

At first, Moses and Aaron are well received by Israel (4:29-31). Everyone is excited about what God is going to do. But instead of getting better, things get harder. Moses and Aaron go to Pharaoh and tell him to let the Israelites hold a festival in the wilderness (**5:1**). Pharaoh refuses. Moses and Aaron seem thrown by this. Their demand becomes a plea in **verse 3**. But Pharaoh refuses any letup to their work (**v 4**). Instead, he makes their task harder. Now the Israelites must collect their own straw for bricks without any change in the quota of bricks they must produce (**v 6-9**). Bricks without straw is a shrewd move designed to divide the Israelites from their leader, Moses.

The orders go down the chain of command—from Pharaoh, to the Egyptian slave drivers, to the Israelites overseers (**v 10-14**). And then the complaints come up the chain of command (**v 15-16**). But Pharaoh is unmoved: "Lazy, that's what you are—lazy! That is why you keep saying, 'Let us go and sacrifice to the Lord.' Now get to work. You will not be given any straw, yet you must produce your full quota of bricks" (**v 17-18**). This is typical of tyrants from leaders of empires to modern gangmasters and workplace bullies: *Get to work. Meet your quota. The fault is yours. Your sufferings are deserved.* "Make the work harder," says Pharaoh (**v 9**). Instead of getting better, things get harder.

Pharaoh versus the Lord

All the time, God is setting up the showdown that will reveal his name. In **verse 9**, Pharaoh portrays God as a liar. God has promised liberation, but Pharaoh says this is false hope. He says, "Make the work harder … so that they keep working and pay no attention to lies". The message that God will deliver his people is a lie, says Pharaoh. It's a lie because Pharaoh reigns in Egypt. This is his empire and his word is law. Who is the Lord, compared with the mighty Pharaoh?

The chapter opened with Moses and Aaron saying to Pharaoh, "This is what the Lord, the God of Israel, says: 'Let my people go'" (**5:1**; see also 4:22-23). In **5:10**, the slave drivers and the overseers go to the people and say, "This is what Pharaoh says …" So, "This is what the Lord … says" and, "This is what Pharaoh says" are pitted against each other—God's word and his claim to rule are up against Pharaoh's word and his rule.

God says Israel should rest more (they should have a three-day break to worship him). Pharaoh says Israel should work more. The words "work" and "worship" are the same in these chapters. We have something similar with the English word "service". To serve is to work, but we also talk about a "church service". So the words translated "work" in **5:9** and **11**, "slave" in **verse 6**, "working" in verse 9 or "servants" in **verses 15-16** are actually the same word (or have the same root) as the word "worship" in 4:23. There, God says to Pharaoh (via Moses): "Let my son go, so that he may serve/worship me". It's the word used to describe Israel's service of God, especially through the worship in the **tabernacle** (12:25-26; 13:5; 27:19; 30:16; 35:24; 36:1, 3, 5; 39:32, 42).

The point is this: both God and Pharaoh think Israel should work, serve, worship. The issue is this: who will they serve? And what will that experience of service be like for them?

One other interesting feature of **5:1** is the question: Why does Moses ask for a festival in the wilderness? God has promised full liberation from Egyptian slavery (3:10). Is this a bit underhand of Moses—a sneaky way of escaping? I think not—I think Pharaoh knows what this request involves. It reflects a typical Near-Eastern way of making a request and entering into a bargain. An initial demand is made which is then increased—but the intent is clear. More significantly, this goes to the heart of the issue. Who is Israel's master? To whom does Israel belong? Three times in **5:15-16**, the Israelites describes themselves to Pharaoh as "your servants" or "your worshippers". That is how they see themselves.

So when, in **6:1**, God replies to Pharaoh's defiance with the statement, "You will see what I will do to Pharaoh", the battle lines are drawn. God and Pharaoh are on a collision course. This conflict is not so much between Egypt and Israel as between Pharaoh and the LORD, with Israel as the prize.

And we should not miss the point for us. Whoever you ultimately work for is the person you ultimately worship. I don't mean you worship your boss (though you might). Ultimately, who are you trying to please through your work? Whose approval are you seeking to gain, or whose disapproval are you desperately working not to lose? Your boss's? Your spouse's? Your friends'? Your parents'? Your own? Or God's? Think about who you fear when you fail. Think about who you're tempted to lie or exaggerate to in order to impress. Think about whose disapproval makes you feel crushed. That will indicate who you truly worship.

Like Pharaoh, like Israel

The surprise in chapter 5 is not Pharaoh's negative response—God had told Moses, "I know that the king of Egypt will not let you go unless a mighty hand compels him" (3:19). No, the surprise, and the disappointment, is Israel's response. If you don't know the LORD, then you won't trust the LORD when you cannot work out what he is doing, when his plans don't match with yours. Instead, you'll complain. That's what the Israelite overseers do when they find Moses and Aaron (**5:19-20**): "May the LORD look upon you and judge you! You have made us obnoxious to Pharaoh and his officials and have put a sword in their hand to kill us" (**v 21**). And Moses himself complains to God, "Why have you brought trouble on this people? Is this why you sent me? Ever since I went to Pharaoh to speak in your name, he has brought trouble upon this people, and you have not rescued your people at all" (**v 22-23**). What does God's name mean? *God's name means trouble*, says Moses. Israel have been in Egypt too long; and while Pharaoh does not see why he should obey the LORD, Israel do not see that they can trust the LORD.

The delay in the fulfilment of God's promises reveals his people's hearts. When they were promised blessing, they were excited. But when they "realised they were in trouble", they started to complain about God (**v 19**). The delay tests them; their complaining displays that they, too, do not know the LORD.

> The delay in the fulfilment of God's promises reveals his people's hearts.

This is a challenge for me, and for you. Does this describe you in any way? When you get what you want you're a passionate Christian. But when you don't get what you want, you complain. When God does not do what you want, when you want, how you want—when you realise you are in trouble in some way—you criticise God. When that happens, the true affections of your heart are revealed—that you love the blessings of Christ more than you love Christ himself. You trust him when he gives you what you want. But you don't trust him when trouble comes. Which means you don't trust him at all. When that happens, lift your eyes to the cross. See God working good from evil. And see his love and commitment to you as he gives you his only Son. As you do that, your affections will be rearranged, so that you love him, and trust him, and live with gratitude and not complaint, even in the hard times.

Questions for reflection

1. When you obey God and things get harder, not better, how do you tend to react? What does this suggest about your affections?

2. "Think about who you fear when you fail. Think about who you're tempted to lie or exaggerate to in order to impress. Think about whose disapproval makes you feel crushed. That will indicate who you truly worship." Think about these things now—what do they indicate?

3. How does the cross cause you to love Christ, and worship him? How will you lift your eyes to the cross next time you are tempted to worship someone else; and next time things get harder, not better?

PART TWO

But God...

Things have got harder for God's people—so that God can reveal his name, his character and his power to them. God's people need to know who the LORD is. Every day spent gathering straw builds up more tension, so that the revelation of God's name when it comes will be crystal clear.

And so we come to God's response in **6:2-8**. At the beginning, in the middle and at the end of this speech are the words "I am the LORD"—that is what God reminds Moses of (**v 2**), what Moses is to start with when he addresses the Israelites (**v 6**), and what he is to end with (**v 8**). But perhaps the key phrase is **verse 7**: "Then you will know that I am the LORD your God, who brought you out from under the **yoke** of the Egyptians."

So far, so simple: but God also says in **verse 3** that "I appeared to Abraham, to Isaac and to Jacob as God Almighty, but by my name the LORD I did not make myself known to them". So what God said to Abraham when he appeared to him in Genesis 17:1 was: "I am God Almighty." Exodus **6:3** suggests that God has previously revealed himself through more **generic** terms like *Elohim* ("God" or "gods") or *El-Shaddai* ("God Almighty"), but that this is the first time he has revealed his personal name, *Yahweh*. Just as I am a man called Tim, he is a God called Yahweh.

But the problem with this understanding of **verse 3** is that the word Yahweh is in fact used in Genesis (see, for example, Genesis 2:4, 5, 7, 8, 9, 15, 16, 18, 19, 21, 22). It could be that the writer of Genesis is reading back into the narrative the name he now knows for God, in just the same way that we would not think it strange for a biographer of Muhammad Ali to refer to him as "Ali" throughout his childhood, even though he only changed his name from Cassius Clay at the age of 22. But a better explanation is this: that the term "Yahweh" was known before, but God is about to give it a new level of meaning through the exodus. The exodus is going to be a revelation of God's character. So, what are we going to see?

The Lord who keeps his promises

The first look is a look back. God made promises to Abraham, Isaac and Jacob—and he will keep those promises. "I am the Lord. I … established my covenant … I have remembered my covenant" (Exodus **6:2-5**). In **5:15**, Israel cried out to Pharaoh, but Pharaoh refused to listen. The Lord is different—he has heard their groaning (2:23-25; 3:7-9). He hears and he remembers—he will act to keep his covenant. (Again, we need to underline that God remembering does not mean that the state of his people or his promises to them had previously slipped his mind. In a similar way, when Jeremiah 31:34 promises that God will remember our sins no more, it doesn't mean God will suffer from amnesia. Jeremiah means God will not act on our sins.) What will be revealed in the exodus is that God keeps his promises—and so we can trust those promises.

The Lord who rules his world

"I am the Lord, and I will bring you out from under the yoke of the Egyptians. I will free you from being slaves to them, and I will redeem you with an outstretched arm and with mighty acts of judgment" (Exodus **6:6**). Chapter 5 has set up what is about to happen as a showdown between Pharaoh and God. And what we will see in the exodus is that God reigns. Put simply, the Lord wins. The rule of the most powerful ruler that the world has ever seen will be broken, because God will stretch out his arm. It's great picture of his power—his arm reaches out to accomplish whatever he purposes. Just as you might stretch out your arm over the dinner table to pick up the salt, so God stretches out his arm to shake up Egypt. His acts of judgment are mighty. We are going to see in the exodus that God is powerful;

he is sovereign; he reigns in his world—so we can trust, and should tremble at, his power.

The LORD who redeems his people

6:6 is one of the first times the word "redeem" is used in the Bible story (in addition to Genesis 48:16, see ESV). It is the word *gā'al*. The **subject** of this verb is a *gō'ēl*: a redeemer. When God's people reached the land, a *gō'ēl* was the kinsman responsible for avenging a murdered relative, redeeming an enslaved relative or providing an heir for a deceased relative. They were a close relative who acted as avenger, protector and provider even if that involved personal loss (Leviticus 25:47-59; Ruth 3:9, 4:1-10). Yahweh has already described himself as Israel's father (Exodus 4:22), their kinsman. **6:6** tells us that he is the kinsman-redeemer of his people. He will act as Israel's avenger, protector and provider—even when that involves personal loss.

But God doesn't just redeem from slavery. He redeems Israel so that they will be his people. Later, Israel will sing to God of how "In your unfailing love you will lead the people you have redeemed. In your strength you will guide them to your holy dwelling" (15:13). Exodus is the story of redemption from Egypt for life in the presence of God (the meeting with God at Sinai and the construction of the tabernacle).

In chapter 6, God continues, "I will take you as my own people, and I will be your God ... I am the LORD" (**6:7-8**). This is the first time this phrase is used in the Bible—but it is going to recur throughout the Bible story. In fact, it is a kind of refrain for the whole Bible. It keeps coming up until we see John's vision of the new creation in Revelation 21:3: "And I heard a loud voice from the throne saying, 'Look! God's dwelling-place is now among the people, and he will dwell with them. They will be his people, and God himself will be with them and be their God.'"

This speech here in Exodus **6:6-8** is a key statement of intent for the whole Bible story—the great history of God redeeming us from slavery to sin and death (**v 6**) so that we might be his people (**v 7**) living in his new world (**v 8**). He redeems us to be his people—so we can trust him to love, lead and care for us.

Israel, it seems, are slumped so deep in discouragement that they are unmoved by this revelation of the Lord's name and purposes (**v 9**). But, as we saw in chapter 3, the ultimate revelation of God's name will be in the exodus itself. So the Lord moves events towards the confrontation that will reveal his power, by again sending Moses to Pharaoh (**6:10-11**).

True Israelites

6:30 repeats **verse 12**—so **verses 13-29** are an aside from the story. Why? In between these two statements, we find an extract from a genealogy authenticating Moses and Aaron as true Israelites. It starts with three sons of Jacob: Reuben (the firstborn, which may link back to 4:21-26), Simeon and Levi. Levi's sons are then the focus, to show the lineage of Moses and Aaron. The text is emphatic: "It was this Aaron and Moses to whom the Lord said, 'Bring the Israelites out of Egypt by their divisions'" (**6:26**).

Why does this need to be here? Remember that Moses has appeared out of the desert, claiming to be the man called by God to lead his people. Aaron has been appointed as his spokesman. But now the people have begun to doubt them. Perhaps people remember Moses' upbringing in the Pharaoh's court, his brief appearance at their workplace, and his long spell in Midian—and doubt his allegiance, or even his heritage. So now there is every reason to demonstrate that they are authentic members of God's people.

Knowing God

I was talking to the wife of a couple who were about to go as missionaries to mainland Europe. She told me with tears of her fears about going. She's worried about taking her young children to a new country. Will she cope? Will her children cope? Will she be desperate to come home after a few months? I was very struck by something she said:

"I imagine an Israelite mother leading her small children out of Egypt. She must have been full of doubt. Was this a good idea— wandering off into the desert with small children? Who is the LORD? Can they trust him? And then they pass through the sea with the walls of water on either side."

And then she added:

"This is what gives me the confidence to go."

The exodus is the revelation of God's name to God's people. He is the LORD who keeps his promises (**6:4-5**), rules his world (**v 6**) and loves his people (**v 6-8**).

I was talking to a young father who is planning to move to the Middle East to plant a church. It's easy to think of missionaries as having some kind of special calling that somehow makes it easy for them. But it's not true. As we prayed together, he prayed, "I'm such a coward. I'm terrified for my family." I found it so challenging. I realised, "This man is no different to me in his fears". But perhaps he, and the woman on her way to the missionfield in Europe, are different to me in this: they know—really trust—that God is the LORD, and that he keeps his promises, rules his world and redeems his people.

If you and I are to follow God—whether that takes us to the Middle East, mainland Europe, or to a nearby school, coffee shop, factory or office—then we must know who he is. And when we know who he is, then we see that we must follow him. Every new day is a day when you can live trusting God and obeying God. You will only do that if you know he is the LORD; and if you know he is the LORD, then you will do that.

You may have become a Christian fairly recently and, instead of getting better, life has got harder. Or your life may not have worked out the way you hoped—your dreams remain mere dreams. So now you complain, just like Moses and the Israelites. What did God say to them? "You will see what I will do ... I am the LORD" (**v 1-2**). And what does

God say to you today? Something *better: You have seen what I have done.* You have seen it in the exodus (or you will as you continue reading). And supremely, you have seen it in the cross and resurrection.

There, you have seen that he is the LORD who keeps his promises: "For no matter how many promises God has made, they are 'Yes' in Christ" (2 Corinthians 1:20). When you're wondering what God is doing, when you doubt his kindness, when you're struggling to trust him, when life gets harder rather than better, look to the wooden cross and the empty tomb. See how God keeps his promises.

You have seen that he is the LORD, who rules his world. It didn't look like that at the cross. It looked like Satan ruled or that chaos won or that evil people triumphed. But in fact "they did what [God's] power and will had decided beforehand should happen" (Acts 4:28). God used the defeat and weakness and folly of the cross to bring salvation. When you're wondering what God is doing, when you doubt his kindness, when you're struggling to trust him: when life gets harder rather than better, look to the cross. See how God brings triumph from defeat.

You have seen that he is the LORD who redeems his people from death, to give them life: "He has rescued us from the dominion of darkness and brought us into the kingdom of the Son he loves, in whom we have redemption" (Colossians 1:13-14). "This is love: not that we loved God, but that he loved us and sent his Son as an **atoning** sacrifice for our sins" (1 John 4:10). It's at the cross that our redemption is secured—at the cross that his loving care is written out in large letters across the canvas of history. God had promised, "I will redeem you with an outstretched arm and with mighty acts of judgment" (Exodus **6:6**). Ultimately, that promise found its

> If you are struggling to obey God, you don't need more willpower. You need to know God more.

fulfilment as Jesus died. The arms of God were both outstretched, on a cross. There was a mighty act of judgment—but the judgment fell not on God's enemies, but on God himself in the person of his Son. Jesus redeems us to be God's people by dying for us. When you're wondering what God is doing, when you doubt his kindness, when you're struggling to trust him, when life gets harder rather than better—look to the cross. See how God himself bears his own judgment out of love for you, to redeem you.

If you're struggling to obey God, you don't need more willpower. You need to know God more. The book of Exodus is a revelation of the name of God—of the character of God—so that we might know him better. So pray as you read it. Delve deep into its pages—not just to get more information, but so you might encounter God. Seek the LORD that you might know him better and so serve him better, both when life gets better and when life gets harder. He is the LORD who keeps his promises, rules his world and redeems his people.

Questions for reflection

1. What do we lose if we think only about what God has redeemed us *from*, and never remember what he has redeemed us *for*?

2. Is there a Christian you know who is slumped in discouragement? How could you remind them who God is, in a way that might both comfort them and challenge them?

3. Identify a way in which you currently feel that God has let you down, or that you keep letting God down. Then re-read the last section, entitled "Knowing God". How do you need to pray that these truths will change the way you feel and the way you live?

4. GOD V PHARAOH

Sometimes we don't know what to do and would like someone just to tell us what to do. But most of the time, we don't like to be bossed about. "I'm my own man or woman," we say. "No one tells me what to do." "You're not the boss of me." And if we don't say these things because we are too polite or don't want to look bad, then we still think them. We resist, or resent, being told what to do.

So how do you react when God tells you what to do? Why should you obey him? Do you resist or resent… or obey without grumble or grudge?

Who is the LORD?

Pharaoh was the most powerful man in the world. No one told him what to do. He was the one who gave the orders. Then Moses and Aaron turn up. "This is what the LORD, the God of Israel, says: 'Let my people go'" (5:1). Pharaoh replies, "Who is the LORD, that I should obey him and let Israel go? I do not know the LORD and I will not let Israel go" (v 2).

"Who is the LORD, that I should obey him?" Authority is tied to the identity of the person making a command. We obey when we recognise a higher authority. We obey gladly when we recognise a higher, trustworthy and good authority. In fact, that's Pharaoh's point. Slaves obey overseers, overseers obey foremen, foremen obey Pharaoh. There's a chain of command and Pharaoh is at the top— not the Hebrew slaves. So Pharaoh's question is really: *What gives this God of slaves a right to issue commands to me, the king of Egypt, a living deity?*

And ultimately it is God, not Moses, that Pharaoh is taking on. In 6:30, Moses asks God, "Why would Pharaoh listen to me?" and God replies, "I have made you like God to Pharaoh" (**7:1**). The issue is not whether Pharaoh will listen to Moses, but whether Pharaoh will listen to God. God's answer may also be another echo of creation; Adam was created in God's image, to be like God, as God's representative on earth. Adam failed to live in that image, to act like God, and to rule as God's representative. Now Moses is "like God". The salvation pictured in the exodus and fulfilled in Christ restores humanity to its God-imaging rule over creation (Hebrews 2:5-9).

But Pharaoh will not listen: "Pharaoh's heart became hard and he would not listen to them, just as the LORD had said" (Exodus **7:13**).

"He would not listen." We tend to use this as a description of children, but in fact it could be a description of our culture. People today will not listen to the word of God. Christians sometimes talk about turning a conversation towards spiritual things as we attempt to share the good news. But the reality is that non-Christians are far more adept at turning a conversation away from spiritual issues. Underlying this is Pharaoh's question: "Who is the LORD, that I should obey him?" Why should I let God meddle in my affairs? Why should I let someone else have the final say in my life? And Christians are not immune. We try to limit our obedience. Instead of throwing ourselves, body and soul, into God's service, we try to limit what we do. "What's the least I can get away with?" "How far do I have to I go?" "Why should I deny my feelings?"

So why should we obey? That's the question answered by the ten plagues.

God is not surprised by Pharaoh's refusal to listen (**v 2-4**). He predicted it (3:19), and now he predicts it will continue: "He will not listen to you. Then I will lay my hand on Egypt and with mighty acts of judgment I will bring out my divisions, my people the Israelites. And the Egyptians will know that I am the LORD when I stretch out my hand against Egypt and bring the Israelites out of it" (**7:4-5**).

The purpose of the plagues is that Egypt might know that "I am the LORD". God's identity and authority will be revealed through the words of two 80-something-year-olds (**v 6-7**) and the mighty deeds of the eternal God.

It's worth asking the question: Why the first nine plagues? The tenth plague was the one that made the difference and saw God's people finally allowed to go. Why not skip straight to the tenth? Why all the bother and suffering of the first nine? The answer comes in **9:15-16**, in the middle of the plague stories: "For by now I could have stretched out my hand and struck you and your people with a plague that would have wiped you off the earth," God tells Moses to inform Pharaoh. "But I have raised you up for this very purpose, that I might show you my power and that my name might be proclaimed in all the earth." God could have liberated his people with just one plague. But the ten plagues are a demonstration of his power. In this sense, they are missional. Their aim is that God's name might be proclaimed in all the earth.

Who hardened Pharaoh's heart?

This is the reason behind the mysterious hardening of Pharaoh's heart. Three times we're told that Pharaoh's heart "became hard", "was hard" and "was unyielding" (**7:22; 8:19; 9:7**). Three times we're told that Pharaoh "hardened his heart" (**8:15, 32; 9:34**). There is a kind of madness to Pharaoh's actions. Calamity after calamity is inflicted on Egypt, but he refuses to submit. At one point his officials beg him to relent (**10:7**)—but he keeps on inviting more suffering on his country. He cannot concede because his pride is at stake. It's insane. After the fourth, eighth and ninth plagues Pharaoh attempts to negotiate with Moses. He offers some concessions to Moses' request, but will not grant it in full (**8:25-28; 10:8-11, 24-28**). After the seventh plague he relents, but then changes his mind again (**9:27-35**).

Eventually, in **10:28**, Pharaoh says to Moses, "Get out of my sight! Make sure you do not appear before me again! The day you see my face you will die." Remember, God had said he would make Moses "like God to Pharaoh" (**7:1**). So Pharaoh is in effect banishing God. And God gives him what he wants. "'Just as you say,' Moses replied. 'I will never appear before you again.'" (**10:29**). The tragedy is that Moses is Pharaoh's only hope. This is God's judgment: to give us what we want, but in so doing to remove from us any hope. We ask God's servant Jesus to get out and stay out of our lives, and we are given what we have asked for—for ever.

Pharaoh is a case study in the deceit of sin. It's like a slow-motion car crash that allows us to see the tragedy unfold. We want to step in to make it stop. But in the real-time action of our own lives, we ourselves too often get caught up in the insanity of sin. Hebrews 3:13 says, "Encourage one another daily, as long as it is called 'Today', so that none of you may be hardened by sin's deceitfulness". The hardening of our hearts overthrows reason. We find excuses for our sinful and proud desires. We find reasons for doing what we want to do. When it all unravels, we wade further into sin, rather than accepting our terrible mistake and backing away from it. We're like Shakespeare's Macbeth, who, having murdered his king, is confronted with the choice of admitting his actions or murdering again, and concludes:

> "I am in blood stepped in so far that should I wade no more, Returning were as tedious as go o'er." (Act 3)

By nature, we go on, deeper and deeper. That is what Pharaoh did. And that is why we need others to encourage us to fight sin, and expose for us the deceit of sin when we cannot see it for ourselves.

But there is more going on than this. Remember that God's purpose in the nine plagues is to reveal his name. God introduces them with

> Pharaoh is a case study in the deceit of sin. He goes on, deeper and deeper.

these words: "I will harden Pharaoh's heart, and though I multiply my signs and wonders in Egypt, he will not listen to you" (Exodus **7:3-4**). So after the sixth, eighth, ninth and tenth plagues, we're told that "the LORD hardened Pharaoh's heart" (**9:12; 10:20, 27; 11:10**). **11:9-10** is a summary statement: "The LORD had said to Moses, 'Pharaoh will refuse to listen to you—so that my wonders may be multiplied in Egypt.' Moses and Aaron performed all these wonders before Pharaoh, but the LORD hardened Pharaoh's heart, and he would not let the Israelites go out of his country."

Pharaoh refuses to listen because Pharaoh hardens his heart. But it is also true that Pharaoh refuses to listen because the LORD hardens Pharaoh's heart. We have to take both of these perspectives seriously. Pharaoh determines Pharaoh's actions, and God determines his actions. To put it another way, Pharaoh freely chooses to do what God had freely chosen that he would do.

What is clear is that God planned ten plagues so he could display his power and glory. That's why he hardened Pharaoh's heart. The workings of this are mysterious. But its purpose is clear.

- "The Egyptians will know that I am the LORD when I stretch out my hand against Egypt and bring the Israelites out of it." (**7:5**)

- "By this you will know that I am the LORD: with the staff that is in my hand I will strike the water of the Nile, and it will be changed into blood." (**v 17**)

- "It will be as you say, so that you may know there is no one like the LORD our God." (**8:10**)

- "I will send the full force of my plagues against you and against your officials and your people, so you may know that there is no one like me in all the earth." (**9:14**)

- "I have raised you up for this very purpose, that I might show you my power and that my name might be proclaimed in all the earth." (**9:16**)

■ "Then the Lord said to Moses, 'Go to Pharaoh, for I have hardened his heart and the hearts of his officials so that I may perform these signs of mine among them that you may tell your children and grandchildren how I dealt harshly with the Egyptians and how I performed my signs among them, and that you may know that I am the Lord.'" (**10:1-2**)

The plagues are an act of revelation. God sends them so that people might know that he is the Lord, that there is no one else like him, and that his name might be revealed in all the earth.

And it seems that people did come to know this, even while Pharaoh remained blind to it. Exodus 12:38 tells us a mixed group left Egypt. Since no other nations other than Israel and Egypt are mentioned in the narrative, it seems that this group included Egyptians—in which case, the plagues had acted for salvation, as well as judgment,

	Passage	Warning	Origin
1. Blood	7:14-24	Yes	
2. Frogs	7:25 – 8:15	Yes	Water
3. Gnats	8:16-19	None	Land
4. Flies	8:20-32	Yes	
5. Livestock	9:1-7	Yes	
6. Boils	9:8-12	None	Soot
7. Hail	9:13-35	Yes	Sky
8. Locusts	10:1-20	Yes	Wind
9. Darkness	10:21-29	None	Sky
10. Death	11:1-10	Yes	

as they revealed to all the great, uncompromising, unchangeable truth: "I am the LORD".

The plagues

In **7:14**, the plagues begin. They take us through to 12:30. And setting them out in a table (see below) helps us see the progression in terms of the seriousness of the plagues and of the response of the people—and the ongoing hardness of Pharaoh's heart.

Remember, what is most important about the ten plagues is what they reveal about the God who sent them. There are four main truths the plagues teach us about him—we'll cover one in this part, and the other three in the next.

Egyptian court	Distinction for Israel?	Pharaoh's heart
Replicate sign		Became hard
Replicate sign		Hardened by Pharaoh
Fail to replicate sign		Was hard
	Yes	Hardened by Pharaoh
	Yes	Was unyielding
Can't stand before Moses		Hardened by the LORD
Harden their hearts	Yes	Hardened by Pharaoh
Ask Pharaoh to submit		Hardened by the LORD
	Yes	Hardened by the LORD
Regard Moses highly	Yes	Hardened by the LORD

The Lᴏʀᴅ is the true God

In one sense, Pharaoh was ahead of his time—he was a thoroughly **postmodern** man. He wasn't an atheist. He believed in a god. Indeed he believed in many gods: sun gods, river gods, harvest gods. Pharaoh himself was seen as a son of the gods. His issue was not: "There is no God". His issue was: "Why should I listen to your God when I've got gods of my own?" As far as Pharaoh is concerned, the Lᴏʀᴅ is simply a local deity. Why should he lose three days' labour at the request of one god among many?

Pharaoh was not offended by the Israelites having their own God, choosing their own religion, or developing their own spirituality. What he took offence at was the suggestion that the God of Israel might have a claim on him. *Don't impose your beliefs on me*, he was saying. In the same way, the reaction of our culture to the claims of Jesus, especially his claim to be unique, is, *Who is the Lord Jesus, that I should obey him?* They replace the **objective** reality of God with a **subjective** choice.

The plagues are God's answer to this way of thinking. God is declaring that he is the only true God and the only relevant God. He is the only God who is worth obeying. Through the plagues, God is saying, "There is no one like the Lᴏʀᴅ our God" (**8:10**). God is going head to head with Pharaoh and Egypt's gods. It is God versus gods. And in the plagues, "the Lᴏʀᴅ … brought judgment on their gods" (Numbers 33:4).

The nine plagues systematically undermine Egypt's pluralist claims. They are a lecture against religious pluralism—the belief that all religions are valid—and personal autonomy—the belief that I have the right to live how I like. It is a curriculum with ten unforgettable lessons. And the message is clear: there is only one God.

The main curriculum is previewed in an introductory unit. In Exodus **7:10**, Aaron's staff turns into a snake, just as God had promised him (**v 8-9**). No problem for Pharaoh—the Egyptian sorcerers can replicate this "trick" (**v 11-12**). But then Moses and Aaron's snake eats their snakes (**v 12**). Snakes were a fundamental part of Egyptian religion. In their belief system, the world was created by the sun-god, who took the form of a snake. So more is happening here than one supernaturally created snake eating another. In this prelude to the plagues—the main event—Egypt's gods are destroyed by God.

This pattern continues. Many of the plagues are attacks on specific Egyptian gods. Hapi, the god of fertility, was closely associated with the Nile. Without the River Nile were was no fertility in Egypt—there was no Egypt. But the LORD turns the Nile to blood (**7:19-21**). It may be that Pharaoh had come to the Nile in the morning to make an offering to Hapi. Heqt or Heket, another fertility goddess, had the head of a frog—but the frogs are the LORD's to command (**8:1-6**). The bull was another symbol of fertility, with shrines across Egypt. The bull-god Apis was worshipped at Memphis and the bull-god Mnevis was worshipped at Heliopolis, while Hathor, the goddess of love, had the head of a cow. None of them could resist the plague on the livestock (**9:1-7**). Sekhmet, the lion-headed goddess of plagues, might have been expected to heal the epidemic of boils (**v 8-11**). Nut, the sky goddess, could not prevent the plague of hail (**v 13-26**), nor stop the east wind which brought the locusts (**10:12-15**). Each day Re, the sun-god, was thought to sail through the celestial sea in a boat. Then at night he would descend into the netherworld before rising victorious again with the dawn. But during the ninth plague (**10:21-23**) he did not rise. Those three days of darkness were a clear sign that he had been defeated.

> Before Israel's God, all other gods are powerless, and all pretenders are defeated.

Before Israel's God—our God—all other gods are powerless, all pretenders are defeated, all blasphemers are silenced.

It is interesting to track the reaction of the Egyptian court. The Egyptian magicians are able to replicate the first two plagues (**7:22; 8:7**).

But they cannot replicate the third plague (**v 18**), and after the third plague they no longer try. "This is the finger of God," they conclude (**v 19**). In **9:11**, the magicians cannot stand before Moses because of their boils. By the eighth plague, Pharaoh's officials are begging him to concede defeat (**10:7**). By **11:3**, Moses was "highly regarded" in Egypt. The plagues dismantle the physical foundations of Egypt and so they explode the religious foundations of Egypt. There is only one God—the God of Israel.

Questions for reflection

1. Do you ever find yourself thinking, in effect, "Who is the LORD, that I should obey him"? When, and with what consequences?

2. Pharaoh is a case study in sin's deceit. Do you recognise the same deceit working in your life in some way? Do you need to get help, and what steps will you take to get it?

3. "Before our God, all other gods are powerless, all pretenders are defeated, all blasphemers are silenced." How will you live in light of this truth today?

PART TWO

The Lord is the mighty Creator

As he unleashes each plague, the Lord is marshalling the powers of creation against Pharaoh, using "weapons" that only the Creator can use. The Lord is unique because he is the Creator.

Sometimes we're told the source of the plague: the frogs come from the waters (**8:6**), the gnats from the dust of the ground (**v 16-17**), and the hail and the darkness from the sky (**9:22-23; 10:21-22**). In **10:21**, for example, the Lord says to Moses, "Stretch out your hand towards the sky so that darkness spreads over Egypt". The idea is that God deploys all of creation—land, sea and sky. From the waters come frogs. From the ground come gnats. From the air come flies. All of creation is mobilised against Pharaoh. In the end, even light and life are extinguished as we move from frogs in the bed to bodies in the street.

Some of the plagues may have been natural phenomena. There may even have been a knock-on effect with the earlier plagues. The Nile is polluted, which sends the frogs into the towns. The frogs die in huge numbers, which brings gnats and flies. These then produce an epidemic of disease, which kills the livestock and spreads boils among humans.

But the timing of the plagues leaves no room for doubt that this is God's doing. Most of the plagues are announced in advance, although every third plague (the third, sixth and ninth) comes without warning. With every third plague (this time the first, fourth and seventh), we are told that Moses appears to Pharaoh in the morning (**7:15; 8:20; 9:13**). Four of the plagues mention "tomorrow" as a start or stop time. Moses grants Pharaoh "the honour" of setting a time for the end of the second plague (**8:9-10**), while Moses himself sets the time of the end of the fourth plague (**v 29**). With the fifth and seventh plagues, the focus shifts. Now the Lord sets the time, and it is a start time (**9:5, 18; 11:4**). With the final plague, the Lord's appointed start time is moved forward to midnight (**11:4**). Aaron is said to be the agent of the first three plagues (**7:19; 8:5, 16-17**) and

Moses is the agent of the sixth to ninth plagues (**9:8, 22-24; 10:13, 21-22**). But God is the direct agent of the fourth, fifth and tenth plagues (**8:24; 9:6; 11:4**). The point is that these plagues did not just happen. They happened in God's timing and at God's instigation, through God's chosen messengers.

Divine sovereignty over these plagues is reinforced after the fourth plague with the introduction of a distinction for God's people (**8:22-23; 9:4, 26; 10:23**; 12:12-13). The Israelites had experienced the first plagues alongside the Egyptians, for often living in a world under God's judgment means God's people suffer alongside those who are rejecting him. But God protects his people from the hail, the darkness and the death. We are left in no doubt. The LORD is the Creator of all the earth and all creation is in his power.

The LORD is the holy Judge

In **9:8**, the boils come from "soot from a furnace"—probably a brick kiln. So the source of Israel's oppression becomes the source of Egypt's judgment. The punishment fits the crime.

In chapter 1, the Hebrews filled the land in fulfilment of God's command in Genesis 1 to fill the earth. But Pharaoh tried to stop this creative energy, becoming a kind of anti-creator. So now, through the plagues, God unravels creation. He sends it into reverse. Water no longer brings life. Animals no longer serve human beings—instead they invade like armies. Light returns to darkness and life to the dust. Creation is heading back into its dark and chaotic state (Genesis 1:2). Everything falls apart. Egypt is unmade. All around Pharaoh the very fabric of his world is falling apart, disintegrating into chaos, darkness and death.

Something similar happens to us. We were made to live in obedience to God and in dependence on him. But Romans 1:18-32 says we have exchanged the truth about God for a lie and worshipped created things rather than the Creator. And when we reject God, we are unmade. Our psychological and physical lives become disordered. The result is emotional darkness, mental breakdown, relational conflict and physical addictions. Sickness has entered the world and we are all heading for death, the ultimate act of un-creation. Egypt is a picture of life in melt-down under God's judgment.

The plagues are a pointer to something bigger and more terrible. God told Pharaoh his judgment would come and it did. And God has told all humanity that judgment is coming. The plagues are a sign that God's coming judgment is real.

The LORD is the gracious Saviour

As creation unravels around Pharaoh, God makes an exception for his people, as we've seen. In the introduction to the fourth plague, he says, "But on that day I will deal differently with the land of Goshen, where my people live; no swarms of flies will be there, so that you will know that I, the LORD, am in this land. I will make a distinction between my people and your people" (Exodus **8:22-23**). This distinction is re-stated with the fifth, seventh, ninth and tenth plagues.

Why? What made them different? Were their desires purer, or their efforts more righteous?

In Romans 9:15-18 Paul comments on this episode. He takes seri-ously the hardening of Pharaoh's heart by God. Quoting Exodus 33:19 and **9:16**, he says:

"For [God] says to Moses, 'I will have mercy on whom I have mercy, and I will have compassion on whom I have compassion.' It does not, therefore, depend on human desire or effort, but on God's mercy. For the Scripture says to Pharaoh: 'I raised you up for this very purpose, that I might display my power in you and that my name might be proclaimed in all the earth.' Therefore God has mercy on whom he wants to have mercy, and he hard-ens whom he wants to harden.'"

Paul conclusion is this: salvation does not depend on human desire or effort. We do not choose to pursue God. God first pursues us. If it were left to us, then we would never turn to God in faith and repentance. So why does God harden the hearts of some or leave them in their hardened state? It is so none of us can ever assume our salvation depends on our desires or our effort:

"What if God, although choosing to show his wrath and make his power known, bore with great patience the objects of his wrath—prepared for destruction? What if he did this to make the riches of his glory known to the objects of his mercy, whom he prepared in advance for glory—even us, whom he also called, not only from the Jews but also from the Gentiles?" (Romans 9:22-24)

There is a reason why we are allowed to see the hardening of Pharaoh's heart. There is a reason why we see people refusing to turn to Christ. It is, says Paul in Romans 9:23, so we might see in utter clarity the riches of God's glory to us on whom he has shown mercy. I cannot claim to be a Christian because of my desire or effort. It is all because of God's mercy from first to last.

And what mercy it is. The ninth plague was not the last time darkness came as a sign and means of judgment. Another day dawned, and then darkened unnaturally, as a man hung dying on a cross while "from noon until three in the afternoon darkness came over all the land" (Matthew 27:45). The three days of darkness over Egypt was mirrored by the three hours of darkness over Jesus—followed by his death. At the cross, the plagues fell on Jesus, the Son of God. At the cross, the Maker came to be unmade so that we can be remade! The Son was unravelled under the judgment of the Father. He experienced chaos, darkness and death. As Jesus died, the rocks split and the earth shook (v 51). It was the ultimate moment of un-creation.

> At the cross, the Maker was unmade so that we can be remade.

Yet as the rocks split, "the tombs broke open [and] the bodies of many holy people who had died were raised to life" (v 52). In that moment re-creation erupted as the dead came back to life. It was an anticipation of the re-creation of Jesus at his resurrection. And the resurrection of Jesus is the promise and beginning of all re-creation. It's the promise of *our* re-creation.

The only place of safety in Egypt was in Goshen, the home of the Israelites—when the darkness fell, still "all the Israelites had light in the places where they lived" (Exodus **10:23**). And the only place of safety in the coming judgment will be in Christ, the true home of God's people. For Christ has already absorbed the plagues of God's judgment.

By what name?

Shortly after the day of **Pentecost**, Peter and John heal a lame man outside the Jerusalem Temple. As a result, they are arrested, imprisoned and then brought before the Jewish Council. The question they are asked is: "By what power or what name did you do this?" (Acts 4:7). What authority? What name? It's an echo of Pharaoh's question: "Who is the LORD, that I should obey him?"

Peter, filled with the Holy Spirit, replies, "Know this, you and all the people of Israel: it is by the name of Jesus Christ of Nazareth, whom you crucified but whom God raised from the dead … Salvation is found in no one else, for there is no other name under heaven given to mankind by which we must be saved" (Acts 4:10-12).

The plagues were signs of God's judgment and salvation. He judged Egypt and he saved his people. God sent the plagues, as we have seen, "so you may know that there is no one like me in all the earth … and that my name might be proclaimed in all the earth" (Exodus **9:14, 16**).

But the plagues were pointers to the cross and resurrection of Jesus—to the ultimate signs of judgment and salvation. On the cross, Jesus experienced the judgment that will fall on all who are outside of him—and he has been raised as Judge of the world to bring that judgment. But his cross also brings salvation to all who are in him, and his resurrection is the promise of our resurrection.

So Jesus is the ultimate sign, and his name is the ultimate name. He died and rose again so that his name might be known in all the earth "for there is no other name".

When you see the signs—the plagues, the cross, the resurrection—you proclaim his name with courage. Acts 4:13 continues, "When [the religious leaders] saw the courage of Peter and John and realised that they were unschooled, ordinary men, they were astonished and they took note that these men had been with Jesus". *These men had been with Jesus.* You may not be theologically trained or express yourself particularly eloquently. You may be a very "ordinary" Christian. But when you grasp the meaning of Christ's cross, when you see God's salvation in Christ's resurrection, when you have "been with Jesus"—you will proclaim Christ's name with courage to those around you, whoever they are and whatever the risk, because "salvation is found in no one else".

It's very easy to be intimidated in our culture. Biblical perspectives on marriage, sex, gender, other religions, self-denial and so on are not only seen as wrong, but increasingly they're seen as a deviant position—unhealthy, unnatural or hateful. None of us want to be thought of in that way. So the temptation is always there to "downplay" or "edit" or "update" Christian teaching as we speak—or to simply keep our heads down and not speak at all.

When you're tempted to do that, remember the plagues. Remember the resurrection. When God goes head to head with the gods and ideologies of this world, there is only one winner. It may not have looked like that on the day before the plague of blood, or on Easter Saturday—it became very clear the day after the final plague, and the day after Easter Sunday. Our God is the true God, the mighty Creator, the holy Judge—and he is our gracious Saviour.

In Exodus **10:1-2**, God says he is sending the plagues so "that you may tell your children and grandchildren". God wants worshippers for generations to come. He sends the plagues to free the Israelites to worship him and to give them reasons to do so. And it's the same for us. He sent his Son to free us to worship him and to give us reasons to do so. The only difference is that we have been given far more reasons to worship. They saw judgment and salvation in the plagues. We have seen judgment and salvation in the cross and resurrection of God's own Son.

Questions for reflection

1. How has this passage caused you to worship God in gratitude for changing your hard heart?

2. How has it caused you to worship Christ in awe at all his death took from you and achieved for you?

3. If you lived at each moment this week truly believing that God's judgment is coming at each moment, what would you say and do differently?

5. LIBERATED FOR SERVICE

The Passover is a significant event for the formation of Israel's identity and in the Bible's story. So it's easy to think of it and teach it as a stand-alone event. But of course it's actually the tenth of ten plagues. It's the climax of the great showdown between Moses and Pharaoh, between the God of Israel and the gods of Egypt. God says, "I will bring judgment on all the gods of Egypt. I am the Lord" (**12:12**). Because of the hardening of Pharaoh's heart, this was always going to be a contest to the death. And Exodus 12 is a chapter of death.

> "At midnight the Lord struck down all the firstborn in Egypt, from the firstborn of Pharaoh, who sat on the throne, to the firstborn of the prisoner, who was in the dungeon, and the firstborn of all the livestock as well. Pharaoh and all his officials and all the Egyptians got up during the night, and there was loud wailing in Egypt, for there was not a house without someone dead." (**v 29-30**)

It could not be more comprehensive. At some point after midnight, a lone voice could be heard in Egypt, lamenting the death of a beloved child. Soon that voice was joined by another. And then another. And the more voices that could be heard, the more people woke up to find their firstborn dead. Through the darkness of the night, "there was loud wailing in Egypt" (**v 30**).

Who has died?

The battle between God and Pharaoh has reached its deadly conclusion. Even before the dawn breaks, Pharaoh summons Moses and

Aaron and pretty much commands the Israelites to leave (**v 31-32**). The entire population of Egypt join this exhortation (**v 33**). So the Israelites leave in haste—a haste symbolised by the fact that there is no time for their dough to rise (**v 34, 39**) just as God has planned (**v 14-20**). Far from reluctantly giving up their Israelite slaves, the Egyptians effectively pay them to leave (**v 35-36**). They give them silver, gold and clothing—victory booty that God has won for his people. About 600,000 men leave, plus women and children (**v 37**). Their numbers are swelled by "many other people" (**v 38**)—possibly some people simply take advantage of the act of liberation, but perhaps others have come to share Israel's faith. After all, God had sent the plagues so "that my name might be proclaimed in all the earth" (**9:16**). All this takes place just as God had promised to Abraham (**12:40-42**; see Genesis 15:12-16).

And if that were that, we would have here a model of socio-political liberation. Certainly, this is not less than that. It is true that we see here God's concern for the oppressed. Much of the legislation in the law he gives to Moses will be concerned with the treatment of the poor and vulnerable. And repeatedly, the rationale given for this is Israel's own experience of liberation (Exodus 22:21; 23:9; Leviticus 25:42, 46, 55; Deuteronomy 5:15; 10:19; 15:15; 24:17-22). In his book *Exodus and Liberation*, historian John Coffey explores the way the exodus story has inspired liberation and emancipation movements throughout Western history from the sixteenth-century Protestant Reformers seeing themselves as liberated from "**Popish** slavery", through the Puritans viewing England as experiencing an exodus in the Civil War of the mid-seventeenth century and then escaping bondage in an exodus to America, to the emancipation movements of the nineteenth century and the Civil Rights movement of the mid-twentieth century.

But there is more to the story than this. We know this because, as we shall see, the rest of the Bible sees the exodus and the Passover as a **paradigm** of salvation from sin and judgment, culminating in redemption through Jesus our Passover Lamb. In Romans 8:12-14, for example,

Paul parallels being led by the pillars of cloud and fire with being led by the Spirit. In this context it is freedom from our own sin that is in view, rather than the oppressive effects of someone else's sin.

There is also a big clue in the story itself that this is more than socio-political liberation. The plague is announced in Exodus 11, and then takes place in **12:29-32**. In between, God gives instructions to Moses that will exempt the Israelites from the plague of death (**v 1-20**), and Moses then passes on these instructions (**v 21-27**), which the people obey (**v 28**). "Each man is to take a lamb for his family … year-old males without defect … all the members of the community of Israel must slaughter them at twilight" (**v 3, 5, 6**, see also **v 21**). Then the blood is to be daubed "on the sides and tops of the door-frames of the houses where they eat the lambs", using a bunch of **hyssop** to wipe it round the frame, and then "that same night they are to eat the meat roasted over the fire" (**v 7-8**, and also **v 22**). The LORD will pass through Egypt, bringing death to every firstborn creature. But "the blood will be a sign for you on the houses where you are; and when I see the blood, I will pass over you. No destructive plague will touch you when I strike Egypt" (**v 13**, see also **23**). The subsequent feast will be called "Passover" because the judgment of God is going to "pass over" his people. They are also to make bread without yeast (**v 14-20**) and eat the lamb dressed to depart (**v 11**) as a sign of their faith that God will liberate them before the night is out.

> The Israelites had to daub blood on the doorposts precisely because they were as guilty as the Egyptians.

The point is this: the Israelites deserve the judgment of death just as much as the Egyptians. If this was simply a story of political liberation, then Israel would be the innocent victims. They wouldn't need to fear judgment. But the truth is that they were sinners deserving of death. The Israelites had to daub the blood on the doorposts precisely because they were as guilty as the Egyptians, and so needed a substitute to die in their place if they were to avoid the judgment of death. The blood is daubed around the doors not because God can't tell who is inside the house, but because he can! He knows there are sinners inside.

In every home throughout Egypt and Goshen, the death count is the same. The following morning there is a corpse. The only question is: is it a lamb or is it a child? Who has died? The lamb is a substitute for the child. If the blood were simply marking out Israelite homes, then red paint would have done the job. But the blood is a sign that a sacrifice has been made, that a substitute has been offered.

So the sacrifice of a lamb means there is unfinished business. After all, who really thinks a lamb is a fair exchange for a human life? The lamb is simply a pointer. It's an embodied promise of a true substitute. The Passover is the sign of a greater act of redemption.

Over a millennium later, with this unfinished business still waiting to be resolved, John the Baptist sees Jesus and says, "Look, the Lamb of God, who takes away the sin of the world" (John 1:29). A few years later, Peter says, "For you know that it was not with perishable things such as silver or gold that you were redeemed from the empty way of life handed down to you from your ancestors, but with the precious blood of Christ, a lamb without blemish or defect" (1 Peter 1:18-19). Paul describes Christ as "our Passover lamb" (1 Corinthians 5:7).

Jesus is our Passover lamb. He was sacrificed as our substitute. We all deserve to die because of our rebellion against God. But Jesus has died in our place. His blood is, as it were, daubed over our lives so that God will "pass over" us when he comes in judgment.

As a result, we are redeemed. Like Israel, we are redeemed from slavery and death—but not from slavery in Egypt, but slavery to sin, and the penalty of death that our sin deserves.

Redemption from the power of sin

When Peter speaks of Jesus as "a lamb without blemish", it is to emphasise liberation from the power of sin (1 Peter 1:18-19). The precious blood of Jesus is given as the reason and motivation for the commands in the preceding verses:

"Therefore, with minds that are alert and fully sober, set your hope on the grace to be brought to you when Jesus Christ is revealed at his coming. As obedient children, do not conform to the evil desires you had when you lived in ignorance. But just as he who called you is holy, so be holy in all you do; for it is written: 'Be holy, because I am holy.' Since you call on a Father who judges each person's work impartially, live out your time as foreigners here in reverent fear." (1 Peter 1:13-17)

We are to be holy because we have been redeemed from slavery to sin through the precious blood of Jesus. We are to be holy because we can be—sin is no longer our slave-master. We are to be holy because this is the Father's purpose in redemption. And we are to be holy because the blood with which we were bought is infinitely precious.

The phrase "with minds that are alert" is literally "gird up the loins of your mind" (KJV). It's an image taken from Exodus **12:11**. The Israelites are to eat the Passover lamb "with your cloak tucked into your belt". It was hard to run in a floor-length cloak, so if you were in a hurry, as the Israelites soon would be, you tucked it into your belt. We, too, are in a hurry—a hurry to be holy. We are always to be ready for action in the service of Christ.

Paul also uses the exodus as a model for our redemption from slavery to sin. "You have been set free from sin," he says in Romans 6:18. Just as Israel passed through the water of the Red Sea to freedom, so we have passed through the waters of baptism to a new life (Romans 6:1-5).

From slavery to slavery

But there is a twist. The exodus is often presented as a movement from slavery to freedom. In fact, through the whole book, the only references to freedom come in the laws describing the circumstances in which an Israelite is to set free an Israelite slave (Exodus 21:2-11). The exodus does not lead to freedom. Quite the opposite.

In 4:22-23, when God tells Pharaoh via Moses, "Let my son go, so that he may worship me", the word for "worship" is (as we've seen) the same word as the word used to describe the slavery of Israel under the Egyptians. 2:23, for example, speaks of how "the Israelites groaned in their slavery". The word is used the describe Israel's slavery under Egypt in 1:14; 2:23; 5:9, 11; 6:6, 9. It is used to describe Israel's service of God, especially through the worship in the tabernacle, in **12:25-26; 13:5**; 27:19; 30:16; 35:24; 36:1, 3, 5; 39:32, 42.

So in 4:23 God literally says, "Let my son go, so that he may serve me". We are presented with competing claims to the service of Israel. To whom does Israel belong? Both God and Pharaoh lay claim to Israel, though the nature of their respective rules is very different. Under Pharaoh's rule the Israelites experienced work without rest, the state-sponsored murder of children, interference in family life and the confiscation of property. In contrast, to serve God is to find true freedom.

> Exodus moves from forced construction for Pharaoh to free construction for God.

So Israel is liberated for obedience; and liberated through obedience— through obeying God by trusting in his rescue plan as they daubed the blood on the doorframes, waited in their houses overnight, and then were "brought ... out of Egypt by their divisions" (**12:22, 28, 50-51**).

The story of the book of Exodus moves from the forced construction of buildings for Pharaoh to the free construction of a building

for God. The freedom in the construction of the tabernacle is typi-
fied by the freewill offering with which it is funded: "All the Israelite
men and women who were willing brought to the LORD freewill offerings for all the work the LORD through Moses had commanded
them to do ... And the people continued to bring freewill offerings
morning after morning" (35:29; 36:3).

It is this theme of service which is actually freedom that is picked up
by Paul in his letter to the church in Rome:

"What then? Shall we sin because we are not under the law but
under grace? By no means! Don't you know that when you offer yourselves to someone as obedient slaves, you are slaves to
the one you obey—whether you are slaves to sin, which leads
to death, or to obedience, which leads to righteousness? But
thanks be to God that, though you used to be slaves to sin, you
have come to obey from your heart the pattern of teaching that
has now claimed your allegiance. You have been set free from
sin and have become slaves to righteousness.

"I am using an example from everyday life because of your human
limitations. Just as you used to offer yourselves as slaves to impu-
rity and to ever-increasing wickedness, so now offer yourselves
as slaves to righteousness leading to holiness. When you were
slaves to sin, you were free from the control of righteousness.
What benefit did you reap at that time from the things you are
now ashamed of? Those things result in death! But now that
you have been set free from sin and have become slaves of God,
the benefit you reap leads to holiness, and the result is eternal
life. For the wages of sin is death, but the gift of God is eternal
life in Christ Jesus our Lord." (Romans 6:15-23)

We are not simply freed from slavery to sin. We are certainly not set
free for a life of self-indulgence (Galatians 5:13). Instead we have become slaves to righteousness. But this service leads to life. This slavery
is freedom for we are liberated to be the people we are meant to be.
We become fit for purpose.

Questions for reflection

1. If someone asked you what the Passover was about, what would you say?

2. Reflect on the idea that God's people are redeemed from slavery, *for* slavery. How does this need to shape your view of yourself as a member of God's redeemed people?

3. "To serve God is to find true freedom." Identify a way in which you struggle with sin. How might this simple truth liberate you to resist that temptation?

PART TWO

Redemption from the penalty of death

All humans are born in Adam (Romans 5:12-21). And that means we are all born as slaves to sin and under the judgment of death. We are children of Adam, who share his sinfulness and his fate.

But God in his grace has promised to create a new humanity free from sin and death. He chose Israel as his firstborn—the first people to be part of this new humanity. Israel was, as it were, the **prototype** of God's new humanity. In Exodus 4:22-23, God told Pharaoh that he must free Israel because Israel were God's firstborn. If Pharaoh refused, then he would face a corresponding retribution—the death of Egypt's firstborn.

The problem was that the Israelites were also part of humanity in Adam. They were the firstborn of God, but they were also enslaved by sin and deserving of death like the rest of humanity. So if they were to be free, then they must first die to humanity in Adam. Only then could they be reborn as God's new humanity.

This is what happens at the Passover, albeit symbolically. Their firstborn die—except that a lamb dies in their place. The lamb bears the death they deserve as their substitute. Their death is symbolically enacted on the lamb. As a result, Israel go free. They die to the old humanity and are reborn as the firstborn of the new humanity. They are free from slavery and free from death. They are free because they have died (symbolically in the death of the lamb). This death has released them from all the obligations of their old life.

This is why the consecration of the firstborn becomes important: "The LORD said to Moses, 'Consecrate to me every firstborn male. The first offspring of every womb among the Israelites belongs to me, whether human or animal'" (**13:1-2**).

Israel died in the Passover so they no longer belonged to Adam and instead belonged to God. Israel's belonging to God as God's firstborn was symbolically marked in the "belonging" of every firstborn Israelite male, whether human or animal. It is as if what was true for the human family (the firstborn son, which was Israel, belonged to God) was mirrored in each Israelite family (the firstborn offspring belonged to God). So each firstborn child had to be bought back (redeemed) from God (**v 11-16**).

But the Passover is only symbolic. The Israelites were free from slavery, but only from slavery to Egypt, not slavery to sin. And they were free from death, but only death on the night of Passover, not from eternal death. The death of the lamb brought life, but not for ever. As a result, while Israel belonged to God, they continued to live as a child of Adam. In other words, they continued to live as a slave to sin. The redemption of the firstborn was a reminder of what God had done, that is, liberate his people from slavery. But the fact that it had to be repeated with each new generation meant it was also a reminder of what God was yet to do—finally and fully liberate his people from sin and death.

If the Passover was a symbol, the reality is Christ. Christ is our Passover Lamb, who died in our place. He is the fulfilment of the promise embodied in the Passover. Christ is "the firstborn from among the dead" (Colossians 1:18). He is the son of Adam who died and was resurrected as the firstborn of a new humanity. All those in Christ by faith have died in Christ to the slavery of sin and condemnation of death. And so we have risen to new life in Christ.

The book of Exodus establishes the pattern of redemption through sacrifice which finds its fulfilment in Christ.

Commemoration

This double liberation from sin and death is, God says, to be commemorated in two festivals. The description of the commemoration is intermingled with the description of the event it commemorates. The story is presented as an explanation of the festivals (Exodus **12:1-2, 14-20, 24-27, 42, 43-49; 13:3-10**). The narrative begins with the reshaping of the Israelite calendar around the story which is about to be described (**12:1-2**). This is to be the defining event for Israel.

Passover starts on the 10th day of the month of Aviv and ends on the 14th day. The Feast of Unleavened Bread starts on the 14th day and ends on the 21st. The key day in both cases is the 14th, the day of liberation. The two festivals essentially take place on the same day and commemorate the same event (as Luke 22:1 suggests). But they each reflect a different aspect of its meaning. The Passover commemorates liberation from death since it re-enacts God's passing over Israel in his bringing of death to Egypt (Exodus **12:24-27, 43-49**). The Feast of Unleavened Bread commemorates liberation from slavery since it re-enacts Israel's hasty departure from Egypt (**12:14-17; 13:3-10**).

There was a further act of remembrance—the consecration of the firstborn (**13:1-2, 11-16**). God had redeemed Israel. As such, they now belonged to him. As we have seen, they were redeemed from slavery to slavery, albeit it a form of slavery which was experienced as freedom. God had bought Israel. So, as his redeemed firstborn son, Israel belonged to God. And this ownership was marked by the consecration or redemption of every firstborn male.

Each of these acts of commemoration includes a moment when future generations are expected to ask about its meaning (**12:26; 13:8, 14**). The festivals do more than merely help Israel to remember a past act. They are re-enactments of the story. People are not simply observers, but participants. So they incorporate future generations into the people of God. As the Passover Festival was kept, the Passover event became an act which future generations were part of. It became an act which continued to shape their identity as God's people.

The exodus was to be a living reality for future generations, never to be forgotten. So it became a cause for shame when Israelites oppressed other Israelites, as the Egyptians had done (Jeremiah 2:6-7; 7:22-26; Amos 2:10; 3:1; Micah 6:4). It became a prompt for prayer, that the God who had liberated his people would act in a similar way in the future (Psalms 44, 77, 80). It became a ground for hope, because God promised to redeem Israel through a new exodus (Isaiah 40; 43:14-21; Jeremiah 23:7-8).

We still commemorate Passover today—we celebrate *the* Passover. Luke recounts one particular Passover: "Then came the day of Unleavened Bread on which the Passover lamb had to be sacrificed. Jesus sent Peter and John, saying, 'Go and make preparations for us to eat the Passover'" (Luke 22:7-8). Luke mentions the Passover six times in his description of the Last Supper (v 1, 7, 8, 11, 13, 15). He portrays the Lord's Supper as the fulfilment of the Passover meal. Just as the redemption of Jesus the Passover Lamb is the fulfilment of the exodus, so the Lord's Supper is the fulfilment of the Feasts of Passover and Unleavened Bread.

And just as the Passover shaped the identity of the Israelites, so the Lord's Supper shapes our identity as Christians. We not only remember the story of the cross and resurrection. We enact it in the breaking of bread and the pouring of wine, and in this sense we participate in it. It becomes our story and our identity, our living reality.

Imagine a slave with a cruel master. One day a new man takes pity on him. He redeems him from his old cruel master at a high price. A week later the old master sees his former slave. He barks out commands as usual and the slave's every instinct is to obey. But he's no longer under the control of the old master. He no longer needs to obey. He no longer should obey. He needs to remember to whom he now belongs. He needs to remember that day of liberation when his old life passed away and his new life began. Remembering that will change everything.

> Communion is our *aide memoire*.

This is what we do every time we take communion. It is our *aide memoire*. It helps us to remember that in Christ, we died to the reign of sin. Sin is no longer our master. We no longer obey its commands. Now we live as slaves to righteousness—a slavery that is true freedom. In communion we remember the day of liberation so that we live as God's children, consecrated to him.

Led by the Spirit

God knows his people lack the faith to face battle: "If they face war, they might change their minds and return to Egypt" (Exodus **13:17**). So he takes them the long way round to avoid confrontation (**v 18**). His claim is proved in 14:10-12, when the Egyptian army come over the horizon and the Israelites immediately despair: "Was it because there were no graves in Egypt that you brought us to the desert to die?" The irony, of course, is that Egypt is known for its graves—its massive pyramids. Sometimes the long way round is the best way. Sometimes what seems to us to be a hard road is God's way of developing our faith.

13:19 is an allusion to Genesis 50:24-26. When Joseph was about to die, he gave specific instructions that his bones should be taken back with the Israelites when God returned to the promised land. It was an act of confidence in God's promise to Abraham that his offspring would inherit the land of **Canaan**. Joseph trusted that God would be faithful to this promise—and so it proved (Joshua 24:32). Hebrews 11:22 recognises this as an act of faith: "By faith Joseph, when his end was near, spoke about the exodus of the Israelites from Egypt and gave instructions concerning the burial of his bones". Faith is believing God's promises. Faith lives in the present in the light of God's promised future.

Near my old home town of Sheffield is a science museum called Magna. One of the exhibits is a column of fire which is lit periodically and then extinguished, leaving a column of smoke. It's very dramatic even though it's only two metres high. God's guiding presence among his people as they travel and camp is symbolised by pillars of cloud and fire (Exodus **13:20-22**). This is the glorious presence of God (16:10; 40:34). And these pillars lead God's people.

Paul has this mind when he says, "all who are led by the Spirit of God are sons of God" (Romans 8:14, ESV). In Romans 6 – 8, Paul retraces the steps of God's people coming out of Egypt to show how the redemption of the exodus is fulfilled in Christ. As we shall see, just as Israel was liberated from slavery in Egypt by being baptised into Moses through the Red Sea (1 Corinthians 10:2), so we have been liberated from slavery to sin through our baptism into Christ through his death and resurrection (Romans 6). Just as Israel came to Mount Sinai to receive God's law, so God's law is written on our hearts by the Spirit (Romans 7). Just as Israel was led by the pillars of cloud and fire to their inheritance in the land, so we are led by the Spirit to our inheritance in the new creation (Romans 8). Just as Israel was God's "firstborn son" (Exodus 4:22), so the Spirit testifies to us that we are children of God (Romans 8:16).

To be led by the Spirit is not a mystical experience in which we receive new revelations from God. It is to live our new, liberated life as we head for life in the new creation. We are being led by the Spirit every time he prompts us to say no to temptation and yes to Jesus (Romans 8:12-13; Galatians 5:16-18). We are being led by the Spirit every time our hearts are set on our heavenly inheritance rather than earthly treasure (Romans 8:16-17, 22-25). So we "live by the Spirit" by putting to death selfish desires (Galatians 5:24-26). If today you refuse to give in to temptation, then you will have been led by the Spirit of God; the same God who led his people in the wilderness.

Questions for reflection

1. How does the Passover in Exodus deepen your appreciation of your Passover Lamb?

2. How will the Passover in Exodus shape how you approach the Lord's Supper, and where you focus your mind as you eat and drink?

3. Why is it exciting to think that the God of the pillar of fire still guides us today through his Spirit?

6. TO THE EASTERN SHORE

The crisis in Egypt began because "the Israelites were exceedingly fruitful; they multiplied greatly, increased in numbers and became so numerous that the land was filled with them" (Exodus 1:7)—because they were fulfilling God's command to humanity in Genesis 1. In the midst of the Egyptian empire, the world was being recreated. But the ruler of that empire became an anti-creator, responding to this explosion of life with a command of death as the newborn Israelite boys were thrown into the waters of the Nile. God rescued Moses from those waters of death as he was placed in, and taken out from, a basket, literally an "ark" (2:3)—Moses, like Noah, escaped death by water in a bitumen-coated ark.

The conflict between God and Pharaoh has continued. God has pulled apart his creation around Pharaoh. Through the plagues, Egypt has returned to a primordial chaos, darkness and death. And yet still Pharaoh has not learned the lesson.

Faithful God to failing people

So we come to chapter 14. Once again, Pharaoh is trying to exert his authority over God's people. Once again, we have a showdown between God and Pharaoh. Once again, God determines to gain glory by demonstrating that he alone is Lord: "I will harden Pharaoh's heart, and he will pursue them. But I will gain glory for myself through Pharaoh and all his army, and the Egyptians will know that I am the LORD ... The

Egyptians will know that I am the LORD when I gain glory through Pharaoh, his chariots and his horsemen" (**14:4, 18**).

Israel appear to be caught in a trap—and it is a trap of the LORD's making (**v 1-3**). The route they take is a terrible military strategy, and as soon as they hear of it, Pharaoh and his officials regret their decision to let God's people go (**v 5**)—just as God had known they would (**v 3**). So now, Israel are caught between the advancing Egyptian army and the Red Sea (**v 6-7, 9**). As so often happens in the Bible, things get worse before they get better. But God was in control even over his enemy's actions (**v 8**)—and things would get much, much better, in an unforgettable way. By parting the sea, says Nehemiah 9:10, God "made a name for [himself], which remains to this day". What happened at the Red Sea would bring the God of Israel "everlasting renown" (Isaiah 63:12).

But while God will establish his name and nature all over again, God's people will once more be found wanting. Psalm 106 recalls this event—and it is a psalm of confession. God's people, centuries later, are confessing that they have doubted and disobeyed God—and the psalmist remembers the unbelief of the Israelites in Exodus **14:10-12**: "We have sinned, even as our ancestors did … they rebelled by the sea, the Red Sea" (Psalm 106:6-7). The psalmist then describes how God "rebuked the Red Sea" and "saved them from the hand of the foe" (v 9-10). The reason he did this was not the merit of his people. They were rebels who deserved to sink with the Egyptians. No—"he saved them for his name's sake, to make his mighty power known" (v 8).

So, what actually happened in history?

What actually happened?

Sceptical scholars reading this story have attacked God's power in two ways.

1. *This is merely a natural phenomenon.* Some people have suggested that a high wind and a low tide might explain the dry ground.

Exodus **14:21-22**, however, talks of two walls of water. This is not water gradually ebbing away. Even if you think the descriptions in Exodus are exaggerated through poetic licence, the timings are supernatural. The parting of the sea happens at Moses' command (**v 15-16, 21-22**) and ends at just the right moment to ensure the last Israelite is safe and the first Egyptian drowns as they "go in after them" (**v 17, 26-28**).

2. *This is the Reed Sea, not the Red Sea.* Some have suggested the name of the sea could be Reed Sea, suggesting a marshy area which the Israelites could cross on foot, but in which the Egyptian chariots became stuck. But the description of two walls of water suggests water of significant depth. And even if we concede that the sea was shallow, the deliverance is still a miracle.

The pastor Donald Bridge tells the story of a liberal preacher visiting an African-American church. As the minister talked about the crossing of the Red Sea, someone shouted, "Praise the Lord. Takin' all them children through the deep waters. What a mighty miracle!" The minister, who did not believe in miracles, was annoyed at this intervention. So rather condescendingly, he told the congregation that the Israelites were probably in marshland with an ebbing tide, so they were simply wading through six inches of water. In response to this, the same voice as before shouted, "Praise the Lord. Drownin' all them Egyptians in six inches of water. What a mighty miracle!" (*Signs and Wonders Today,* page 17).

Wherever it happened and however it happened, it was a mighty miracle. Attempts to "explain" it away as anything less than the act of God reveal more about us and our closed view of the world than the events in Exodus 14. The Bible is unambiguous: this is a supernatural act of God. (For more on these issues, see Tremper Longman III, *How To Read Exodus*, pages 113-114.) And once again, God brings salvation through an act of new creation.

"Then Moses stretched out his hand over the sea, and all that night the Lᴏʀᴅ drove the sea back with a strong east wind and

turned it into dry land. The waters were divided, and the Israelites went through the sea on dry ground, with a wall of water on
their right and on their left." (**v 21-22**)

This is the story of creation all over again. At creation, the waters separated to create dry land. In Genesis 1:9, we read, "And God said, 'Let
the water under the sky be gathered to one place, and let dry ground
appear.' And it was so." At the Red Sea, this happens again. Again the
waters separate to create dry land. Taming the sea is seen throughout
the Bible as an act of creation (Job 26:10-13; Psalm 74:12-14; 89:9;
Isaiah 27:1; 51:9-11).

God separates the waters through a "wind". "Wind", "blast" and
"breath" in Exodus **14:21**, **15:8** and **10** respectively are all the same
word, *ruach*—the word used for "Spirit". The wind blowing over the
waters echoes the Spirit at creation, where the *ruach* of God hovered
over the waters (Genesis 1:2). It was the same in the story of Noah.
Floating on an endless sea of watery judgment, Noah had no future.
"But God remembered Noah and all the wild animals and the livestock
that were with him in the ark, and he sent a wind over the earth, and
the waters receded" (Genesis 8:1). God rescues his people from death
by sending his Spirit-wind to repeat creation as he separates the waters to create dry ground.

But in Exodus 14, when the Egyptian army tries to follow the Israelites, the waters close over them (Exodus **14:23-28**)—"not one of
them survived" (**v 28**), in stark contrast to the Israelites, who walked
between the walls of water (**v 29**). Again, judgment takes the form of
un-creation. Water and land un-separate, just as they did when God
sent judgment during the time of Noah. Judgment takes the form of
water. In 10:19 the Spirit-wind of God carried away the locust army
into the Red Sea. Now the Spirit-wind of God carries away the Egyptian army into the same sea. In response, Moses sings, "By the blast
of your nostrils the waters piled up ... But you blew with your breath,
and the sea covered them" (**15:8, 10**). God pulls apart his creation
around the Egyptian army.

This may seem harsh to us, but the men of Egypt are drowned for drowning the boys of Israel (1:22). And they are drowned at daybreak (**14:24**)—which is when Ra, the sun god, should have risen to their aid. But Ra was unable to save them. For "the Egyptians will know that I am the Lord when I gain glory through Pharaoh, his chariots and his horsemen" (**v 18**). According to one ancient Egyptian inscription:

> "He whom the king has loved will be a revered one, but there is no tomb for a rebel against his majesty, and his corpse is cast into the water."
>
> (Philip Graham Ryken, *Exodus: Saved for God's Glory,* page 396)

The corpses in the water were a sign to Egypt that God is God.

> The men of Egypt are drowned for drowning the boys of Israel.

Pulling creation apart

At creation, and then again at the time of Noah, and then again during the exodus, God conquered chaos. He brought life out of death. His judgment came as an act of un-creation, as creation went into reverse. But he bought salvation out of judgment. He recreated his people from the waters of death. God did it again in Joshua 3 – 4 when he parted the River Jordan to lead his people into the promised land. He did it again in 2 Kings 2:7-14, when Elijah and Elisha crossed through the River Jordan on dry ground.

What God is doing in all these stories is setting up a pattern. Isaiah 43:16-19 says:

> "This is what the Lord says—
> he who made a way through the sea,
> a path through the mighty waters,
> who drew out the chariots and horses,
> the army and reinforcements together,
> and they lay there, never to rise again,

extinguished, snuffed out like a wick:
'Forget the former things;
　do not dwell on the past.
See, I am doing a new thing!
　Now it springs up; do you not perceive it?
I am making a way in the desert
　and streams in the wasteland.'"

Isaiah reminds the people of how God liberated the Israelites through the sea. But then God says, in effect, *Forget about that. I'm going to do it again—bigger and better.* Isaiah repeatedly speaks of a coming new exodus (Isaiah 4:5-6; 11:15-16; 35:6-10; 40:3-5; 43:14-19; 48:20-21; 50:2; 51:9-11; 63:11-14; see also Jeremiah 16:14-15; 23:7-8; 31:31-33). And this coming act of liberation is described as an act of new creation (Isaiah 25:6-8; 42:5; 44:24; 45:11-12; 65:17-25).

Echoes of this promise are all over the New Testament. Jesus is baptised in the waters of the River Jordan. Again and again in the Bible story, water has represented judgment—now Jesus is immersed in water. He immerses himself in judgment. It's a picture of the cross—in Mark 10:38, he describes his death as a baptism. Water is the symbol of judgment. The cross is the reality. At **Calvary**, the waters of judgment engulfed Jesus. And the land was covered in darkness. God pulled apart creation around Jesus, and Jesus sank into the tomb.

But on the third day Jesus rose again. God brings life out of death, salvation out of judgment, light out of darkness. All the stories of rescue from water have been building up to this moment. They have been preparing us to understand the cross and resurrection. God brings his people through the waters of death in the person of his Son. God unravels his creation in order to recreate his people.

Imagine the walls of waters collapsing in on one another, with people and horses being tossed about and dragged down into the depths. This is what Jesus stepped into at the cross. Jesus plunged into the chaos of the waters of judgment so that we can walk through on dry ground. Imagine the people of God standing, safe on the shore, watching God's judgment unfold before their eyes. This is what we are doing as we watch, with the eyes of faith, God's Son hanging on the cross.

When the Israelites saw God deliver them, they "put their trust in him and in Moses his servant" (Exodus **14:30-31**). How much more should we, when we see our deliverance in the cross and resurrection, put our trust in God, by putting our trust in Jesus his servant.

Questions for reflection

1. God led Israel into a "trap" in order that he might show his own glory. How does this give us a helpful perspective on the difficulties of our own churches and lives?

2. Why is it good that God acts for the sake of his name, rather than in response to our merit?

3. How did imagining the walls of water collapsing in, and seeing that this is what Jesus stepped into at the cross, make you feel about him?

PART TWO

Jesus has entered the waters of death and has passed through to new life. And we passed through with him if we are "in" Christ by faith. This is what is symbolised in baptism. And so what happened to Israel at the Red Sea has happened to us in our baptisms:

> "I do not want you to be ignorant of the fact, brothers and sisters, that our ancestors were all under the cloud and that they all passed through the sea. They were all baptised into Moses in the cloud and in the sea." (1 Corinthians 10:1-2)

"They were all baptised," says Paul. They went into water and then came out of water. They passed through the waters of death and came out to freedom. On the western side of the Red Sea they were runaway slaves. On the eastern side, they were a liberated people.

> We walk through life with our judgment behind us.

And this is what happened at the cross and resurrection. On Good Friday we were slaves, under the authority of sin and facing divine judgment. On Easter morning we were a liberated people, free from sin, free from judgment. Christ passed through the waters of death on our behalf. So our baptism is the pledge and promise that we are liberated people on the eastern side of judgment. We walk through life with our judgment behind us. Paul says:

> "Or don't you know that all of us who were baptised into Christ Jesus were baptised into his death? We were therefore buried with him through baptism into death in order that, just as Christ was raised from the dead through the glory of the Father, we too may live a new life." (Romans 6:3-4)

How to respond on the eastern side

So what are we to do in response? In Exodus **14:10-12**, the Israelites are full of doubt and despair. Maybe you see sin and judgment on the horizon, just as the Israelites saw the Egyptian army on the horizon. And you're afraid, as they were. Will sin overtake you? What will stop you being crushed by it? "Leave us alone," they say. "Let us serve the Egyptians" (**v 12**). Maybe life for you is indeed harder, not better—and what you left behind suddenly looks very attractive. "It would have been better for us to serve the Egyptians," they say, "than to die in the desert!" Maybe you're tempted to return to your pre-conversion life.

In **verses 13-14**, Moses tells God's people, "Do not be afraid. Stand firm and you will see the deliverance the LORD will bring you today. The Egyptians you see today you will never see again. The LORD will fight for you; you need only to be still."

There are three exhortations here, all of which we need to hear.

Do not be afraid

Sin can pull us down to the waters of death. Judgment can overwhelm us. How do we respond to these fears? Not by pretending our sin is not a problem. Not by pretending we don't deserve judgment. We are sinners. We do deserve judgment. So what is the antidote to this fear?

We tell ourselves this. We have already been pulled down to death, and judgment has already overwhelmed us—in the person of Jesus. We died with him and we have risen with him. We need not fear death and judgment because we have already passed through the waters in Christ. "The LORD will fight for you," says Moses (**v 14**). Christ has taken on sin and death, and has given us the victory. He fought, for you.

Stand firm

The Israelites faced an army, and so they wanted to capitulate and return to slavery. In the same way, we face an army. But "our struggle," says Paul, "is not against flesh and blood, but against the rulers, against the authorities, against the powers of this dark world and against the spiritual forces of evil in the heavenly realms" (Ephesians 6:12). We face the temptations of the world, the flesh and the devil. And maybe we're tempted to capitulate and return to slavery. Moses' word to us and Paul's word to us are the same: *Stand firm.* "Put on the full armour of God, so that when the day of evil comes, you may be able to stand your ground, and after you have done everything, to stand" (v 13).

Our armour is the gospel. It is faith in the finished work of Christ. Satan says, *You cannot resist me* or *You are mine.* And we say, *No— I can, and I'm not. I am Christ's. I am on the east side of the sea. I am no longer under the power of sin. I have gone through death and resurrection in Christ. And so I have risen to a new life—and I am going to stand firm, whatever lies you may whisper to me.*

Be still

Can you imagine what it's like to stand still as the greatest army in the world bears down on you? Every instinct in you is telling you either to fight or flee. Do you instinctively want to stand and fight your weaknesses and your problems with your own strength, in your own way? Or do you naturally tend to flee from your problems and hope that if you ignore your weaknesses they will disappear? Maybe you're in the midst of conflict or uncertainty. Maybe you fear exposure or shame. Maybe you feel as if your world is falling apart. You will want to come out fighting or you will want to run away.

And God says, "Be still".

That doesn't mean you can abdicate responsibility and do nothing. It means you take responsibility for what is your responsibility—but that you leave the rest to God. Our problem is often that we take responsibility for what is not our responsibility. I'm responsible for being a good parent, but I'm not responsible for the choices of my children—I must leave that to God and be still. I'm responsible for being a good employee, but I'm not responsible for the actions of my boss—I must leave that to God and be still. I'm responsible for telling others the gospel, but I'm not responsible for their salvation—I must leave that to God and be still. And ultimately, while I'm responsible for my sin, I am not responsible for achieving my forgiveness—I must leave that to God too, and be still.

When we try to take control of our world or of our eternal future, we're in effect saying, *God's not doing a good job so I'm going to step in.* The result is over-busyness, stress and unwise decisions, because it turns out that we're not very good at doing God's job for him. And God graciously says, "The LORD will fight for you; you need only to be still" (Exodus **14:14**).

There was a period of his life when Martin Luther, the great Reformer, was in hiding in a castle. He spent his time translating the Bible into German, but it was a dark time for him. He struggled with doubt and discouragement.

> It turns out that we're not very good at doing God's job for him.

He felt attacked by the devil—on one occasion, he famously threw an inkpot at him. But his more successful strategy was this. He was heard shouting in the grounds of the castle, "Baptisatus sum": "I am baptised". How Luther felt was up and down. His circumstances looked bleak. But his baptism was a fact and it was a fact that embodied the promise of God. He felt he had little fight left, but the truth was that, in all the ways that eternally mattered, the fight was not his—God had already fought for him, and won for him.

In his *Large Catechism*, Luther wrote:

"Thus we must regard Baptism and make it profitable to ourselves, that when our sins and conscience oppress us, we strengthen ourselves and take comfort and say: Nevertheless I am baptised; but if I am baptised, it is promised me that I shall be saved and have eternal life, both in soul and body." (Part Four)

When we are afraid—when we feel the weight of our sin or the power of the enemy, we can say, "I am baptised". In other words, *I have received a promise from God. God is for me. And if God is for me, who can be against me? I will not be afraid. I will stand firm. I will be still.*

Responding with song

In Exodus 15, Moses responds to the Lord's deliverance with a song of praise. When he has finished, Miriam (his sister) and all the women of Israel take up the chorus with their tambourines and dancing (**15:19-21**). We echo this act every time when we join to praise God. We sing songs that celebrate his salvation. We celebrate Jesus passing through the waters of death to liberate us from sin and judgment. Even in heaven, God's people join in singing the song of Moses (Revelation 15:2-4).

The opening verses of the song are about God (Exodus **15:1-5**). That is, they are not addressed directly to God—instead, they describe him. They are a call to praise God because of who he is and what he has done. This distinguishes them from **verses 6-17**, in which God is addressed directly. They are also marked by an "inclusio"—the technical term for a section that begins and ends in a similar way. This section begins and ends with the enemy being hurled into the sea (**v 1, 4-5**).

Perhaps the key phrase is **verse 3**: "The Lord is a warrior; the Lord is his name". "I will praise him" (**v 2**) is literally "I will decorate him", as in a solider being decorated for his courage. There are twelve references to "chariots" and twelve references to horses or horsemen in chapters 14 – 15. Israel faced cutting-edge military technology sweeping down on them and their children. But that Egyptian army was no match for the Lord: the Warrior.

The section ends with the enemy covered by the water of judgment: "The deep waters have covered them; they sank to the depths like a stone" (**15:5**). They have sunk down to death—but God's people have been rescued through these waters. For us, as we think of our baptism, we can say, "The Lord is my strength and my defence; he has become my salvation. He is my God, and I will praise him, my father's God, and I will exalt him" (**v 2**).

From verse 6 onwards the language about God shifts from "he" and "him" to "you". Now Moses addresses God directly. This section is marked by another inclusio—both **verses 6** and **12** refer to "your right hand". It is a picture of God's personal power. God himself has rescued his people.

So the story of chapter 14 is retold in **15:7-10**, with the emphasis on God's personal and powerful intervention. The pillars of cloud and fire that separated the Egyptians and Israelites in **14:19-20** are described as "your burning anger" (**15:7**). The "wind" that separated the waters in **14:21-22** is "the blast of your nostrils" (**15:8**) and "your breath" (**v 10**). The conclusion is clear: "Who among the gods is like you, Lord? Who is like you—majestic in holiness, awesome in glory, working wonders?" (**v 11**).

Then comes the final section, from **verses 13-17**, and again, it is marked off by an inclusio. "In your strength you will guide them to your holy dwelling ... You will bring them [to] ... the place, Lord, you made for your dwelling" (**v 13, 17**). These verses anticipate how the story of the exodus will continue. The news of the exodus will bring fear to the surrounding nations (**v 14-15**). That this is what happened is clear from Joshua 2:9-11. So God will lead his people through foreign lands (Exodus **15:16**) until they reach the promised land, the place of God's dwelling (**v 17**).

The theme of God's dwelling also anticipates a key theme of the remainder of the book of Exodus. The theme of Exodus 1 – 14 is that God's people, then and now, are saved from slavery and death. The theme of Exodus 15 – 40 is that God's people, then and now, are saved for a relationship with God. This transition in the song mirrors the transition in the book as a whole. We are saved so that we might enjoy the presence of God and dwell with him. Not only are we saved from the sin of Genesis 3—we are saved to walk with God in the cool of the evening as Adam and Eve did in the Garden of Eden in Genesis 2. We are saved to enjoy and live under the reign of the eternal LORD (Exodus **15:18**).

Looking back

Psalm 77 recalls the story of the parting of the Red Sea. The psalm begins by describing intense personal pain (v 1-6), including a crisis of confidence in God (v 7-9). But then in verses 10-12 the psalmist makes a determined decision: "I will remember the deeds of the LORD" (v 11). The dominant **pronoun** in verses 1-12 is "I"—these verses are all about what the psalmist feels. But in verses 13-20, the dominant pronoun is "you". Now the psalmist is focusing on who God is and what he has done—and what the psalmist remembers most of all is the exodus (v 13-19). That past event is the sign that gives him confidence in God's shepherding of him in the here and now (v 20). The objective reality of salvation gives him confidence to face the present struggle.

In the same way, we look back to God's redemptive acts. But we look back to the cross and resurrection—the deliverance to which the exodus pointed. The exodus, the cross and resurrection are the objective demonstrations in history that God is for us, however we feel and whatever is happening. Whatever our circumstances, we can still sing of God's goodness, for we stand on the eastern side of the sea.

In Revelation 15:1-4, God's people again stand beside a sea, celebrating God's victory. Revelation 12 – 14 have pictured history as a prolonged battle between Christ and the dragon, or Satan. This cosmic battle has a counterpart on earth, in the battle between the church and the two beasts (the personification of idolatrous state power). Tellingly, the song that the people of God sing is "the song of God's servant Moses and of the Lamb" (Revelation 15:3). In Revelation 15 we are clearly looking over the whole of history, but the rescue of Exodus 14 is also in view. The point is that the threat to God's people at the Red Sea was one manifestation of this ongoing war—and the defeat of the Egyptian army is therefore a sign of God's overall victory. And so we sing:

"Great and marvellous are your deeds,
    Lord God Almighty.
Just and true are your ways,
    King of the nations.
Who will not fear you, Lord,
    and bring glory to your name?
For you alone are holy.
All nations will come
    and worship before you,
for your righteous acts have been revealed." (Revelation 15:3-4)

We have been judged in Christ, and saved in Christ. We have passed through the waters in him, and now we stand on the eastern shore, on our way home… and we sing.

Questions for reflection

1. What difference does it, and should it, make that we stand on the eastern side, not the western side, of the waters of chaos and death?

2. Do not be afraid … stand firm … be still. Which of these exhortations particularly speaks to you today?

3. "Whatever our circumstances, we can still sing of God's goodness, for we stand on the eastern side of the sea." How and what will you sing today, and when will you most need to sing it?

7. GRUMBLING OR GRATITUDE?

People who moan really annoy me. People who go on about their petty problems or the failings of the government or the state of the roads or the behaviour of young people—or old people. Don't they realise how privileged they are? It really annoys me. The worst are those people who moan about people who moan.

Let me make my irony explicit. As I grumble about grumblers, I turn out to be the biggest grumbler of all.

But, of course, that's what we often do. We think of grumbling as something other people do. What we do is make justified complaints or offer constructive criticism, but we don't grumble. We make ourselves the exception—but the reality is that most of us grumble and some of us grumble most of the time.

And this section of Exodus, out on the eastern shore of the sea, is about grumbling. In Exodus 15:22 – 17:7, we get three stories of grumbling:

■ "So the people grumbled against Moses, saying, "What are we to drink?" (**15:24**)

■ "In the desert the whole community grumbled against Moses and Aaron." (**16:2**)

■ "But the people were thirsty for water there, and they grumbled against Moses." (**17:3**)

These chapters reveal the dangers of grumbling, but also point to the solution. We need to hear both, without making excuses for ourselves.

The story of Marah

It's sometimes said that most Western societies are three days of empty shelves from civil disorder. We appear to live peacefully together—but if something went wrong with food supplies, then it would only take three days before rioting and looting broke out. That's certainly how it was among the Israelites. They travel for three days from the Red Sea without finding water (**15:22**). Then on the third day, they find water, but it is undrinkable (**v 23**). They call the place Marah, which means "bitter". It is not only the water that is bitter—so are they. And so they grumble (**v 24**).

The Israelites have been rescued from Egyptian slavery in the most dramatic fashion. They have seen the hand of God parting the Red Sea and defeating the Egyptian army. They have sung, "The LORD is my strength and my defence … In your unfailing love you will lead the people you have redeemed" (v 2, 13). But all that was three days ago. Today they are hungry and they are grumbling.

> Perhaps you sing of God's love on a Sunday. But days—or maybe hours—later, you are grumbling.

When we think of it like this, the Israelites' grumbling is ridiculous and inexcusable. But then think about your own life. Perhaps you sing of God's unfailing love on a Sunday morning. But three days later—or maybe three hours later—you are grumbling. Think of all the things that God has done for you. Think of all he has promised to you. But think, too, how easily you lose a sense of perspective. Think how much better you are at seeing what you do not have than what you do have. All we see is bitter water. All we see is our problem or lack. And so we say, "Ma-rah"—*my life is bitter.*

How does God respond? God graciously shows Moses a piece of wood which makes the water fit to drink (**v 25**). This story is a promise.

If we trust God, we will find he is the God "who heals you" just as he "healed" the bitter water (**v 26**).

The story of manna

But Israel do not learn the lesson. After a brief stop in Elim, "where there were twelve springs" (**v 27**)—natural water that does not require the Israelites to trust God and look to him for provision—they begin to travel through the desert (**16:1**). Again they grumble (**v 2, 7-8**). "If only we had died by the LORD's hand in Egypt! There we sat round pots of meat and ate all the food we wanted, but you have brought us out into this desert to starve this entire assembly to death" (**v 3**). It's a stinging complaint—a horrendous claim. They are saying that they were better off in Egypt—that the exodus has actually made things *worse*. The people are effectively telling God, *We wish you hadn't bothered rescuing us. We wish you'd left us as we were.*

One of the characteristics of grumbling is that it often posits idealised and unrealistic alternatives. In chapter 2, the people were groaning and crying out. Now, all of a sudden they think of Egypt as a wonderful place to live! The Egyptian slave-drivers are forgotten. Indeed, they suggest that it was God who oppressed them in Egypt ("if only we had died by the LORD's hand in Egypt", **16:3**). And they claim God's intentions are malign ("you have brought us out … to starve this entire assembly").

What would your response be?

God's response is manna from heaven: "I will rain down bread from heaven for you" (**v 4**). God will reveal his glory by providing for his people (**v 6-10**). In the evenings quail come and are easily caught so that the people have meat (**v 13**). In the morning the dew leaves behind "thin flakes like frost" (**v 14**). The people call it "manna", which sounds like the Hebrew for "What is it?" because that's what they ask when they first see it (**v 15, 31**). The answer to the question is, "It is the bread the LORD has given you to eat. This is what the LORD has commanded: 'Everyone is to gather as much as they need'" (**v 15-16**).

Verse 18 reiterates this: "Everyone had gathered just as much as they needed".

God is generously providing for his people. As at Marah, manna is an invitation to trust God and his provision. But now, with the manna, this trust takes a particular form:

"Then the LORD said to Moses, 'I will rain down bread from heaven for you. The people are to go out each day and gather enough for that day. In this way I will test them and see whether they will follow my instructions. On the sixth day they are to prepare what they bring in, and that is to be twice as much as they gather on the other days.'" (**16:4-5**)

Manna requires you to trust that God will provide today and then again tomorrow and then again the day after. You have to trust God one day at a time (**v 19**). This is why the "leftover" manna "melted away" once "everyone [had] gathered as much as they needed" (**v 21**).

This is a hard lesson for the Israelites to pay attention to (**v 20**). Some people gather more than they need and "kept part of it until morning". They trust their efforts, their savings, their provision. They go to bed looking at the pot of manna saved for tomorrow and that makes them feel secure. But the next morning, it is full of maggots and has started to smell. There is no alternative but to trust that God will provide tomorrow.

The exception is the seventh day. The Sabbath is to be a day of rest, so the people are to gather twice as much on the sixth day. On this day and this day alone, the extra will keep for the next day (**v 5, 22-30**). So the Sabbath, too, is an invitation to trust God. And the Sabbath, too, is a hard lesson for the Israelites to listen to—"some of the people went out on the seventh day to gather it, but they found none" (**v 27**).

One of the ways in which we demonstrate our trust in God is in our ability to rest. We can rest because we are trusting God to provide. Let me turn that around. If you can't rest—if you're always busy with your work or your family or your ministry—it is because you're not trusting God. You're trying to secure your own future or create your own identity or provide your own justification. You can make excuses, but that's all they are—excuses.

In the desert, God is schooling his people to trust him with daily trust. As a permanent reminder of this lesson, a jar of manna is "to be kept for the generations to come" (**v 32-36**). If we had enough manna for a year, we would trust our stores for 364 days and then turn to God on day 365. But we have to learn to trust him every day. Hence the Lord's prayer: "Give us today our daily bread" (Matthew 6:11).

This is so very helpful when we are in the midst of a crisis. Jesus says, "Therefore do not worry about tomorrow, for tomorrow will worry about itself. Each day has enough trouble of its own" (Matthew 6:34). *Tomorrow is my worry,* says Jesus.

Recently, a five-year-old girl in our church was diagnosed with a brain tumour. She was diagnosed on a Tuesday and spent nine hours in surgery on the Wednesday. Now she is in the midst of a year-long process of treatment. As I talked with her parents, it was so helpful to be able to say, "We don't have to worry about how we will cope in three months' time. We can just take one day at a time. We trust God for today. And we trust that he will enable us to trust him tomorrow and in three months' time."

> You are not given grace for tomorrow, for ifs and maybes— you are given grace for today.

God doesn't give grace today for tomorrow. Don't worry how you would cope if ... Don't play scenarios. You are not given grace for ifs and maybes. You will be given grace for today. You will have the grace for the next day when it comes—and it will not come till tomorrow. Look not to your version of the jar of manna when you go to bed each night and tell yourself you have gained what you need—look instead to the providing God and tell him that you trust him to give you what you need.

The story of Massah

The manna is meant to teach Israel, so that they would "know that it was the LORD who brought you out of Egypt, and … see the glory of the LORD" as he provides for them each day (Exodus **16:6-7**). But they will not learn: still the Israelites do not trust God. Again they grumble against Moses. Again they demand water. Again they want to return to Egypt (**17:1-3**).

In the first two stories we are told that God tested Israel. **15:25** says, "There the LORD issued a ruling and instruction for them and put them to the test". **16:4** says, "In this way I will test them and see whether they will follow my instructions". God is not trying to trip them up (James 1:13-15). He is revealing their allegiance and refining their trust in him (1 Peter 1:6-7). Imagine an employer exposing a new recruit to a difficult situation (in a controlled way) to strengthen their ability to perform their job. That's what God is doing.

But in this third story, the Israelites test God (perhaps because the situation at Massah so closely resembles that at Marah). When they complain, "Moses replied, 'Why do you quarrel with me? Why do you put the LORD to the test?'" (Exodus **17:2**). Moses is by now despairing of the people (**v 4**)—he understands what they are doing, which is why he names the two places as he does: they were testing God, "saying, 'Is the LORD among us or not?'" (**v 7**).

We can all too easily think of grumbling as harmless. But grumbling—all grumbling, including yours—is toxic. It's toxic for two reasons:

First, grumbling grows because it spreads to others. It's infectious. Think how those grumbling conversations unfold. We spread discontent. We reinforce one another's grumbles. This is why it's so important to cut it off at the root. We need to challenge one another when we grumble. We need to say, "Stop. Don't talk to me about it. Go and talk to the person concerned" or "Go and talk to God, since he's sent the circumstance about which you are concerned." None of us are immune to the contagion—someone else's grumbling gives us all the excuse our hearts need to indulge in it ourselves. Notice there's a suggestion in **verse 4** that even Moses caught the grumbling bug.

Second, grumbling grows because it hardens our hearts. Grumbling presumes to put God to the test. It scrutinises God. It questions his goodness. We become the judge and God is in the dock. Grumbling puts God on trial and finds him guilty. "He has failed to deliver the life I want ... I deserve more than this ... I need better than this." Think about that for a moment. When you grumble, *you are judging God*. Is that really what you want to be doing?

Psalm 95 is God's reflections on these episodes in the wilderness:

"Do not harden your hearts as you did at Meribah, as you did that day at Massah in the wilderness, where your ancestors tested me; they tried me, though they had seen what I did." (Psalm 95:8-9)

In the New Testament, Hebrews 3 quotes from the psalm and makes the same application:

"See to it, brothers and sisters, that none of you has a sinful, unbelieving heart that turns away from the living God. But encourage one another daily, as long as it is called 'Today', so that none of you may be hardened by sin's deceitfulness." (Hebrews 3:12-13)

Both Psalm 95 and Hebrews 3 suggest that what started as grumbling at Massah led to outright rebellion on the borders of the promised land, and forty years of judgment in the wilderness. When we presume to judge God, we are in great danger of being deceived by sin and so facing God's judgment.

In the Lord's Prayer, when Jesus teaches us to say, "Lead us not into temptation" (Matthew 6:13), it's the same word as "testing" in Exodus 15 – 17 in the Septuagint, the Greek translation of the Old Testament. We are to ask God to help us not to test God, so that we trust God. How do we test God? By putting him on trial for not running the world the way we would like.

God sent the plagues on Egypt so that Egypt might learn that, "I am the LORD" (Exodus 7:5). This is the refrain of the story of the plagues. Egypt failed to learn that lesson and was ruined as a result.

Now Israel is having to learn the same lesson, that "I am the LORD" (**15:26; 16:12**). They must learn what Pharaoh failed to learn—otherwise they will receive the judgment Pharaoh received. Ultimately and tragically, the generation that left Egypt failed to learn that lesson and died in the wilderness.

A central theme in the story of the plagues is the hardening of Pharaoh's heart. Here, we find what leads to a hardened heart. Grumbling may seem a small thing. But it leads to a hardened heart. And a hardened heart leads to ruin. When God provides in a manner that does not accord with your preferences or your timing, be careful. You will want to grumble. Instead, take the opportunity to trust God, rather than to test him.

Questions for reflection

1. How do you need to learn the lesson of the manna?

2. When do you grumble, and why? What does it say about your view of, and faith in, God? How seriously do you take it?

3. Are you able to rest? What does this suggest about your view of, and faith in, God? What will help you to rest well?

PART TWO

Perhaps, since you read Part One of this chapter, you've tried to grumble less, either verbally or inwardly. And I guess you've noticed it more, and tried hard, and struggled to stop. Grumbling is a spiritual problem that can lead to catastrophe. So what is the solution to your grumbling?

Jesus meets our needs

As we have seen, God graciously responded to the grumbling of the Israelites by generously providing for their needs. He is the same God today.

John 6:1-15 describes how Jesus feeds 5,000 men with five loaves and two fish in a wilderness. The people recognise the echoes of Moses providing manna in the wilderness. Moses had promised that "the LORD your God will raise up for you a prophet like me from among you" (Deuteronomy 18:15). And so the people wonder if Jesus might be "the Prophet who is to come into the world" (John 6:14). If Jesus is the new Moses, then maybe he will provide free food on a regular basis (v 30-31)!

But Jesus is more than a new type of Moses, providing bread from heaven. Moses was merely a type of Jesus. Jesus is "the bread of life. Whoever comes to me will never go hungry, and whoever believes in me will never be thirsty" (6:35). Jesus himself has come down from heaven like manna to satisfy God's people. He satisfies our hunger and quenches our thirst, just as God did for Israel in Exodus 15 – 17. Jesus satisfies in a way that goes far beyond the provision of bread. Jesus gives eternal life to his people.

Jesus doesn't always give us what we want. But he meets our deepest needs. He gives us identity, fulfilment, forgiveness and relationship. Above all, he gives us life. He gives us a future—an eternal future in God's presence. Jesus gives us himself, and that is a gift that endures beyond death. We look for satisfaction in wealth, but wealth corrodes.

We look for satisfaction in our careers, but at best, careers end in retirement. We look for satisfaction in the admiration of others, but our looks fade or our powers decline or someone more admirable comes along. We look for satisfaction in relationships, but people betray us or we are left bereaved. Even when these things endure, we don't. We die; and death robs us of all the things for which we have lived, for we take none of it with us. There is only one exception and that is Jesus. Death does not rob of Jesus. Quite the opposite. It opens the door to a greater experience of his glory. Look to Jesus to be enough for you, and there will never, ever come a day when he is not enough.

> Let Jesus be enough for you, and there will never, ever come a day when he is not enough.

How do Jesus' hearers respond to this offer? They *grumble*: "At this the Jews there began to grumble about him because he said, 'I am the bread that came down from heaven'" (6:41). It's as if we are back in Exodus 16! *He's the carpenter's son*, they say: *How can he have come from heaven?* Jesus' words in John 6 are full of invitations to come to him to find satisfaction and life. But among all these invitations there is one command and it is this: "Stop grumbling" (John 6:43).

We grumble when we lose perspective. We shrink our horizons until they are filled by our problem. We take our eyes off Jesus. We seek satisfaction elsewhere. And in those moments, Jesus invites us to look at our lives from the perspective of the cross and from the perspective of eternity. Here is what we need to see:

- *The cross is the measure of his generosity.* Jesus has given everything for us. He left heaven for us. He knew hunger and thirst so we could be satisfied. He sweated blood in Gethsemane for us. He was betrayed, mocked, beaten and ultimately crucified. This is how generous he is. He gave up his life for his people. Do we really think the One who gave everything he had for us would not give everything we need to us?

■ *Eternity is the measure of his gift.* What he gives is eternal life. This really is the gift that goes on giving! This gift never runs out and never wears out. Our life now may not be the life we would have chosen. But "our light and momentary troubles are achieving for us an eternal glory that far outweighs them all" (2 Corinthians 4:17). Jesus will give us all we need today; and he will give us all he has one day.

So Jesus responds to his grumbling listeners this way:

"I am the bread of life. Your ancestors ate the manna in the wilderness, yet they died. But here is the bread that comes down from heaven, which anyone may eat and not die. I am the living bread that came down from heaven. Whoever eats this bread will live for ever. This bread is my flesh, which I will give for the life of the world." (John 6:48-51)

Jesus is using wonderful imagery here. But… what does this mean for Brian? Brian is 35, single and longs to be married. And he could become bitter, because his life is not the life he would have chosen. He could become desperate and look for romance with a non-Christian, or turn to porn. Or he can say, "I have Christ. I have life with God. I have forgiveness, adoption, community in him. And that is enough."

Jesus' words here are wonderfully evocative. But… what does this mean for Clare? Clare's husband has cancer. Her days switch between slowly waiting by hospital beds and rushing after her children. Her future is uncertain. How will she survive as a single mother? How will she deal with the loneliness and all the practicalities? Her heart is breaking as she sees her lovely husband wasting away. Some days she feels overwhelmed. This isn't what she dreamed of. She can say, "I have Christ, and so I am never alone. He gives me grace for today and that is enough."

Jesus' words here are often quoted. But… what does this mean for Tim? When Tim—and yes, it's me—is in the middle of conflict, he often gets stewed up by it, frustrated that he's being ignored. He could replay conversations over and over in his head, being more and more vindicated in his imaginary scenarios. He can grow more and more annoyed about how he is being treated or under-appreciated. Or he can say, "I have Christ. I don't need other people's approval. I can feast richly on Christ. Besides which, it's Christ glory that matters. My glory is nothing. I can let it go."

I realise this is easy to say and hard to do. But Jesus has given us a regular reminder of his generous provision. When Brian, Clare and Tim receive the bread and wine at communion, it is a reminder that they have Christ—taking that bread and wine is a visual reminder that Christ satisfies their needs and gives them life.

That's a wonderful promise. But it may also feel—very possibly *should* also feel—like a stinging rebuke, because we have not always, or often, found him to be enough. You and I have grumbled, have judged him and his plans, and have lived as though we needed something else, something more. Don't underestimate what your grumbling is saying to your God. We are guilty. What does God do with guilty grumblers?

Striking the Rock

Come back with me to Massah and look at what happens. The choreography is very significant. The Israelites have put God on trial through their grumbling. And so the courtroom is arranged. The representatives of Israel are on one side (Exodus **17:5**). God says, "I will stand there before you by the rock at Horeb" (**v 6**). So God is on the other side. This is the case of "Israel versus God". In the middle is Moses with his staff, and we're reminded that this is the staff that brought judgment on Egypt (**v 5**). So Moses is, as it were, the judge. All this takes place "in front of the people"—they are in the public gallery, so that everyone can see what happens.

We know that Israel are guilty and deserve to be condemned. We know that God is innocent and deserves to be vindicated. But God tells Moses, "Strike the rock"—the rock where God is standing (**v 6**). It is the most dramatic and surprising moment. Moses brings down the rod of judgment on... God. God takes the judgment that his people deserve—and as a result, blessing flows to the people, as the water comes out from the rock to quench the people's thirst.

Coming after the Red Sea parted, and before God came down on Sinai in fire and thunder (14:21-22; 19:16-19), this may seem to us like a small detail. But it did not seem like that to Moses—this moment was so formative for Moses that when he sang his final song for Israel, it was full of the image of God as the Rock (Deuteronomy 32:4, 15, 18, 30).

And, for us, there is more. "That rock was Christ." In 1 Corinthians 10:4 Paul says, "For [the Israelites] drank from the spiritual rock that accompanied them, and that rock was Christ". What happened at Massah was a picture of, and a pointer to, the cross. At the cross, the great court case between God and humanity came to its climax. On one side was guilty humanity deserving condemnation. On the other side was the perfect, sinless Son of God, Christ the Rock. And God the Father said, "Strike the rock". The rod of his judgment fell on Jesus. Jesus is both the Bread who satisfies our needs and the Rock who bears our judgment.

As a result, blessing flows to God's people. Jesus said, "Whoever believes in me, as the Scripture has said, rivers of living water will flow from within him" (John 7:38). Water flows from Jesus to his people— but this time, the water is symbolic: "By this [Jesus] meant the Spirit, whom those who believed in him were later to receive" (v 39).

Jesus-the-Bread-of-life was all well and good for those who were there, we might suppose. They saw him and heard him. But the feeding of the 5,000 took place a long time ago in a faraway place. How does Jesus-the-Bread-of-life satisfy me today? The answer is that, through the death of Jesus, the Spirit flows to God's people. And the Spirit brings us the presence of Christ. Through the Spirit, Christ speaks to us in the Bible. Through the Spirit, we call on God as our Father in prayer. Through the Spirit, we are assured of Christ's love and rely on his provision and direction. Our thirst is quenched. Our hunger is satisfied. Our guilt is removed.

Here is the truth, however it looks to you today: God is working everything for your good as you love him (Romans 8:28-30). God's understanding of "good" may be different from what you would like for your life. But you can trust him. He has not withheld anything good from you, for he has given you his Son. There is nothing else to give. There is no greater good that God could have given to you.

And now he works for your good by conforming you to the image of that Son. You get to be like *him*! In *all* things, God is providing for you and working in you so that you would become more like him. It might be in the big circumstances, and sadnesses, of your life—your singleness or illness, perhaps. It might be in the small details—the traffic jam in which you find yourself, perhaps. Whether it is a big, life-shaping issue or a momentary inconvenience, think of it as something God intends for your Christ-likeness, trust him to know what he is doing, rely on his provision, and live in gratitude rather than with grumbling.

William McEwen, the eighteenth-century Scottish preacher, wrote:

"The water flowed when the rock was smitten not in scanty measure, but in large abundance. The miraculous stream was not exhausted, though many hundred thousand men, with their herds, drank it. Nor were the dry places of that sandy desert able to imbibe the copious moisture. So inexhausted is the fulness of Jesus Christ, from whom all sorts of men, the Jews, the Gentiles, the barbarians, the Scythians, the bond, and the free, may receive all sorts of blessings. You are not straitened [restricted] in him, O children of men; this river of God, which is full of water, can never run dry, nor be exhausted, how abundantly soever we drink of its refreshing streams."

(*Grace and Truth or, The Glory and Fulness of the Redeemer Displayed,* page 116)

Don't grumble. Look at the cross and think, *He is enough. He has provided, and he will provide.*

Questions for reflection

1. How have you experienced Jesus being enough for you in the past? To which parts of your life do you need to apply this experience now? (Hint: think about what you grumble about.)

2. Are you anything like Brian, Clare or Tim on pages 125-126. What do you need to preach to yourself?

3. How would trusting that God is working to make you more like Jesus today reshape your reaction to momentary inconveniences, and to any life-shaping issues you are wrestling with?

8. FATHER-IN-LAW: MISSION AND WISDOM

Exodus 18 is an odd chapter in many ways. It starts with a family reunion. That's all very touching, but it feels like a distraction from the main story. This is followed by some advice on delegation. The wonderful, exciting story of tense confrontations and dramatic plagues and powerful rescues and parting seas suddenly feels like a management manual. Can't we just skip this chapter and move on to more exciting stuff at Mount Sinai?

But actually this chapter is really important. It takes us right to the heart of the story of the book of Exodus. In fact, it's something of a hinge. It links together the two main halves of the book. It's the climax of the story of the exodus, and it's the introduction to what comes next—the giving of the law.

And right at the centre of this central chapter is a Gentile: Jethro. He's there as a representative of the nations. This chapter demonstrates that the goal of God's salvation and the goal of God's people is that the nations come to worship the LORD.

More than a tribal squabble

But first, in **17:8-16** we see God's judgment on the nations. The Amalekites "came and attacked the Israelites" (**v 8**), provoking a battle (**v 9**).

This story is often taken as a reference to prayer. The thinking goes that while Moses prays on the mountain, the battle goes well. But actually, there is no reference to prayer in this section. Moses does not say in **verse 9** that he is going to pray. Instead, he's going to hold up "the staff of God" (see 4:17, 20). The NIV translates **17:11** as, "As long as Moses held up his hands, the Israelites were winning, but whenever he lowered his hands, the Amalekites were winning." But it is actually "hand" (singular)—the hand that held the staff of God. In **verse 12** it is "hands" (plural), presumably because now Moses cannot hold the staff with one hand. This is the staff with which he struck Egypt in judgment (7:15-19; 8:5-6, 17; 9:3, 15, 22; 10:22; 14:16, 21, 26-27). This is the staff with which he struck God in 17:6 as a sign that God himself would take the judgment his people deserve. Now this staff of judgment is lifted up against the Amalekites. As long as God's judgment is (symbolically) directed against the Amalekites, the battle goes well—and as Moses' hands steadily hold aloft his staff, "Joshua overcame the Amalekite army" (**17:13**). This is a story of judgment.

Why does Moses say, "Tomorrow I will stand on top of the hill with the staff of God in my hands" (**v 9**)? Why the delay? Perhaps it is because throughout the account of the plagues on Egypt, "tomorrow" was the time when God would act in judgment (8:23, 29; 9:5, 18; 10:4). In 9:22 and 10:12 Moses raised his hand in an act of judgment against Egypt. And Israel was saved at the sea through an act of judgment, again when Moses raised his hand (14:16-17). All of this suggests that in this story Moses raises the staff in an act of divine judgment akin to God's judgment on Egypt.

And this is how the story is explained in **17:14-16**. God tells Moses to "write this on a scroll as something to be remembered"—and it is particularly important that Joshua remembers that "[God] will completely blot out the name of Amalek from under heaven" (**v 14**). Joshua will continue this judgment when he leads the Israelites into the promised land—he needs to remember whose judgment it is.

The enmity between Israel and Amalek is a running theme through the next centuries of history. A year later, the Amalekites again attacked Israel, this time in alliance with the Canaanites (Numbers 14:45). The

Amalekites were part of the reason why the people turned back from entering the promised land (Numbers 13:29; 14:25, 43, 45), which led to a whole generation dying in the wilderness. The Amalekites went on to oppose God's people in the land (Judges 3:13; 6:3, 33; 7:12; 10:12; 1 Samuel 15:1-8; 30:1-20)—just as Exodus **17:16** predicts.

In his final sermon, Moses called on the people to wipe out the Amalekites (Deuteronomy 25:17-19). The Amalekites were defeated by Gideon (Judges 6:3; 7:12) and Saul (1 Samuel 14:48; 15:8), but not finally completely destroyed until the reign of Hezekiah (1 Chronicles 4:42-43). Indeed, it seems that **Esther**'s enemy, Haman the Agagite, was named after the Amalekite king, Agag, whom Samuel had killed in 1 Samuel 15:32-33. So the final Amalekites may not have been killed until the time of Esther (Esther 9:7-10).

But the enmity does not only stretch forward from Exodus 17; it has roots back in the past, too. The Amalekites were descended from Amalek, a grandson of Esau (Genesis 36:12, 15-16). The Israelites were descended from Jacob (also called Israel), the brother of Esau. So Exodus 17 is the latest manifestation of an ancient enmity between Esau and Jacob. The enmity itself reflects a more fundamental enmity which stretches back to **Cain and Abel** and beyond that to God and Satan. And it stretches forwards to Babylon and Israel, to the world and the church. This is the true significance of Moses' words: "The LORD will be at war against the Amalekites from generation to genera-tion" (Exodus **17:16**). This war between the people of God and the people of Satan runs throughout history. "Do not be like Cain", says 1 John 3:12-13, "who belonged to the evil one and murdered his brother. And why did he murder him? Because his own actions were evil and his brother's were righteous. Do not be surprised, my brothers and sisters, if the world hates you." This battle at Rephidim in Exodus 17 is not a

> This battle in Exodus 17 is not a small tribal conflict; it is a picture of the battle that rages still today.

small tribal conflict; it is a picture of the battle that has raged since the fall, and rages still today.

With victory secured, Moses builds an altar. He calls the altar, "The Lord is my Banner" (Exodus **17:15**). A banner or standard was what soldiers looked to in battle. It was the rallying point, the sign by which the army stood firm. But the banner to which Israel looks is not held by Joshua on the battlefield, but by Moses on the hill. The banner is God himself. God in Christ is our rallying point, our standard, our sign of victory.

The beginning of **verse 16** is ambiguous. It literally reads, "Hand towards / against the throne of the Lord". It could refer to Moses lifting up his hands in prayer to the throne of God—but the story has not focused on lifting up hands (plural) in prayer, but rather on lifting up the staff of God. Nor is it clear how this connects with the rest of the verse. So it is better to read it (as the NIV does) as a reference to the defiance of the Amalekites: "Because hands were lifted up against the throne of the Lord…"

The point is that it was not Moses who first lifted up hands. The Amalekites initiated this conflict (**v 8**). They lifted up their hands against Israel, and only then did God respond with his own uplifted hand—the hand of Moses, holding the staff—as a sign of his judgment. And Moses does not say that the Amalekites lifted up their hands against Israel; instead, their hands were lifted "against the throne of the Lord". In other words, by opposing Israel, it was God they were fighting.

The sobering message of this story is this: when we lift up our hands against the throne of the Lord, he lifts up his hands against us (symbolically in this story through the raised hands of Moses). And God does not bring his hands down until judgment is complete.

So this story leads to another hill and another man with his hands outstretched and another story of judgment. God's people are again liberated through the judgment of God. Their enemies are defeated. But there is an important difference. Moses spread out his hands to dispense judgment. Jesus spread out his hands to receive judgment.

So the end of chapter 17 shows us what the nations face because they oppose God's people and so lift hands against God—judgment. Then chapter 18 comes as a contrast—because next, we witness a representative of the nations joining God's people to worship God.

Family reunion

Jethro, the "priest of Midian" and Moses' father-in-law, has heard of what God has done (**18:1**). It seems that Moses' wife, Zipporah, has been "sent away" by Moses and has been living with her father and her two sons (**v 2-4**), and now they send word and then come to meet Moses "where he was camped near the mountain of God" (**v 5**). This family reunion frames the story of the exodus. Moses was called away from his family to liberate God's people, and now that liberation is complete, he is reunited with his family. Moses may have sent Zipporah back to her father after the incident in 4:24-26 for her safety; or because they were estranged; or he may have sent her to her father to prepare for his own coming after the exodus.

We have met Moses' son Gershom before. His name sounds like the Hebrew for "a foreigner there". His name is probably Moses' way of saying that Egypt had become a foreign land to him, and Midian had become home (see page 19). **18:4** introduces the second son of Moses: Eliezer. His name means "my God is helper". Moses explains, "My father's God was my helper; he saved me from the sword of Pharaoh". Perhaps Eliezer was conceived before Zipporah returned to her father, but was born after her departure—in which case, this is the first opportunity Moses has had to name him and so his name marks the help that God has given during the exodus. Alternatively, Moses could have previously called him "my God is helper", and now testifies to the way that the name has been fulfilled in the events since he last saw his son.

This episode with Jethro may have been brought forward in the narrative, since it sounds as though the body of laws Israel is about to receive in the next chapters have in fact already been given (**v 16, 20**).

Deuteronomy 1:9-18 suggests that the delegation described in Exodus **18:17-26** took place after the events at Mount Sinai (called Mount Horeb in Deuteronomy 1). In other words, it may well be that Jethro actually arrived after Moses had received the law from God in chapters 19 – 24, but before Israel moved on from Sinai. If the story has been moved forward in this way, it is because it functions as bridge between the story of the exodus and the receiving of the law. In **18:11**, Jethro rounds off one of the key themes of the exodus story—that God is revealing himself to the nations through his judgment against Egypt. Then **verses 13-27** pave the way for the giving of the law by setting in place the judicial framework.

The Amalekites and the Midianite

There are a number of links between the story of the Amalekites in chapter 17 and the story of Jethro in chapter 18:

- In **17:8** the Amalekites "came" and "attacked"; in **18:5-7** Jethro "came" and "greeted".

- In both **17:9** and **18:25**, men are "chosen" for a specific task.

- In both **17:12** and **18:13**, Moses "sits" to judge.

- In both episodes, Moses commences his judging the "next day" (**17:9; 18:13**) and it lasts "all day" until evening (**17:12; 18:13-14**).

- In both **17:12** and **18:18**, Moses is said to be "tired" so that he requires assistance.

Both stories are about the impact of God's people on the nations. But the impact in each is very different. As "Moses told his father-in-law about everything the LORD had done to Pharaoh" (**v 8**), he fulfilled God's purposes, which he had announced to Moses back in 9:16, of raising up Pharaoh so that his "name might be proclaimed in all the earth". The word "proclaimed" in 9:16 is the same word as the word "told" in **18:8**. This is what mission is: the people of God proclaiming or telling in all the earth everything God has done.

A number of times, God says people will "know" that he is the Lᴏʀᴅ as a result of the exodus (6:7; 8:10; 9:29; 10:1-2; 14:4, 18). That same word "know" is used by Jethro here: Jethro knows the Lᴏʀᴅ because the Lᴏʀᴅ rescued his people from the Egyptians (**18:10**), "I know that the Lᴏʀᴅ is greater than all other gods" (**v 11**). God rescued Israel from Egypt so that his name might be "proclaimed" among the nations— and now his name is proclaimed among the nations. And God rescued Israel from Egypt so that his name might be "known" among the nations—and now his name is known among the nations.

Jethro's response contrasts with that of the people of other nations. Exodus 15:14-15 said that "the nations" would "tremble … be terrified … melt away" as they heard what had happened and as they encountered God's people; on the other hand, "Jethro was delighted to hear about all the good things the Lᴏʀᴅ had done for Israel in rescuing them from the hand of the Egyptians" (**18:9**).

What is the result of God's name being made known to the nations? "Jethro, Moses' father-in-law, brought a burnt offering and other sacrifices to God, and Aaron came with all the elders of Israel to eat a meal with Moses' father-in-law in the presence of God" (**v 12**). The nations (Jew and Gentile) are brought together by a sacrifice to eat a meal in the presence of God.

Don't rush past this moment. This is the climax of the exodus. So far in the story we've had people treading on holy ground. We've had spectacular plagues of blood, frogs, gnats and hail. We've seen the death of every firstborn Egyptian. We've had pillars of cloud and fire connecting earth and sky. We've seen a road through the sea with walls of water on either side. We've had manna appearing from heaven.

But the climax of all this astonishing drama is a meal—a meal in the presence of God (see also 24:8-11) to which the nations are invited. And this is the climax because this is what endures. The dramas come and go. They live on only in the memory. But the meal continues. The presence of God continues.

The exodus is a pointer to a greater exodus, a greater act of deliverance from sin and death through the death and resurrection of God's own Son. And the climax of that great exodus is an eternal banquet. People from every nation will be brought together by the blood of Christ to eat in the presence of God. And that moment will continue for ever.

Midianite and Israelite are brought together to eat in the presence of God. It wouldn't always be like this—later, the Midianites would plot the ruin of Israel (Numbers 25) and would oppress and exploit Israel (Judges 6 – 7). In the same way, today there are tensions between people of different nations. Nations war against nations. At a personal level we experience racism, prejudice and mistrust. But across the world, there are communities of light in which the nations are brought together by the sacrifice of Jesus to eat in the presence of God.

This moment, which brings the story of the exodus to a climax, is replicated whenever the people in your church eat a meal together. We look back to the exodus and we look forward to the eternal banquet. As we share bread and wine, the differences between us are redeemed. Division becomes diversity as we're united in Christ—"we, who are many, are one body, for we all share the one loaf" (1 Corinthians 10:17). Christ's sacrifice brings us together and the fruit of that sacrifice is a meal in the presence of God. We don't get plagues and miraculous signs every week—because they were just the means. What we get is their goal: a meal in the presence of God to which the nations are invited.

> Division becomes diversity when we are united in Christ.

Questions for reflection

1. How does holding chapters 17 and 18 together help us to view our communities in a way that is both realistic and optimistic?

2. Are you surprised when the world hates you? Or do you seek to make sure as a priority that the world never hates you? How does Exodus 17 both reshape your expectations and challenge your behaviour?

3. How does Exodus 18 excite you about the next time you share the Lord's Supper with your church?

PART TWO

Preparing for the law

The narrative takes a strange turn in **18:13-27**. Jethro sees Moses hearing all the cases brought to him by the people (**v 14-16**). It is clearly too much for Moses. Twice we're told that people "stood round [Moses] from morning till evening" (**v 13, 15**). Jethro, very understandably, warns Moses, "What you are doing is not good. You and these people who come to you will only wear yourselves out. The work is too heavy for you; you cannot handle it alone" (**v 17-18**). So Jethro tells Moses to take his advice and do two things: "Teach them [God's] decrees and instructions, and show them the way they are to live and how they are to behave" (**v 20**); and then he tells him to appoint representatives of the people to share the load of judging (**v 21-22**). Then only the difficult cases need to come to Moses (**v 22**).

At one level, this is a simple example of the wisdom of delegating responsibility. And it is striking that Moses, the man of God, is happy to adopt this wisdom from the Gentile world. But the book of Exodus is not a book on management practice! This story is here because it paves the way for the giving of the law. Israel needs a system for resolving legal disputes because Israel is about to become a nation governed by the rule of law, the rule of God's law.

This in turn paves the way for one of the great hidden blessings that most Western countries enjoy—the rule of law, with its governing principles that no one is above the law and the law applies equally to all. Though it's not perfect, we can largely trust that our laws will be implemented by the police and courts without bribery, **nepotism** or corruption.

More importantly, Israel is a picture of the church, which is the beginning of the new humanity. We are a people living under the rule of God rather than the rule of self. We do not lift up our hands against the throne of the LORD as the Amalekites did (**17:16**). What is the result? "All these people will go home satisfied" (**18:23**).

What the law does

But there is another outcome. Living under God's law does not only satisfy his people; it also displays God to those who are not his people. God has made his name known through the exodus. At Sinai, Israel is constituted as God's covenant people with a calling to continue to make God's name known to the nations. God intends not only to make himself known to Israel but also through Israel. The law is given to shape Israel's life so that they display the character of God. It is missional in intent.

"You shall not take the name of the LORD your God in vain," says the third commandment (20:7, ESV). The work "take" is better translated as "bear" or "carry"; and the word "vain" can also mean "falsely". So the third command is not so much about not swearing, as a call not to carry God's name in a way that damages his reputation (notably, this is the sin that Paul accuses Israel of in Romans 2:24). Paraphrasing Chris Wright, Ross Blackburn describes Israel as "stewards of the LORD's name" (*The God who Makes Himself Known*, page 102).

This is made explicit in Exodus **19:3-6**, the preface to the Ten Commandments. Don't miss the significance of **verses 1-2**—it is the moment that God keeps his promise, made to a single man in 3:12, to bring out of Egypt a whole people to worship him at Mount Horeb, also called Sinai. These verses say, *God always keeps his promises to his people*. And the next verses say, *God sends his people to his world.* These are wonderful words:

"You yourselves have seen what I did to Egypt, and how I carried you on eagles' wings and brought you to myself. Now if you obey me fully and keep my covenant, then out of all nations you will be my treasured possession. Although the whole earth is mine, you will be for me a kingdom of priests and a holy nation." (**19:4-6**)

Here, God says three things about Israel.

First, Israel was *God's treasured possession* (**v 5**). This phrase is used elsewhere of a king's private treasury (1 Chronicles 29:3; Ecclesiastes 2:8).

Israel was God's special possession. Israel was chosen from the world. But they were also chosen *for* the world.

Second, Israel was a *kingdom of priests* (Exodus **19:5**). Israel were to be a kingdom which, as a whole, had a priestly function similar to the priests in tabernacle. The priests represented the LORD. Aaron's garments were made of the same material as the curtain of the Most Holy Place (Exodus 26:31; 28:5-6)—the word "glory" is only used in Exodus of the LORD, with the significant exception of Aaron's garments (Exodus 28:2, 40, see ESV). In this sense, Aaron bore God's glory to the people. They could not go into the Most Holy Place to witness God's glory there, but they could see Aaron and witness his glory there.

The priests also represented Israel. Aaron's ephod carried stones representing the tribes of Israel (28:6-28). When he stood before God, Israel stood before God; when he presented the blood of the sacrifice which secured forgiveness, Israel presented it and benefited from it.

The presence and activity of priests therefore creates the possibility of a relationship between God and his people. In the same way, Israel as a priestly kingdom created the possibility of a relationship. As a priestly kingdom, Israel was to represent God to the world through mission, and represent the world to God through prayer. The world could not see God, but the world could see Israel and should have seen his glory in them. Today, the world cannot see God, but the world can see the church, and should be able to see his glory there, in us. It's a great encouragement to us to pray for the nations as they appear in the news, to pray for missionaries taking the glory of God around his world, and to pray for our own witness to those across the street.

Third, Israel was a *holy nation* (**19:6**). They were to be holy as God is holy. Indeed the phrase "holy nation" would be arrogant and blasphemous, were it not being said by God. The word "holy" is often used for a tabernacle and priestly function, so it reiterates the idea that Israel was a priestly kingdom. In other words, God's people, today as then, are to reflect God's distinctive character in their distinctive life so that the character of God is displayed to the nations. They are to be a light to the nations.

These words are God's preface to the Ten Commandments, which he gives to Israel in chapter 20. What we are meant to understand is that the Ten Commandments are missional. They were given to shape the life of Israel so that as a nation they displayed the goodness of God. God was creating one area in the world where the goodness of his rule could be seen. His people were his prototype, his working model, his proof of concept.

And we are his people today. Writing to Christians, Peter tells them, "You are a chosen people, a royal priesthood [another way of saying "a kingdom of priests"], a holy nation, God's special possession, that you may declare the praises of him who called you out of darkness into his wonderful light" (1 Peter 2:9). This, of course, is the language of Exodus 19. The missional identity which Israel received at Mount Sinai is fulfilled in the church. The church is the people chosen to be a kingdom of priests who make God known to the world. The church, Peter says, is the nation which is holy as God is holy so that it displays his character (1 Peter 1:14-15). We are the people who declare the praises of God and display the holiness of God to the nations.

This requires us to live distinctive lives (2:11). We want to make connections with people around us. But what will attract people to our message is not our similarities with them, but our distinctives.

> What will attract people to our message is not our similarities with them, but our distinctives.

It is the difference that the gospel makes to our communal life that provokes their questions (3:8-16). This is who you are. Peter is reminding us of our identity in Christ. And one key feature of that identity is that we are a missional community. Peter then applies this in 2:12: "Live such good lives among the **pagans** that, though they accuse you of doing wrong, they may see your good deeds and glorify God on the day he visits us."

Why did God rescue you?

Why did God rescue Israel? He rescued them so that through his rescue, the nations might know that he is the LORD. And he rescued them so that they might be a people who continued to make him known to the nations.

Why did God rescue you? He rescued you so that the nations might know that he is the LORD. And he rescued you so that you might continue to declare his praises to the nations. He rescued us from the nations for the nations.

This is the song they sing in heaven.

"You are worthy to take the scroll and to open its seals,
  because you were slain,
  and with your blood you purchased for God
  persons from every tribe and language and people and nation.
  You have made them to be a kingdom and priests to serve
  our God,
  and they will reign on the earth." (Revelation 5:9-10)

Why did Jesus die? Why was he slain? Why was his blood spilt? There are two reasons.

First, he died to purchase people "from every tribe and language and people and nation" (v 9). God's staff of judgment hangs over the nations. But at the cross, it fell on Christ so that all those in Christ might be saved from the nations.

But second, Jesus died so that we might be "a kingdom and priests" (v 10), making God known to the nations. He died for you so you could be a missionary, declaring the praises of him who called you out of darkness into his wonderful light.

This is our identity, whoever we are and wherever we are. But don't miss God's concern for the nations. They're the goal of God's salvation and they're the goal of our mission. Depending on your context, you may express this concern for the nations in work among refugees, different ethnicities or international students. But you also express it by sending people to the nations. You might like to ask who in your church or home group could be sent. They may not be ready to go now, but who could you be preparing to be sent? We are all part of this worldwide mission. This is our identity in Christ. Christ shed his blood for the nations. And he shed his blood that we might be a priestly kingdom for the nations—that we might be either sent or senders.

World mission matters. It is not peripheral. It is not for super-keen Christians on the margins of the church. It is central to who we are and what we're about. And that's because reaching the nations is central to God's purposes in the world. And it's central to the Bible story. It's central to the story of Exodus. Is it central for you?

Questions for reflection

1. How have you experienced the blessing of living under God's rule, rather than your own?

2. Which aspect of the identity of Israel, and of the church today, most excited you?

3. Why did God rescue you? And how is that being shown in the way you think about, feel about, and go about your life?

9. MEETING AT THE MOUNTAIN OF GOD

Think back to last Sunday's meeting of your church. Were you looking forward to it?

Maybe you were having a lie-in. Perhaps you left it as long as possible to leave your bed or suddenly realised what the time was, and so everything became a big rush.

Maybe getting the children ready in time and trying to chivvy them out of the house made it all seem like a big hassle. Maybe coming to the meeting seemed all very routine, even mundane. You went because it's what Christians are supposed to do. If you didn't turn up, then someone would probably be on your back about it. And so you went through the motions, and then you were glad to get home and enjoy the rest of your day.

In Exodus 19, we come to the very first gathering or assembly or congregation (it's all the same word in Hebrew and Greek) of God's people. Moses describes it as "the day of the assembly" (Deuteronomy 9:10; 10:4; 18:16). And looking at this first "day of the assembly" may transform our attitude to our Sunday meetings. We'll look at the three main players in this story, starting with the most important; the LORD.

Relational holiness

In Exodus **19:9** God says to Moses, "I am going to come to you in a dense cloud, so that the people will hear me speaking with you and will always put their trust in you". God will come, and God will speak. The whole arrangement is designed so that the people can hear God speak.

Indeed, it seems the people literally heard his voice. It is easy to think of God speaking to Moses as some kind of telepathy—but at Mount Sinai, God spoke and all the Israelites heard it. His voice rang out across the plain beneath the mountain. In Deuteronomy 4:12 Moses reminded the people of this day: "The LORD spoke to you out of the fire. You heard the sound of words but saw no form; there was only a voice." The Ten Commandments are heard by the people. God is not a silent God; he is a speaking God.

But there's more. "As the sound of the trumpet grew louder and louder, Moses spoke and the voice of God answered him" (Exodus **19:19**). What's intriguing here is that we're not told what they said. The point seems to be simply this: Moses spoke, and God answered. There is a voice, and there is a conversation. There is a relationship. If you asked people what is the key to a good relationship, the most common answer, I suspect, would be communication. And that's what we see here: communication between God and humanity.

God doesn't simply save the Israelites from slavery and death. He saves them *for* something. He saves for relationship—a two-way relationship with speaking and listening. He saves them so they can enjoy his presence. God says in **verse 9**, "I am going to come to you"; they must be ready "by the third day, because on that day the LORD will come down" (**v 11**); sure enough, we're then told that, on the morning of the third day (**v 16**), as the people stood at the foot of the mountain (**v 17**), "the LORD descended" (**v 18, 20**). God has come to enter into a relationship with his people.

Union and communion

The seventeenth-century English Puritan John Owen talked about the Christian life as "union" and "communion". Our union with Christ is all done by him. We don't contribute anything. It's all by God's grace. But union with God leads to communion with God. And communion with God is a two-way relationship:

"Communion is the mutual sharing of those good things which delight all those in that fellowship ... Our communion with God lies in his giving himself to us and our giving ourselves and all that he requires to him. This communion with God flows from that union which is in Christ Jesus."

(*Of Communion with God*, pages 2-3)

Our union with God through Christ means our salvation is always secure because it doesn't depend on us. But our experience of that union in communion with God does require us to love God, trust God, hear God, speak to God and serve God.

Yet a relationship with God is not straightforward, because God is holy. God cannot be approached lightly. Israel camp "in front of the mountain" (v 2). This is an odd expression, because mountains don't really have fronts. But thrones do—and there is a sense in which the Israelites are approaching the mountain in the way a subject might approach a throne.

In **verse 10**, God tells Moses, "Go to the people and consecrate them". We don't know all that this involved, but it included washing their clothes and abstaining from sex (**v 10-11, 15**). There must be consecration. In verse 6, Israel are called to be "a kingdom of priests and a holy nation" and the next thing that happens is that they are "consecrated" (**v 10**). "Holy" and "consecrated" are from the same root word—the word used of the consecration of priests (28:3, 38, 41; 29:1, 21). Israel must be consecrated as a priestly kingdom and a holy nation.

There must be consecration; and there must be limits. **19:12** says, "Put limits for the people around the mountain and tell them, 'Be careful that you do not approach the mountain or touch the foot of it. Whoever touches the mountain is to be put to death.'" These limits are a kind of safety barrier. God gives these instructions in **verses 12-13**. Then in **verses 20-22** God calls Moses up the mountain to repeat the instructions. Moses says, *We've already done all you told us* (**v 23**). But it's not enough. God must reiterate the importance of this consecration and these limits (**v 24**). These are not suggestions. This is serious. Why?

The problem is spelt out in **verses 22** and **24**:

- ◼ "Even the priests, who approach the Lord, must consecrate themselves, or the Lord will break out against them" (**v 22**).

- ◼ "But the priests and the people must not force their way through to come up to the Lord, or he will break out against them" (**v 24**).

It's as if the holiness of God is nuclear. If you want to approach a nuclear reactor, then you must put on protective clothing, and even then you must not get too close. In the same way, if the people want to approach God they must come prepared through consecration, and even then they must not come too close. A nuclear reactor must be encased in layers of concrete. And as the glory of the Lord descends on Mount Sinai, the mountain is split into three zones of increasing holiness and therefore danger (just as, later, the tabernacle would be). Only Moses may ascend to the top. Aaron and the seventy elders may go on the slopes (**v 22**). The third zone is the border of the mountain, where the people must remain. Transgressing these boundaries leads to death.

Sinai leaves Israel, and us, in no doubt. God wants a relationship with his people. But God is also dangerously holy.

The people

So the first character is the Lord. Now we need to trace the reactions of the people? "On the morning of the third day there was thunder and lightning, with a thick cloud over the mountain, and a very loud trumpet blast. Everyone in the camp trembled" (**v 16**). This is not entirely surprising, because "Mount Sinai was covered with smoke, because the LORD descended on it in fire. The smoke billowed up from it like smoke from a furnace, and the whole mountain trembled violently" (**v 18**). The people trembled with fear because the mountain trembled with violence. The reaction of the people in **20:18**, after God has spoken the Ten Commandments, is the same: "When the people saw the thunder and lightning and heard the trumpet and saw the mountain in smoke, they trembled with fear".

> Moses is saying, *Don't be afraid of feeling fear, because fear is the right response to God.*

This is the right response. In **verse 20**, Moses says to the people, "Do not be afraid. God has come to test you, so that the fear of God will be with you to keep you from sinning". At first sight, it's an odd thing to say. In effect, Moses is saying, *Don't be afraid, but be afraid*! What he seems to be expressing is, *Don't be afraid of feeling fear, because fear is the right response to God. You're doing the right thing. And this fear will keep you loyal to God.* The people who should really be afraid are those who feel no fear and so take God lightly. They should be afraid, because they are heading for disaster.

The heart of what it means to "keep … from sinning" (**v 20**) is spelt out in **verses 22-26**. It is not just about obeying individual laws. What drives true obedience is a whole-hearted allegiance to God. So in **verses 22-23**, God reiterates the first and second commandments (see v 3-6). All sin starts with wanting something or someone more than God. This is what makes breaking God's law seem worthwhile to us. I lie (my sin) to get the admiration I crave (my idol). I look at porn (my sin) to feel powerful (my idol). I use others (my sin) to get my own way (my idol).

And so these verses show us that God is gracious. Even as he reminds the people to keep from sin, he also reminds them of his provision for sin (**v 24**). Through sacrifice comes blessing. But why the instruction not to build with dressed stone (**v 25**)? And why no steps (**v 26**)? Part of the answer is probably that Israel was not to copy the worship patterns of the surrounding nations, with their shaped altars and pyramid-like plinths. Another part is probably that nothing was to distract from a focus on God. The aim was to avoid gasps of amazement as people admired the human craftsmanship of the altar (**v 25**) and to avoid sniggers of amusement as a priest exposed too much or tripped on his robe as he climbed the altar steps (**v 26**). They remain good principles to apply to our gathered worship. Are we copying the patterns of the world around us? Are we drawing attention away from God? Consider the music in your church, for example. Is it so good that people are distracted with amazement? Or is it so bad that people are distracted with amusement or embarrassment?

The mediator

The third player is the mediator, Moses. In some ways this whole episode is set up to confirm his role.

First, Moses' role is confirmed to the people. "The Lᴏʀᴅ said to Moses, 'I am going to come to you in a dense cloud, so that the people will hear me speaking with you and will always put their trust in you'" (**19:9**). Perhaps the point of the conversation between Moses and God here (the full content of which we're not told) was simply that it happened, and so confirmed Moses as God's spokesman.

Second, Moses' role is confirmed to Moses himself. Back in 3:12, when Moses first encountered God at Mount Sinai, God had said to him, "I will be with you. And this will be the sign to you that it is I who have sent you: when you have brought the people out of Egypt, you will worship God on this mountain.'" What is that role? In **20:19** the people say to Moses, "Speak to us yourself and we will listen. But do not let God speak to us or we will die." Then in **verse 21** we're told that, "The people remained at a distance, while Moses approached the thick darkness where God was". Moses is going to be a mediator between God and his people. He will approach God on their behalf. He will speak to God on their behalf. He will hear from God on their behalf.

This role is confirmed by all the ups and downs in chapter 19:

- Verse 3: Moses goes up the mountain.

- **Verse 7**: Moses goes down the mountain.

- **Verse 8**: Moses goes up the mountain.

- **Verse 14**: Moses goes down the mountain.

- **Verse 20**: Moses goes up the mountain (and the first thing God says to him is "Go down" again, **v 21**!).

- **Verse 25**: Moses goes down the mountain.

Then in **20:21**, Moses approaches God. This is his fourth journey up the mountain. Altogether, he makes seven journeys up this mountain while Israel is camped at Mount Sinai. And he's not a young man—he's around 80 years old at this point. We don't know for sure the location of Mount Sinai, but our best guess is that it was Jebel Musa, which is 7,363 feet high. The good news for Moses is that Israel were probably camped on a plateau at about 5,000 feet. But that still leaves over 2,000 feet for Moses to climb each time. Moses is literally a go-between. He is constantly going between the people and God.

Where do we go today if we want to meet with God? Must we travel up to heaven (symbolised by Mount Sinai)? At the end of his life, Moses said:

"Now what I am commanding you today is not too difficult for you or beyond your reach. It is not up in heaven, so that you have to ask, 'Who will ascend into heaven to get it and proclaim it to us so that we may obey it?' ... No, the word is very near you; it is in your mouth and in your heart so that you may obey it." (Deuteronomy 30:11-12, 14)

We don't need to go on a physical pilgrimage to a mountain to discover God in some holy place. Nor do we have to undertake a spiritual journey to discover God within. Instead, Christ our mediator has come down and made God known to us (Romans 10:6-10—Paul is quoting Moses here). If you want to meet with God today, you need only open your Bible and meet him in the word of Jesus. It is that wonderfully simple.

Questions for reflection

1. How do the ideas of "union" and "communion" help you think about your own relationship with God?

2. How does your relationship with God take account of his dangerous holiness?

3. When was the last time you trembled in awe at God's might and purity? How does meditating on what happened at this mountain inspire you to fear him rightly?

PART TWO

Not changed, but everything has changed

We live a long time past Sinai, and a long way from Sinai. So what are we to make of this today? How does it transform what goes on in our hearts next Sunday morning?

First, we must remember that God has not changed. He still wants a relationship with his people; but he is also still holy. He is still nuclear, as it were. He still cannot be approached lightly. God has not turned down the heat of his holiness. He has not been tamed. If we are to feel the wonder of God's grace to us in Christ Jesus, then we must first feel the terror of his holiness.

Second, people have not changed. We still need to be consecrated—made holy. Why? Because we are unholy. We are still in danger of God breaking out against us (**19:22, 24**). Were we to come into God's presence, we would be like tissue paper in the midst of a bonfire. Imagine approaching a large fire with a piece of tissue paper to put into the fire. It would be consumed before you got near. So would you be, in God's presence.

In one sense, what happened at Mount Sinai (which was later replicated in the tabernacle) was a huge visual aid to teach these truths. God's invitation to come near and warning not to come near are both expressed in the choreography of what happens at Mount Sinai. God's desire for a relationship with his people along with the problem of divine holiness for his sinful people are both on display in the events of Exodus 19.

So how can we have a relationship with the God from whom we must be kept separate? Hebrews 12 reflects on Exodus 19 from a post-cross perspective:

> "You have not come to a mountain that can be touched and that is burning with fire; to darkness, gloom and storm; to a trumpet blast or to such a voice speaking words that those who heard it begged that no further word be spoken to them, because they could not bear what was commanded: 'If even an animal touches

the mountain, it must be stoned to death.' The sight was so terrifying that Moses said, 'I am trembling with fear.'

"But you have come to **Mount Zion**, to the city of the living God, the heavenly Jerusalem. You have come to thousands upon thousands of angels in joyful assembly, to the church of the firstborn, whose names are written in heaven. You have come to God, the Judge of all, to the spirits of the righteous made perfect, to Jesus the mediator of a new covenant, and to the sprinkled blood that speaks a better word than the blood of Abel." (Hebrews 12:18-24)

We have not come to Mount Sinai. We have come to Mount Zion. Mount Zion is a picture of heaven. Just as Moses ascended through the clouds to the top of Mount Sinai, so we ascend with Jesus through the clouds into heaven (Hebrews 4:14-16).

The experience of Sinai was full of awe: a mountain burning with fire; the blast of a trumpet that grew louder and louder; the voice of God himself. It was like a volcanic eruption, but with so much more drama. Maybe you wish you could have been there—except, of course, that everyone who actually was there was terrified. Even Moses was trembling with fear.

But each Sunday we come to something more wonderful. We step into the heavenly gathering. The word "assembly" in Hebrews 12:22 means "gathering" or "congregation". By faith, we step into heaven and around us are thousands of angels (v 22) and all the Christians who have died now made perfect (v 23). There are angels standing next to you when you sing. I'm not playing with **metaphors** here. And I realise this sounds strange to us. But this physical world is not all there is—there is a heavenly realm that is separate from our earthly realm, but which intersects with it. We're linked to it because we're linked to Jesus. We stand there with him. So whenever we gather on earth, we are also simultaneously gathering in heaven. Above all, we gather in the presence of God: "You have come to Mount Zion … You have come to God."

What is the mood of this gathering? Not fear, but joy. The writer of Hebrews captures the mood at Mount Sinai: "gloom and storm" (v 18), "terrifying" and "trembling" (v 21). The mood is very different among those who come to Mount Zion. It is a "joyful assembly" (v 22).

The greater mediator

What makes the difference? God has not changed. People have not changed. What's changed is the mediator. Hebrews 12:24 says we have come "to Jesus the mediator of a new covenant".

Remember, Moses had to shuttle backwards and forwards. Moses could only meet God in a dense cloud because Moses was human, so he couldn't directly look at the face of God. He could convey the words of God; but he couldn't reform the people or deal with their sin. So God promised a new and greater prophet. And we're told in Deuteronomy that God makes this promise precisely because the people asked for a mediator at Mount Sinai:

"The LORD your God will raise up for you a prophet like me from among … your fellow Israelites. You must listen to him. For this is what you asked of the LORD your God at Horeb on the day of the assembly when you said, 'Let us not hear the voice of the LORD our God nor see this great fire any more, or we will die.'" (Deuteronomy 18:15-16)

Notice that Moses quotes directly from Exodus 19. In response to their request for a mediator on that day, the people got Moses, and Moses was a great prophet. But Moses wasn't enough; so in response to their request for a mediator, God would one day send a prophet-mediator greater than Moses.

Jesus is the mediator from God who is God. He is the true God and the true man. He perfectly represents both parties. At Mount Sinai, God descended from heaven to the top of the mountain, and Moses ascended from the valley floor to the mountain. They met halfway, as it were. But in Jesus, something much more far-reaching and long-lasting has taken place. Jesus the true God descended to be with humanity. In Jesus, God descended to earth. He came to live among us. Jesus is Immanuel: "God with us". And Jesus the true man ascended to be with God. He ascended into the clouds just as Moses ascended into the clouds. But Jesus passed through the clouds in heaven to appear before the throne of God. In Jesus, humanity has ascended to the presence of God. In Jesus, humanity has entered the nuclear presence of God and survives.

Humanity survives this encounter because the blood of Jesus deals with our sin. We have come "to Jesus the mediator of a new covenant, and to the sprinkled blood that speaks a better word than the blood of Abel" (Hebrews 12:24). Abel was the second son of Adam and Eve, and he was killed by Cain, his brother. Abel epitomises those who cry out for justice, because he was the first person to be wrongly treated by another human being. His cry for justice rises from the ground. And over the years it has been joined by millions and millions of other cries. We, too, cry out for justice. We are all Abel.

But we are also all Cain, the brother who killed him. The cry of Abel— and the countless cries that echo his first cry, including yours— cries out against you and me. It is a din of noise and pain—and it's directed at you. Maybe there are times when you hear it ringing in your ears.

But listen. Listen by faith. Above all the din is the word of Jesus. And it's a better word. It's a word of reassurance. The blood of Jesus satisfies all the demands of justice.

The sinner-consuming holiness of God consumed the body of Jesus as he hung in our place on the cross. God broke out against his own Son so that we can come before God—not with fear, but with joy. We come to angels and saints and God himself to join the joyful assembly.

Warning

But we must end with a note of warning, for that is how the commentary of Exodus 19 in Hebrews 12 ends. The writer highlights two ways in which the events of Sinai are repeated.

First, the voice is repeated in the present. The voice that spoke from Mount Sinai speaks to you today. The voice that made the Israelites tremble with fear addresses you. It speaks as God's word is read and preached and sung. The only difference is that today God speaks from his throne in heaven. Hebrews 12:25 says, "See to it that you do not refuse him who speaks. If they did not escape when they refused him who warned them on earth, how much less will we, if we turn away from him who warns us from heaven?"

When we gather with God's people to hear God's word, we should do it with seriousness. We are not coming together to be entertained. We are coming to tremble before the holy word of our holy God. The great Reformer Martin Luther said:

"Would to God that we would gradually train our hearts to believe that the preacher's words are God's Word ... It is not an angel or a hundred thousand angels but the Divine Majesty Himself that is preaching there. To be sure, I do not hear this with my ears or see it with my eyes; all I hear is the voice of the preacher ... and I behold only a man before me. But I view the picture correctly if I add that the voice and words of [the] pastor are not his own words and doctrine but those of our Lord and God."

("Sermons on the Gospel of St. John" in *Luther's Works*, Volume 22, pages 526-527)

Second, the shaking of Mount Sinai will be repeated in the future. At Mount Sinai "the whole mountain trembled violently" (Exodus **19:18**). It was like a localised earthquake—and it was terrifying. But Hebrews 12:26-27 tells us that, "At that time his voice shook the earth, but now he has promised, 'Once more I will shake not only the earth but also the heavens.' The words 'once more' indicate the removing of what can be shaken—that is, created things—so that what cannot be shaken may remain."

A time is coming when not only with the earth will shake, but the heavens as well. God is going to come down again; and this time he will shake up the whole of creation. This is the final day of judgment, when God wraps up history and remakes the world. It will be a day when everyone will assemble before God—and the Bible says it will be a day when people tremble with fear.

So Hebrews 12 concludes, "Therefore, since we are receiving a kingdom that cannot be shaken, let us be thankful, and so worship God acceptably with reverence and awe, for our 'God is a consuming fire'" (Hebrews 12:28-29). If you put your trust and keep your trust in Jesus—the better mediator with a better word—you will be part of a kingdom that cannot be shaken. There is a place of safety when God shakes up this world, and there is only one—and that place of safety is in Jesus and his kingdom.

God has not changed. So we worship him with reverence and awe. But Christ has come as our mediator. And so we worship him with joy. Next Sunday morning when you are putting off getting out of bed or your family breakfast has descended into chaos or your church gathering feels dull, remember this. Each time you gather as a church, you are standing with angels in the presence of God. And so participate not as a hassled parent or bored church-goer. Participate as a member of the congregation of heaven—the "joyful assembly".

Questions for reflection

1. How will the truths of this passage shape what you think when you wake up on Sunday morning, and what you think as you walk into your church?

2. How does identifying both with Abel and with Cain enable you more deeply to understand and appreciate the cross of Christ?

3. Do you need to heed the warning set out on the previous two pages? How?

10. THE LAW OF GOD AND LIFE IN CHRIST

Here are five chapters of law, quite a lot of which are about livestock disputes. If you're not a farmer, you might wonder how this applies to you. Or what about laws governing slavery when we don't own slaves? Or what about these commands?

- "Anyone who curses their father or mother is to be put to death" (**21:17**). Is executing your children an application of this passage?

- "If you lend money to one of my people among you who is needy, do not treat it like a business deal; charge no interest" (**22:25**). Is it wrong to have a mortgage?

- "Celebrate the Feast of Unleavened Bread" (**23:15**). Should we keep Jewish festivals?

- "Do not cook a young goat in its mother's milk" (**23:19**). What has that got to do with anything?

These are not flippant questions, because they get to the central question of how Christians today should respond to the laws of the Old Testament. If we love God, we will desire to obey him—and so we will read chapters like these and ask, "Should Christians obey these commands? Should we try to enforce them in society? How should we relate to the law of Moses?"

A different historical culture

First, we need to recognise these laws were given to people at a different time in a different culture. Many of them assume an **agrarian economy**. Some seem designed to avoid any confusion or contamination with Canaanite religions, which isn't an issue for us. The law against charging interest assumes people are in debt because of poverty, rather than because they're buying a house or growing a business. The laws of slavery are regulating what was then a fact of life to ensure it was conducted in a humane way. The Bible contains the seeds that would eventually lead to the abolition of the slave trade—in the meantime, it ensured slaves were well-treated. Likewise the divorce laws, as Jesus makes clear in Mark 10:2-9, accept the realities of life in a fallen world (without actually condoning fallen behaviour) to ensure the vulnerable are protected. There is an accommodation to the realities of life in a fallen world with an attempt to limit the harm caused by sin.

A different redemptive moment

Even more significantly, the law of Moses was given to people at a different stage in the history of redemption. The covenant with God confirmed in Exodus 24 is not the covenant under which we live. We live under what Jesus calls "the new covenant" (Luke 22:20). In Exodus 24, Moses relates these laws to the people, who commit to keeping them (**v 1-3, 7**). Then they sacrifice bulls on an altar (**v 3-6**) and Moses sprinkles the blood on the people (**v 8**). So the covenant of Moses was made through blood. But this "old" covenant gave way to a new covenant when Jesus was sacrificed. That is why, when Jesus gave his disciples the wine during the Last Supper, he said, "This cup is the new covenant in my blood, which is poured out for you" (Luke 22:20).

In the new covenant, the law of Moses written on tablets of stone is replaced by the law of the Spirit written on our hearts (Jeremiah 31:31-34; Hebrews 8:7-13). Augustine of Hippo, the fourth-century African theologian, highlighted the link between Sinai and Pentecost (in *Against Faustus*, 32.12, and Letter 55). Israel came to Sinai fifty days after offering the Passover lamb. The Spirit came at Pentecost fifty days after Jesus had been offered as the Passover Lamb. Both events took place fifty days after the Passover. Both involved violence—a violent shaking or a violent wind. Both involved fire. Both involved God writing his law. The difference is that the fire at Pentecost was intimate and personal. We're no longer confronted by God's power. We're now indwelled by God's power. Now God writes his law on our hearts through the Holy Spirit. And so, Augustine wrote, we must...

> We're no longer confronted by God's power; we are indwelled by it.

"Notice how it happened there and how it happened here. There, the people stood a long way off; there was an atmosphere of dread, not of love. I mean, they were so terrified that they said to Moses, 'Speak to us yourself, and do not let the Lord speak to us, lest we die.' So God came down, as it was written, on Sinai in fire; but he was terrifying the people who stood a long way off, and 'writing with his finger on stone,' not on the heart [Exodus 31:18].

"Here, however, when the Holy Spirit came, the faithful were gathered together as one; and he didn't terrify them on a mountain but came in to them in a house. There came a sudden sound, indeed, from heaven, as of a fierce squall rushing upon them; it made a noise, but nobody panicked. You have heard the sound, now see the fire too, because each was there on the mountain also, both fire and sound; but there, there was smoke as well, here, though, the fire was clear. 'There appeared to them,' the Scriptures says, you see, 'divided tongues, as of fire.' Terrifying them from a long way off? Far from it. Because 'it settled upon each one of them, and they began to talk in languages, as the

Spirit gave them utterance.' [Acts 2:1-4] Hear a person speaking a language, and understand the Spirit writing not on stone but on the heart." (Augustine, *Sermon 155.6*)

This means, in short, that Jesus and the Spirit replace the law of Moses.

The Son, the Spirit, and the will of God

In his letter to the Galatian Christians, Paul addresses some false teachers who were turning back to the law of Moses and enforcing it as a guide for Christians. He says to his readers, "My dear children, for whom I am again in the pains of childbirth until Christ is formed in you…" (Galatians 4:19). It's not the law of Moses that gives shape to the Christian life, but Jesus. We're called to be Christ-like, not law-keepers. Or, as Paul puts it in Galatians 6:2, we're to keep "the law of Christ".

The law of Christ is not codified in a serious of rules or axioms. Romans 7:6 says, "But now, by dying to what once bound us, we have been released from the law so that we serve in the new way of the Spirit, and not in the old way of the written code". The Spirit now illuminates God's word so that we know God's will.

So after writing that "the fruit of the Spirit is love, joy, peace, forbearance, kindness, goodness, faithfulness, gentleness and self-control," Paul adds, "Against such things there is no law" (Galatians 5:22-23). In other words, the Spirit grows in us virtues that cannot be created or even expressed by any law. You can't codify patience or kindness or goodness. Parents know all too well that you can't create patience by diclat. The best you can do is make your child's impatience slightly less wearing. But the Spirit writes virtues into our hearts as he glorifies the example of Jesus.

Think of it like this. When you were a child, your parents imposed lots of rules on you. "Don't go out of my sight." "Ask before you leave the table." As an adult you no longer live by obeying those rules. You move out of the sight of your parents. You don't ask permission to leave the table. There was nothing wrong with those laws. They were good laws for your five-year-old self. But they're no longer relevant because (hopefully) you've internalised the principles which they were teaching. You're no longer bound by the rule to remain in the sight of your parents because you've learnt how to be safe. You no longer ask their permission to leave the table because you've learnt for yourself when it's appropriate to do so. In a similar way, the law of Moses is no longer necessary because the Spirit internalises for us the will of God.

More than that, the Spirit empowers us so we can obey God's will. The great symbol of membership of the old covenant law of Moses was circumcision. But now, Paul says, "Circumcision is circumcision of the heart, by the Spirit, not by the written code" (Romans 2:29). In other words, we belong to God's people and we fulfil God's will "by the Spirit, not by the written code".

So the words of the law of Moses no longer apply to Christians as they did to Israel. For example, Exodus **20:8-10** says, "Remember the Sabbath day by keeping it holy. Six days you shall labour and do all your work, but the seventh day is a sabbath to the LORD your God. On it you shall not do any work, neither you, nor your son or daughter, nor your male or female servant, nor your animals, nor any foreigner residing in your towns." **23:12** says it again: "Six days do your work, but on the seventh day do not work, so that your ox and your donkey may rest, and so that the slave born in your household and the foreigner living among you may be refreshed".

But in the New Testament, Paul says this has become a matter of indifference: "One person considers one day more sacred than another; another considers every day alike. Each of them should be fully convinced in their own mind" (Romans 14:5). Indeed, in Galatians 4:8-11 Paul says that imposing special days on people is to enslave them all over again. It pushes people back not to Sinai, but to Egypt! "Therefore," he says in Colossians 2:16, "do not let anyone judge you … with regard to a religious festival, a **New Moon celebration** or a Sabbath day."

The writer to the Hebrews expresses this even more strongly. Talking about the new covenant, which the Spirit writes on our hearts, he says in Hebrews 8:13, "By calling this covenant 'new', he has made the first one obsolete; and what is obsolete and outdated will soon disappear". The laws of Exodus 20 – 23, confirmed in the covenant in Exodus 24, are now obsolete.

People have often tried to make a distinction between the **moral, ceremonial and civic aspects** of the Law of Moses. The ceremonial and civic regulations no longer apply to Christians, they say, but the moral regulations do. There is some truth in this, as we shall see. But dividing up the law in this way has proved notoriously hard to do in practice. More importantly, the Bible itself never makes these distinctions.

So can we tear these pages out of our Bibles? If they're "obsolete" and they no longer apply, can we dispose of them? Can we skip them in our Bible-reading programmes?

The answer is emphatically no. Paul says, "For everything that was written in the past was written to teach us, so that through the endurance taught in the Scriptures and the encouragement they provide we might have hope" (Romans 15:4). What's interesting about this is that he writes these words in the context of discussing how the law of the Sabbath has become a matter of indifference. We may not have to obey the letter of the law, but the law still matters. It still informs our understanding as Christians. And it does so in three ways—one of which we will look at in this part, with the other two in focus in the next.

The law points to God's will

The Law of Moses may no longer define God's will for us, but it does point to God's will. God is not arbitrary or changeable. It's not that he approved one set of behaviours in the Old Testament and then changed his mind by the time of the New Testament. His will is fixed and eternal.

But how that will is expressed does vary. The Law of Moses expressed God's will to a specific people in a specific context at a specific moment. Those conditions no longer apply. Nevertheless, the Law of Moses did express something of God's eternal will (which is why so many of its moral regulations clearly continue to apply today).

So we can work backwards, as it were, from the Law of Moses to understand God's eternal will, and then work forwards to apply it to our own situation.

For example, take Exodus **21:28-29**: "If a bull gores a man or woman to death, the bull is to be stoned to death, and its meat must not be eaten. But the owner of the bull will not be held responsible. If, however, the bull has had the habit of goring and the owner has been warned but has not kept it penned up and it kills a man or woman, the bull is to be stoned and its owner also is to be put to death." Most of us don't own bulls, so in one sense this law is irrelevant to us. But it is nevertheless also expressing something that is timeless. Accidents happen, and people shouldn't be held responsible for something that was an accident. But you can be culpable for an accident if you didn't takes steps to prevent what could have been anticipated. So I learn two things from this passage:

- ■ I shouldn't blame someone if they accidentally harm me.

- ■ If I can anticipate an accident, then I should take steps to prevent it.

In fact, it's not difficult to distil what is timeless and universal in the Law of Moses. Jesus said there are really only two commands: love God and love your neighbour (Mark 12:28-34). Paul wrote, "The entire law is fulfilled in keeping this one command: 'Love your neighbour as yourself'" (Galatians 5:14). In Romans 13:9-10 he says, "The commandments, 'You shall not commit adultery,' 'You shall not murder,' 'You shall not steal,' 'You shall not covet,' and whatever other commandment there may be, are summed up in this one command: 'Love your neighbour as yourself.' Love does no harm to a neighbour. Therefore love is the fulfilment of the law."

It's all too easy for us to think of "law" in a negative way. We see it as something restrictive. But the rule of law is a great blessing in any society. The alternative is **anarchy**, in which the strong exploit the weak with impunity. Just 50 days before these chapters, the Israelites had been oppressed slaves. Now they stood before Mount Sinai and heard the Ten Commandments. To former slaves, these commandments would have sounded like a declaration of liberation, not a decree of imposition:

Pharaoh's rule	God's exodus rule
The powerful have complete power over others	God's authority prevents people claiming complete power (first commandment, **20:3**)
The gods are used to support the powerful	An imageless God cannot be co-opted and the divine name cannot be used for gain (second and third commandments, **v 4-7**)
Production and consumption is unrestrained	The Sabbath sets limits to production and consumption (fourth commandment, **v 8-11**)
Vulnerable workers are exploited and overworked	Rest for all with protection for vulnerable workers (fourth commandment, **v 8-11**)
Family life is subject to destructive interference	Respect for parental authority and marital integrity (fifth and seventh commandments, **v 12, 14**)
The weak are vulnerable to violence with state-organised genocide	Respect for human life (sixth commandment, **v 13**)
The weak are vulnerable to economic exploitation	The weak are protected from the greed of the powerful (eighth and tenth commandments, **v 15, 17**)
The weak have no effective legal protection	Integrity and impartiality of judicial system (ninth commandment, **v 16**)

What the Law of Moses does—along with the rest of the Bible and supremely the Lord Jesus himself—is to show us what it means to love God and other people in different situations. The Law of Moses defined what it meant to love your neighbour back then. In so doing, it gives us lots of pointers to what it means for us now. So we should think of the Law of Moses as case law—case studies or applied wisdom which points us to God's will. Indeed, the commentator John Mackay believes this was how it was intended even in its original context; that chapters 21 – 23 contain...

"... illustrative decisions which show how the principles embodied in the Ten Commandments may be worked out in specific everyday situations that Israel would have to face. No attempt is made to develop an all-embracing law code. Instead God provides paradigms, authoritative patterns which would allow Israel (and the church still) to think through how to apply basic **ethical** principles in a variety of situations." (*Exodus*, page 364)

When we begin to see the law in this way, we realise that we may not have a goat to milk or a bull that enjoys goring people—but we do have many varied situations in life where as God's people we desire to live for him, and where as God's people we can use these laws to show us principles that enable us to live for him.

Questions for reflection

How has this section helped you to:

1. understand the place of God's law in a Christian's life?

2. appreciate the goodness and blessing of God's law?

3. be motivated to live in obedience to God's law?

PART TWO

The law points to our Saviour

As we've seen, the Old Testament law points us to God's will, and it is immensely precious for that. But there is more. Second, we turn to the Law of Moses because it points us to our Saviour. Romans 3:20-22 says:

"Therefore no one will be declared righteous in God's sight by the works of the law; rather, through the law we become conscious of our sin. But now apart from the law the righteousness of God has been made known, to which the Law and the Prophets testify. This righteousness is given through faith in Jesus Christ to all who believe."

This is anticipated in the Ten Commandments themselves. They are introduced in Exodus **20:1-2** with God reminding the people that he brought them out of slavery. The law is not given as a means of redemption, for God has already redeemed his people.

And so the law points in two ways to the Saviour whom God sent to make his people righteous:

1. *Our need is exposed.* The law makes us conscious of our problem. "Through the law we become conscious of our sin" (Romans 3:20). We all have embarked upon a deep-seated rebellion against God, and what the law does is expose that hidden rejection of God. Suppose a child hates their teacher. How would you know? You would know as soon as the teacher expresses their will in a rule and the child refuses to keep that rule. That's what would reveal the child's heart-hatred. In the same way, the law reveals the state of our hearts—and what it reveals is a rebellious attitude towards God.

2. *Christ's salvation is promised.* Paul says something striking in Romans 3:21—that a righteousness from God "has been made known, to which the Law and the Prophets testify". The law condemns us. It says we're in the wrong. But the law also points to a

way in which we can be made right. And that rightness before God is found through faith in Jesus Christ.

Shortly before his death, Moses gathered the people together, and outlined the blessings that would come if they kept God's law and the curses that would fall if they disobeyed God's law (Deuteronomy 27 – 28). Those curses culminated in exile and death. Jesus alone has kept the law of God—has been righteous—and the blessings he merited come to us because we are in him. On the other hand, we've broken God's law, but the curse we deserve fell on Jesus as he died in our place. So Jesus sets us free from the condemnation of the law.

These pointers to what Jesus would do became obsolete when Jesus came because the picture gave way to the reality. We no longer have to obey these laws, because they've been fulfilled in Jesus. But neither do we ditch them, because they help us understand what Jesus has accomplished. (What this looks like for our approach to the law and how we live is what the rest of this chapter is about.)

A model of God's future

The exodus is an act of re-creation, as we have seen. Exodus 1:7 closely resembles the story of creation in Genesis 1:28. The people literally "swarm" across Egypt, recalling Genesis 1:21 and 8:17. When the mother of Moses sees him she declares him "good", echoing God's verdict on creation in Genesis 1. Among the Israelites we see the **mandate** of creation being fulfilled. When Pharaoh tries to impede this creative fruitfulness, God "de-creates" his world around him through the plagues. When Pharaoh pursues Israel to the Red Sea, God separates the waters to create dry land as he did at creation through his Spirit-wind. But when the Egyptian army follows them, the waters "un-separate". Creation goes into reverse in an act of judgment. And as we shall see, the tabernacle is designed to echo the temple-garden of Eden and is therefore a blueprint for a new creation.

So Exodus presents us with a re-created people in recreated space in re-created time. The exodus is the blueprint for a new creation in both...

- the method—redemption through sacrifice, and

- the content—a unified cosmos with God at the centre.

In Exodus 20, God has led his people to Mount Sinai to give them his law. Here he creates his people as his people. And through his law he orders or re-orders them. The word "justice" or "judgment" was not just a legal term. It also has the sense of restoring everything to its proper place. God is creating the blueprint for his new creation through the law of his re-created people.

> God is creating the blueprint for his new creation through his law.

In particular, the law symbolises the re-ordering of creation. The separation of light and darkness, water and water, water and land, and day and night in creation (Genesis 1:3-19) is replicated in the law. Animals that span the separation of earth and land are unclean. So animals with both scales and feet or aquatic animals without scales are unclean. Mixtures of cloth are unclean (Leviticus 19:19). This is also why "anyone who has sexual relations with an animal is to be put to death" (Exodus **22:19**). They are transgressing the boundaries separating an ordered creation. The life-giving and death are separated. So birds that feed on carrion are unclean. Things that are defective are unclean. A goat should not be cooked in its mother's milk because what gives life should not bring death (**23:19**).

These distinctions are symbolic—but their symbolism is important. These laws are a testimony that the work of Christ re-orders a cosmos jumbled by sin. In God's new world, everything will be made new.

In the meantime, many of these symbolic separations no longer apply in the New Testament (Mark 7:19; Acts 10; Colossians 2:20-23).

But the fundamental principle of separating from what is sinful or anti-creation is continued (2 Corinthians 6:14-17).

In his book *Paul and the Law,* Brian Rosner identifies four ways in which Paul uses the Law of Moses: repudiation, replacement, reappropriation as prophecy, and reappropriation as wisdom. Paul *repudiates* the law as a moral code, for it is replaced by Christ as the standard of Christian behaviour. But the law still matters. So Paul also *reappropriates* the Mosaic law as wisdom and prophecy. These two ways of reappropriating the law map onto our two main points—the law points to God's will (the law as wisdom) and the law points to God's Saviour (the law as prophecy).

Jesus fulfils the law

Jesus said, "Do not think that I have come to abolish the Law or the Prophets; I have not come to abolish them but to fulfil them" (Matthew 5:17). The big question this raises is: *What does it actually mean for Jesus to fulfil the law?!*

We've seen how the law points to God's will, and the law points to God's Saviour. These two truths help us understand how Jesus fulfils the law.

First, Jesus fulfils the law by embodying love for God and love for others (the law as wisdom). Jesus is the epitome of the law. He is the law in action. The affection which the Old Testament saints have for God's law is striking (see, for example, Psalm 119:16, 20). They love the idealised life it describes. For us, that same love is transferred to Christ, for in Christ idealism gives way to reality. He is the embodiment of the good life.

In particular, Jesus shows that obeying God is more than outward conformity to a rule. He teaches that it is about the inward attitude of our hearts. This is precisely how Jesus expands his claim that he fulfils the law in Matthew 5. The law against murder becomes a call not to harbour murderous thoughts (Matthew 5:21-26); the law against adultery is a call not to harbour lustful thoughts (v 27-30), and so on.

This move was already anticipated in the law itself. The theologian Andrew Cameron argues that the Ten Commandments are about managing competing desires in society. Every society needs to assist proper longings and resist desire's worst excesses:

"The Ten Words are a workable, memorable sketch of what we really need against what we think we need, and although it is not necessarily comprehensive or exhaustive it is a more than adequate guide for how to manage desire within a society."

("The Logic of Law in Exodus and Beyond"
in *Exploring Exodus*, page 131)

The tenth commandment against covetousness (Exodus **20:17**) can seem out of place among the others, not least because a society cannot enforce it. The prominent atheist writer Christopher Hitchens labelled it "absurd":

"One may be forcibly restrained from wicked actions, or barred from committing them, but to forbid people from *contemplating* them is too much." (*God is Not Great*, page 100)

But, if the ten commandments are about managing desires, then as Cameron continues...

"the tenth word reveals what has been at work all along: the problem of the inner world that drives perjury, theft, adultery, murder, contempt for loving authority, overwork and false or absent worship."

This is precisely the point Jesus makes in Mark 7:14-23 after he has debated the keeping of the law with the Pharisees (v 1-13):

"Nothing outside a person can defile them by going into them. Rather, it is what comes out of a person that defiles them ... all ... evils come from inside and defile a person." (v 15, 23)

Second, Jesus fulfils the law by bringing its promises to fulfilment (the law as prophecy). He meets the need the law exposes. So the law itself contains picture after picture of this salvation. Jesus fulfils these pictures embedded in the law. Exodus 21 – 24 contains a sample selection of laws that will get repeated and expanded in Leviticus and Deuteronomy:

- In Exodus **21:2-4**, we find laws about freeing slaves because Israel had been redeemed from slavery. They point us to Jesus setting us free from the slavery of sin.

- **Verses 23-24** say, "Life for life, eye for eye, tooth for tooth". The punishment must not exceed the crime, but a punishment must pay for the crime. It's the principle that underlies the death of Jesus in our place. He paid the penalty we deserve, and so no more punishment can be required.

- **23:10-13** talks about giving both the land and people rest through the Sabbath. It's a pointer to the rest that we find in Jesus.

So, as you read extracts from the Law of Moses, the following questions will help apply it to you as a follower of Jesus Christ today:

1. How does this law express love for God or love for neighbour? How might the same principles be expressed today?

2. How does this law expose my sinfulness and need?

3. How did Jesus perfectly keep this law or the principles it embodies?

4. Does this law picture his work of salvation in some way?

Questions for reflection

Reflect on the same questions as you did at the end of Part One: how has this section helped you to:

1. understand the place of God's law in a Christian's life?

2. appreciate the goodness and blessing of God's law?

3. be motivated to live in obedience to God's law?

PART THREE

Checklist

In the Law of Moses, we see both our sinfulness and our solution. We see ourselves as we really are in all the ugliness of our sin. And we see Jesus in all the glorious beauty of his righteousness, and all his bountiful provision in giving us that righteousness.

Think about the Ten Commandments. We cannot explore them in detail within the scope of this book. But what we must do as we read these commandments is to think of them in two ways.

First, see them as a checklist by which you can assess your life.

1. "You shall have no other gods before me" (Exodus **20:3**). This first commandment is the root of all the others because whatever matters most to us is what will determine our behaviour and emotions. Have you ever made something more important than God? Or have you ever loved yourself more than God?

2. "You shall not make for yourself an image" (v 4). This is to reduce God to something of our own making—not to replace him, but to make him manageable, to understand him according to our notions rather than according to his revelation in his word. Have you ever judged God, or reduced him?

3. "You shall not misuse the name of the Lord your God" (**v 7**). This is literally to "carry the Lord your God's name wrongly". We're his image-bearers, made to reflect his glory. We're his people, called to reveal his goodness. The ESV translates this verse, "You shall not take the name of the Lord your God in vain"—the word "vain" can also mean "falsely"—do not carry God's name in a way that damages his reputation. Have you ever damaged God's reputation, through what you have done or said, or what you have not done or said?

4. "Remember the Sabbath day by keeping it holy" (**v 8**). This is to work, or to place demands on others that force them to work, as

if we determine our future and it all depends on us. Have you ever looked to yourself for identity or security?

5. "Honour your father and your mother, so that you may live long in the land the LORD your God is giving you" (**v 12**). This command has a promise attached, because obeying parental authority is the beginning of respecting authority in general. If children don't learn to respect authority in the home, then society will be chaotic. Even more significantly, we will reject the authority of our heavenly Father. Breaking this command will lead to the curse of exile. Have you ever bristled under authority? Ever completely rejected authority?

6. "You shall not murder" (**v 13**). In the Sermon on the Mount, Jesus said God's will is not about mere outward conformity, but the attitude of our hearts. We can murder people in our hearts—"anyone who is angry with a brother or a sister" has done it (Matthew 5:22). Have you ever harboured violent thoughts, or plotted or imagined another's downfall—whether or not you ever acted on them?

7. "You shall not commit adultery" (Exodus **20:14**). Again, Jesus says, "Anyone who looks at a woman lustfully has already committed adultery with her in his heart" (Matthew 5:28). Have you ever harboured lustful thoughts? Ever looked at someone who is not your spouse and imagined what sex with them might be like?

8. "You shall not steal" (Exodus **20:15**). Remember, Jesus teaches that our hearts matter as much as our hands. Have you ever harboured greedy thoughts?

9. "You shall not give false testimony against your neighbour" (**v 16**). Have you ever deceived or dissembled?

10. "You shall not covet" (**v 17**). Have you ever been discontented? Have you ever wished your life was different? Ever wished that someone else didn't have something because you don't have it, disliked them because they do, or grown bitter with God because he chose to give a blessing to someone else and not to you?

For me—for all of us—the answer to each of these questions the Ten Commandments pose is: *Yes*. This is who we are. Though we are capable of great good, we are not good people who occasionally slip up. You are not a good person who occasionally bristles under authority or occasionally looks at porn or occasionally feels discontented. You and I are God-rejecters, God-reducers, God-disgracers and God-replacers. We are rebels, murderers, adulterers, thieves, liars and enviers. People sometimes ask, "Have you kept all of God's Ten Commandments?" In fact, the sobering fact is that we have not kept *any* of God's Ten Commandments.

> Denial of sin is no way forward and it is no way out.

You will never know forgiveness and freedom from sin until you face up to this reality. Denial is no way forward and it is no way out. Some people are stuck in sin because they refuse to recognise that sin is the problem—that *they* are the problem.

Western culture utterly rejects this. It finds it deeply offensive. Our culture busily promotes self-esteem so that people can feel good about themselves. To talk about sin is seen as an assault on "project me". But the irony is the more we promote our self-esteem, the more neurotic and insecure we become. A great gap has been grown between image and reality—and every day people are falling into the void it's created.

Christ's checklist

Once we accept the depth of our sin, then we are in a position to see the glory of God's glorious solution. And that solution is Jesus. Let's assess Jesus against this checklist.

1. "You shall have no other gods before me" (**v 3**). Jesus said to his Father, "I have brought you glory on earth by finishing the work you gave me to do" (John 17:4).

2. "You shall not make for yourself an image" (Exodus **20:4**). Jesus didn't reduce God or re-imagine God. He said, "The Son can do nothing by himself; he can do only what he sees his Father doing, because whatever the Father does the Son also does" (John 5:19).

3. "You shall not misuse the name of the LORD your God" (Exodus **20:7**). Jesus said, "I have revealed your name to those whom you gave me" (John 17:6, see NIV footnote).

4. "Remember the Sabbath day by keeping it holy" (Exodus **20:8**). Jesus brought wholeness on the Sabbath. He re-created. He said, "Why are you angry with me for healing a man's whole body on the Sabbath?" (John 7:23). Each time he healed someone on the Sabbath, he provided a picture of both sabbath re-creation, and sabbath dependence.

5. "Honour your father and your mother" (Exodus **20:12**). Jesus said, "I love the Father and I do exactly what my Father has commanded me" (John 14:31).

6. "You shall not murder" (Exodus **20:13**). Even as his enemies nailed him to the cross, Christ's heart was not filled with hatred. Instead he prayed, "Father, forgive" (Luke 23:34). He didn't take life—his plans were dominated by his desire to gives his own life in order to give others life: "I am the good shepherd. The good shepherd lays down his life for the sheep" (John 10:11).

7. "You shall not commit adultery" (Exodus **20:14**). John 13:1 says, "Having loved his own who were in the world, he loved them to the end". Jesus gives his life for his bride (John 3:29).

8. "You shall not steal" (Exodus **20:15**). Jesus came to give, not take: "The thief comes [to the sheep] only to steal and kill and destroy; I have come that they may have life, and have it to the full … No one takes [my life] from me, but I lay it down of my own accord" (John 10:10, 18).

9. "You shall not give false testimony" (Exodus **20:16**). Jesus said, "I do nothing on my own but speak just what the Father has taught me" (John 8:28; 14:10). Indeed, Jesus is "the truth" (John 14:6)—"there is nothing false about him" (John 7:18).

10. "You shall not covet" (Exodus **20:17**). Jesus is content with God's will, even when that meant the cross. He said, "Now my soul is troubled, and what shall I say? 'Father, save me from this hour'? No, it was for this very reason I came to this hour" (John 12:27). He had a right to more riches, influence and praise than any other human; yet instead he freely, joyfully chose to become poor, for our good and his Father's glory.

Jesus is both the Law-Giver and the Law-Keeper. He is the Righteous One. He is the perfect embodiment of God's will. He is Love incarnate. When we read the Ten Commandments and consider Christ, we can only respond in awe and with worship.

Now realise that all that goodness and beauty is ours in Christ. His record is now our record. We're redeemed by the death and resurrection of Jesus—we've seen that in the Passover—but we're also redeemed by the obedience of Jesus.

Kept on our behalf

Exodus **21:12 – 23:9** outlines penalties for various crimes. If you track these penalties, what emerges is that they come in two parts:

- a restitution of what is lost

- a punishment equivalent to the intended harm

If it's accidental damage, then there's restitution, but no punishment. If your crime is only attempted, then there's no restitution, but there is punishment. And if your crime is deliberate and committed, then there is both.

So what of our crime against God? There must be a punishment—and that is what Jesus took for us through his death. But there must also be restitution—and that is what Jesus gives on our behalf through his life.

It is significant that the laws of restitution in **21:12 – 23:9** are preceded and followed by "laws of jubilee". **21:1-11** makes provision for slaves to be liberated, just as Israel had been liberated from slavery by God (**20:1-2**). **23:10-13** makes provision for rest for the land and for workers. This is no accident: the restitution and punishment paid by Christ at the cross produces liberation and rest for his people.

Jesus kept the law on our behalf. And that is such good news. Maybe this week you've tried so hard to be a good mother. But at some point this week—maybe at many points—you've felt utterly defeated. Or maybe you've looked at porn this week. And so you hide a deep sense of shame. You've failed so many times that you've pretty much given up. Or maybe you're desperate to be a good church leader—reaching the lost and pastoring your people. But it feels so precarious. And setbacks bring you crashing down. Or maybe you're full of envy and discontent. You don't like your life. You feel let down by God. And so he seems a million miles away.

When you're measured against God's law as fulfilled and embodied in Christ, the verdict is: you fail. Acknowledge that. Feel that. And then turn to the Gospels. Read the life of Jesus. Every act of love, every act of obedience, every right word he spoke—he did that for you. And if you have faith in Christ, then God places you in Christ, and all those things are credited to you. "It is because of [God] that you are in Christ Jesus, who has become for us wisdom from God—that is, our righteousness, holiness and redemption. Therefore, as it is written: 'Let the one who boasts boast in the Lord'" (1 Corinthians 1:31).

So every time you break God's law, remember this: Jesus kept that law for you. Every time you fail to do God's will, remember this: Jesus perfectly obeyed God's will for you. Say to yourself, "The law I've just broken, Jesus kept on my behalf". The Father has put you in Jesus and he treats you as Jesus' record deserves. And so the verdict he writes across your life is, *You are my child, whom I love; with you I am well pleased*—just as he said to Jesus (Luke 3:22). Righteous in Christ, empowered by his Spirit and loved by his Father, today you can begin again to do God's will. And tomorrow. And the day after.

Covenant confirmation

The laws end with promises: "See, I am sending an angel ahead of you to guard you along the way and to bring you to the place I have prepared" (Exodus **23:20**). The Israelites must listen to what he says and worship God alone (**v 21, 24-26**). If they do, the angel of the LORD will defeat their enemies (**v 22**) and give them the promised land (**v 22-23, 31**). God says, "I will send my terror ahead of you" (**v 27**) and, "I will send my hornet ahead of you" (**v 28**)—two evocative images of the destructive power of the angel of the LORD. But God will not immediately displace the inhabitants of the promised land, for that would leave it desolate (**v 30**). So it will be a gradual process (**v 30**), which will test the loyalty of Israel (**v 32-33**). This is exactly what we see in Judges 1 and especially in Judges 2:22 – 3:4. The threat of the nations would provoke each new generation of Israelites to trust God for themselves, just as the trials of this world prove and refine the faith of Christians (1 Peter 1:6-9).

In Exodus 24, the covenant is confirmed. Moses relays all that God has said and the people respond with one voice, "Everything the LORD has said we will do" (Exodus **24:3**). Moses then writes everything down to create a permanent record, which we still have to this day (**v 4**). The covenant is confirmed in two ways. First, it is confirmed through blood (**v 4-8**). Moses reads the law; the people affirm their intention to obey; and then the blood of sacrifice is sprinkled on the people. The sprinkling of blood is only used elsewhere in Exodus for the sanctifying of the priests (29:20-21). So this act in chapter 24 enacts and reinforces the identity of Israel as a priestly kingdom (19:3-6). As Israel live under God's rule expressed in God's law, they will make God known to the nations (Deuteronomy 4:5-8).

Second, the covenant is confirmed through a meal. Already God has provided regular festivals to remind Israel of his redemption

(Exodus **23:14-19**). Now the representatives of Israel go up the mountain with Moses (Exodus **24:1-2, 9-12**). This is an extraordinary moment, given the dire warnings against approaching the mountain in 19:20-24. Though they still have to stand at a distance, apart from Moses (**24:1-2**), nevertheless they see "the God of Israel. Under his feet was something like a pavement made of lapis lazuli, as bright blue as the sky itself. But God did not raise his hand against these leaders of the Israelites; they saw God, and they ate and drank" (**v 10-11**). God might have been expected to "break out against them" (19:22). But he doesn't raise his hand against them—instead they eat a meal in the presence of God. The shed blood and the covenant promises lead to this moment—a meal in the presence of God.

As we have seen before in Exodus meals matter, because in the story of the gospel meals matter. This moment on the mountain was repeated on the night before Jesus died: "After the supper [Jesus] took the cup, saying, 'This cup is the new covenant in my blood, which is poured out for you'" (Luke 22:20). Jesus made a new covenant with his people. Again, it was a covenant confirmed through blood. But this time it was his own blood that was shed, as symbolised in the wine. His sacrificial death would appease divine wrath and so reconcile us to God. And the covenant was confirmed in a meal. This is salvation: to eat in the presence of God (as we also saw in Exodus 18:12). This is what we are looking forward to. At the Last Supper Jesus said, "I tell you, I will not eat it again until it finds fulfilment in the kingdom of God" (Luke 22:16). Salvation is described as a perpetual feast with God, and every time we celebrate communion, we look back to the shed blood of Christ, which reconciles us to God; and therefore we are able to look forward to the eternal meal which embodies that

> In Exodus meals matter, because in the story of the gospel meals matter.

reconciliation, enjoyed in the full and glorious presence of God. We will not stand at a distance—we will sit with him.

Exodus 24 ends with Moses and Joshua, his "assistant" (and, one day, his successor), once again returning up the mountain to hear from God (Exodus **24:13-16**). This time Moses will be there for 40 days, receiving instructions for the construction of the tabernacle (**v 18**). A cloud descends on Mount Sinai and the Israelites: "To the Israelites the glory of the LORD looked like a consuming fire on top of the mountain" (**v 17**). This is a repeat of chapter 19, but it also anticipates 40:34-35, when the cloud of God's glory will fill the completed tabernacle. The representatives of Israel have, as it were, visited God for a meal. But now God is going to lay out his plans to come down from the mountain and make his home among his people.

Questions for reflection

1. How did reflecting on your answers to the questions on pages 176-177 reshape your view of yourself?

2. How did reflecting on Christ's life in terms of the commandments move you to praise and worship him?

3. God is at work to transform you from your natural self into someone who is just like Christ. Given your answers to Questions One and Two, how does that make you feel? How are you motivated to live for Christ, in obedience to God?

11. FINDING OUR WAY HOME

Are you a wanderer or a nester?

By a wanderer, I mean someone who is always looking for the new thing, always on the move, restless and rootless, never settled—someone who loves to travel, to go to new places and try new things.

By a nester, I mean someone who loves creating a nest or homemaking. You love baking or DIY. You love curling up on the sofa. You always look forward to coming home.

Perhaps you're a bit of both. There's a bit of the wanderer in me. I love stepping into open country. Every footpath beckons me to be explored. But only in Britain—because actually, mainly I'm a nester. If you told me I would never again leave Britain, I would receive that as good news. It's not that I think Britain is a better country. It's just that it's my country. It's home. Whenever I'm away, I look forward to coming home.

These two contrasting instincts probably actually reflect the same desire—a longing for home. Wanderers go looking for home, while nesters try to create it. Deep in the heart of every person is a longing for home.

This longing for home reflects the human story. Humanity suffers a deep sense of dislocation. We feel homeless. That's because we were cast out of our first home.

Leaving home

God placed the first man and woman in the garden-home of Eden. It was a place of provision and plenty, of safety and security. It was home. In the middle of this home was the tree of life, and the best thing about this home was that God was present with them. Humanity was at home with God.

But when the first humans rejected God, they were exiled from Eden:

"The LORD God banished [the man] from the Garden of Eden to work the ground from which he had been taken. After he drove the man out, he placed on the east side of the Garden of Eden **cherubim** and a flaming sword flashing back and forth to guard the way to the tree of life." (Genesis 3:23-24)

Adam and Eve found themselves east of Eden. Then, when Cain killed his brother, he "went out from the LORD's presence and lived in the land of Nod, east of Eden" (4:16). Humans are further from God and further east of Eden. And we've never returned. So ever since, we've had a deep longing for home, and a deep sense of dislocation and rootlessness. Some of us feel that sense more keenly than others, and at some times of life and in some circumstances it's more acute than at others. But it's there—that longing to get home.

Israel is, in one sense, a nation on the way home—to the land God has promised to give them and be present with them in. But they are not there yet—and when they get there, they will discover that the land is only a glimmer of and pointer to their true, eternal home. The dislocation and rootlessness will continue, to a greater or lesser extent; and it is to address this that God provides the plan for the tabernacle (or tent) that Israel is to build "exactly like the pattern I will show you" (Exodus **25:9**).

Map home

The tabernacle is a map showing us the way back home. So it is full of echoes of Eden. The clues are all embedded in the architecture and furnishings.

First, the list of materials for the tabernacle begins with gold and ends with **onyx** (Exodus **25:3-7**). Compare this to the description of

Eden in Genesis 2:12: "The gold of that land is good; aromatic resin and onyx are also there".

Second, Exodus **25:31-39** describes the lampstand in the tabernacle. With all its buds and blossoms, it looks like a tree. The tabernacle will look like a garden with a tree that gives light. It is an echo of the tree of life at the centre of the Garden of Eden.

Third, seven times in the account of creation we read "God said" (Genesis 1:3, 6, 9, 14, 20, 24, 26). And seven times in the tabernacle instructions we read, "The LORD said to Moses" (Exodus **25:1**; 30:11, 17, 22, 34; 31:1, 12). Moreover, both accounts culminate in a description of the Sabbath (Genesis 2:1-3; Exodus 31:12-18). The building of the tabernacle is like the building of our garden-home in Eden.

Fourth, before the fall, Eden was a temple-mountain with Adam as its priest. Now, in the tabernacle, the temple-mountain is being re-created. Adam's charge "to till and keep" (Genesis 2:15, RSV) is only used again of priests (Numbers 3:7-8; 8:26; 18:5-6). What is striking is that Adam in Eden is described in ways similar to the priests in Exodus 28 – 29, and Eden is described as the "mount of God" (Ezekiel 28:13, 14, 16). And in Ezekiel 28:11-19, God condemns the King of Tyre in language that sees him as another embodiment of either Adam or Satan.

Above all, God is there. What Israel are told to build is a *tent* (Exodus **26:15-29**). Constructing a tent seems odd to us. Perhaps you start thinking of a wedding marquee. But to the Israelites a tent meant only one thing: home. They were a people on the move, living in tents. God had come down to visit on Mount Sinai; now, he was moving into the neighbourhood. He was going to dwell among his people. He commanded them to "make a sanctuary for me" so that he would "dwell among them" (Exodus **25:8**). The New Testament scholar Vern Poythress writes:

"His tent had rooms and a yard and a fireplace like their own."
(*The Shadow of Christ in the Law of Moses*, page 11)

Let's think again about the lampstand. It is a tree that permanently burns—so it burns, but is never consumed. It's an echo of the burning bush that Moses encountered in Exodus 3. His experience of encountering the presence of God on holy ground is replicated in the tabernacle. The theme of God's presence runs throughout the account of the tabernacle (**25:8, 22, 30**; 29:45; 30:6; 40:38).

Moreover, all the pieces of furniture have rings and poles permanently built into them (**25:14-15, 26-28; 27:4-7**). The tabernacle and courtyard are built so they can readily be dismantled. This is a tent, not a building. God dwells in a tent so he can travel with his people. As he did in Eden, God lives among his people.

> The tabernacle is an echo back to Eden and a pointer forward to our true home.

So the tabernacle is an echo back to Eden and a pointer forward to our true home. And what is our true home like? Again, the clues are embedded in the furniture. The items of furniture are like signposts.

Ark: home is where we live under God's reign

The ark has the same proportions as the footstool of an ancient king (**25:10-13**). When a king sat in judgment, he sat on his throne and put his feet on a footstool. But Israel is not ruled by a human king. God is her King. And God reigns from heaven. So he is, as it were, seated on his throne in heaven with the ark as his footstool on earth.

In Isaiah 6, God's throneroom is in the temple, but all that can be seen of God is the train of his robe, because God reigns from heaven with his feet touching the earth in the temple. In Isaiah 66:1, the LORD says, "Heaven is my throne, and the earth is my footstool. Where is the house you will build for me? Where will my resting place be?" Moreover, a number of passages speak of God being enthroned between the cherubim (1 Samuel 4:4; 2 Samuel 6:2; Psalms 80:1; 99:1). (Jeremiah 3:16-17 equates the ark with a throne when it says the ark will be forgotten when Jerusalem becomes God's throne.) This is the point where God's throne in heaven touches the earth.

This is why Exodus **25:21** says, "Place the cover on top of the ark and put in the ark the tablets of the covenant law that I will give you" (a repetition of **verse 16**, showing the importance of this detail). God will rule his people through his law, and the rule of his law is symbolised by the tablets of stone. In some ways, the covenant between God and his people reflects the covenant treaties of the ancient Near East. A powerful king (a suzerain) made a treaty with a subject nation (a vassal) offering protection in return for loyalty. Two copies of the treaty were made and deposited in the temple of their gods. Two copies of the treaty between God and Israel are inscribed on two tablets of stone. But since God and Israel share the same tabernacle, both copies are deposited in the ark. Placing "the tablets of the covenant law" in the tabernacle symbolised that God was King and Israel was his vassal, and that both God and the people recognised this.

And so it is the ark from where God reigns over his people: "There, above the cover between the two cherubim that are over the ark of the covenant law, I will meet with you and give you all my commands for the Israelites" (**v 22**, see also **v 18-20**). In Eden humanity rejected the authority of our heavenly Father. The result has been chaos, conflict and condemnation. But in God's new home he will restore his life-giving rule of love.

The word "atonement" in **verse 17** translates the Hebrew word *kapporet,* which literally means "cover". Following Martin Luther, the translator of the Bible that was the forerunner of the King James Version, William Tyndale, translated this as "mercy seat" ("seat" meaning "place" rather than "chair"). This is the place where mercy is found (see Leviticus 16:14-15). But what is being covered? This spot is above the tablets of stone in the ark. So what is being covered is the penalty of the law. (We see something similar in the phrase "This'll cover the cost".) God's rule not only brings justice; it also means mercy. When Jesus, God's King, comes to fully restore God's rule at his second coming, justice will be done. But at his first coming, justice did not fall. Or rather, it fell on the King himself, at the cross. Jesus was the sacrifice of atonement, who covers the penalty of our sin so we can receive mercy.

Table: home is where we eat with God

Most homes have a meal table. Nothing symbolises home more powerfully than a meal table, where a family gathers, sometimes with guests, to share food and friendship. And here in God's prototype home is a table (Exodus **25:23-25**) laid up for a meal (**v 29**) and spread with food: "Put the bread of the Presence on this table to be before me at all times" (**v 30**). It's not there because God is hungry! It's there as a permanent sign that God invites us to enjoy community with him. This is the bread of his Presence.

In Leviticus 24:5-9, we are told that the bread of Presence involved twelve loaves in two rows of six and was replaced each week. There was one for each of the twelve tribes, to indicate that all God's people were welcome to eat with him. In ancient hospitality the host provided protection as well as provision for his guests. So God will protect and provide for his people. He provides with manna in the desert, but will provide through the blessings of the land when Israel enters Canaan.

In Exodus 24:9-11, the elders of Israel went up the mountain into the presence of God. There they "saw the God of Israel ... But God did not raise his hand against" them. Instead "they saw God, and they ate and drank". A meal in the presence of God is the goal of salvation. And that promise was permanently embodied in the tabernacle table and bread.

Lamp: home is where we walk in the light of God

The lampstand may resemble the tree of life, but it is still a lamp. It provides light in God's new home. God's prototype of home is a place of both life and light.

Once the tabernacle is built (**26:1-33**), the altar, table and lamp-stand are to be placed within it (**v 34-37**). God's home is open for mercy (represented by the ark), fellowship (represented by the table) and light (represented by the lampstand).

If these are signposts, showing us the way home, where do they point? John 1:14 says, "The Word became flesh and made his dwelling among us". It is literally "pitched his tent among us". The word for "dwelling" (skēroō) is the word used in the Septuagint, the Greek translation of the Old Testament, for the tabernacle. Jesus the Word "tabernacled" among us. Jesus is our home and he is the way home. God made his home among us in the person of Jesus so that he could bring us home to live with Jesus. Jesus is the point where heaven touches earth. Jesus is where the tabernacle points:

■ Jesus is the true ark. He is the person or place where we live under the reign of God. He is the King through whom God reigns.

■ Jesus is the true bread. He is the bread through whom we eat in the presence of God. He said, "I am the bread of life. Whoever comes to me will never go hungry" (John 6:35).

■ Jesus is the true lamp. He is the light of God in whom we walk. He said, "I am the light of the world. Whoever follows me will never walk in darkness, but will have the light of life" (John 8:12; see also John 1:4.)

Our longing for home is met in Jesus. He is our true home. He is our true destination. Every wanderer is actually propelled by the desire for Jesus. Of course, they probably will not articulate it in those terms. But the longing that propels us over the horizon is a longing that is only truly met in Christ. And every nester is trying to create what we only truly find in Jesus. All the signposts of the tabernacle point to him. Augustine of Hippo was right when he prayed:

"Our hearts are restless until they find their rest in you."

Questions for reflection

1. Look back on the time before you became a Christian, or to times when you have wandered from following Christ. How did you experience the truth of the quote above from Augustine?

2. Are you naturally a wanderer or a nester, and how can this aspect of your character enable you to be excited about your future home?

3. How has your view of the relevance of the tabernacle to your Christian life today been changed as you've read this section?

PART TWO

The guards

The tabernacle was a picture of home; but it wasn't home itself. The tabernacle was not Eden. It was a map, but there was still a journey to travel. Humanity was still east of Eden. The people were still exiled from God because of their sin, and so are we.

This, too, is echoed in the architecture of the tabernacle. God instructed Moses to…

> "Make a curtain of blue, purple and scarlet yarn and finely twisted linen, with cherubim woven into it by a skilled worker. Hang it with gold hooks on four posts of acacia wood overlaid with gold and standing on four silver bases. Hang the curtain from the clasps and place the ark of the covenant law behind the curtain. The curtain will separate the Holy Place from the Most Holy Place." (Exodus **26:31-33**)

As you entered the tabernacle, right before you was this thick curtain, barring the way to God's holy presence. And how is that curtain decorated? It has "cherubim woven into it by a skilled craftsman" (**v 31**). This is an echo of Genesis 3:24: "After [the LORD God] drove the man out, he placed on the east side of the Garden of Eden cherubim and a flaming sword flashing back and forth to guard the way to the tree of life." Here in the fabric of the curtain, cherubim were still guarding the way back to God.

The architecture of the tabernacle reflects the geography of Mount Sinai. The tabernacle replaces and repeats Sinai as the place where God meets with his people. Mount Sinai was divided into three zones. The area where the people stood corresponds to the courtyard of the tabernacle. The mountain where the elders could meet God corresponds to the Holy Place. And the top of the mountain, where God descended, corresponds to the Most Holy Place. In Exodus 19, we saw those limits were put in place to protect the people from God's holy presence "or the LORD will break out against them" (Exodus 19:22, 24). The cherubim do not protect God from us. They protect us from God.

So while the tabernacle shows how wonderful it is to live at home with God, it also bars the way to God. The layout of the tabernacle underlines the problem.

The way home

The descriptions of the furniture are not in order. You might expect instructions on building the tabernacle and then a list of furniture, or maybe a list of furniture and then somewhere to put it. But the order is broken up. First the ark, table and lamp are described. They are the promise of a new home. Then the tabernacle itself is described, embodying the problem of God's holiness and our sin, as we find the route home barred by the curtain and the cherubim. Then, in chapter 27, we're back to descriptions of furniture. The altar is described (**27:1-8**). And it's described here because it represents the solution to the problem: the way back to God is through the blood of sacrifice.

Again, this truth is embedded in the architecture. As they entered the courtyard, the first thing an Israelite would encounter was the altar. This dominated the way in. He or she deserved to die for their sins. They deserved to be eternally excluded from God's presence (which is what hell is). But in a sacrifice, an animal died in place of the Israelite. It took the punishment they deserved for the sins they had committed. It died in their place.

The tabernacle itself perhaps also embodies this. It is built of four layers. The inner layer is blue (**26:1-6**) to represent the heavens. The second layer is made of goat skins (**v 7-13**) to represent the covering God provided to cover the shame of Adam and Eve (Genesis 3:21). The third layer is ram skins dyed red (Exodus **26:14**) to represent the sacrifices and blood required to provide a covering for sin. It is not entirely clear from what the final layer is made, but it seems that this layer was designed to protect everything from the elements.

Of course, like everything else, the altar is only a picture. **27:3** describes the utensils needed "to remove the ashes". **Verses 4-5** describe a grating enabling the ashes to fall to the bottom. This altar is built to be reused. These sacrifices are going to be repeated hundreds and hundreds of times. The sacrifices are pointers to God's solution for sin, but they are not the solution itself.

Opening the way

On the night before he died, Jesus said to his disciples, "My Father's house has many rooms; if that were not so, would I have told you that I am going there to prepare a place for you? And if I go and prepare a place for you, I will come back and take you to be with me that you also may be where I am" (John 14:2-3). Jesus was going to prepare a place for us in God's home. The disciples didn't get it: "Lord, we don't know where you are going, so how can we know the way?" And Jesus replied, "I am the way" (John 14:5-6). Jesus is the way home.

Why? Jesus is the way because Jesus is the sacrifice. He is the sacrifice to end all sacrifices. He is the sacrifice to which all the thousands of sacrifices that had been offered on the altar pointed. When he died on the cross, he took our sins and bore the punishment we deserve. Jesus prepared a place in God's home by dying in our place.

Embodied in the architecture of the tabernacle, and the temple that replaced it, was the curtain, that great symbol of God's inaccessibility (Exodus **26:31-33**). As you stood before it, there on your right was "the bread of the Presence" and on your left was the lampstand, both promising a relationship with God. But there in front of you was the curtain preventing a relationship with God. It hung there to protect you from God, because sinful people cannot survive an encounter with the holy God. So as you stood before the curtain, home was so close and so far away. Where you needed to be and longed to be was both showcased and blocked off. The tabernacle was so full of promise and so full of danger.

Now listen to Matthew's description of the death of Jesus. "When Jesus had cried out again in a loud voice, he gave up his spirit. At that moment the curtain of the temple was torn in two from top to bottom" (Matthew 27:50-51). As Jesus died, the architecture of the tabernacle was radically rearranged. The way home to God is open.

Come back with me to Exodus. The next thing which is described is the courtyard of the tabernacle (Exodus **27:9-19**). "Make a court-yard for the tabernacle. The south side shall be a hundred cubits long and is to have curtains of finely twisted linen, with twenty posts and twenty bronze bases and with silver hooks and bands on the posts" (**v 9-10**). Similar instructions are given for the other sides (**v 11-15**). The courtyard of the tabernacle is surrounded by 100 cubits of curtain on the south and north sides, and 50 cubits on the west side. But on the east side, there are two curtains of 15 cubits with a 20-cubit gap with its own special curtain (**v 16**). That's because this is the entrance. The point is that the tabernacle and courtyard are oriented towards the east. **27:13-15** makes this explicit: the entrance is to be "on the east end, towards the sunrise" (**v 13**).

And where is humanity? As we have mapped out the symbolic geography of humanity's relationship with God, where are we? We are east of Eden, east of home. So the tabernacle is open towards us. It faces towards us, inviting us home.

And when we come home, there's a light on. Someone is waiting for us. Have you ever had the experience of coming home late at night. Maybe it's dark and cold, and you're looking forward to seeing your family again. But will anyone be in when you come home? Will they have waited up for you? Will there be a meal waiting for you? As you walk up the street, you're hoping to see a light on.

In **verses 20-21**, God gives instructions to ensure there is a light burning "from evening till morning". You would expect these verses to come after the description of the lampstand at the end of chapter 25. But in fact, they come after the description of the altar and the courtyard facing east. The point is that in the tabernacle, there is always light, and that light faces east—towards us, in this symbolic universe. The lights are on because God is at home. There is a welcome waiting for you and there is a bread on the table (**25:30**).

If you are far from God, then come home today. The light is on. God is at home. He has pitched his tent among us through Jesus. And there is bread on the table. God invites you to eat with him, to befriend him, to know him. And if you feel far from him, then if you have put your faith in Christ, he has died to bring you home. Don't allow your feelings to shout louder than God's "Welcome home" message. The whole tabernacle was designed to reassure you of this.

Are you a wanderer or a nester? When we find our home in Jesus, that will change our priorities. It will change your sense of home. If you're a wanderer, then by all means harness your love of adventure for the glory of Christ. Go and make disciples of all nations. But wherever you go, be content there. Don't think contentment is just over the horizon. Don't be someone who is always going to new places or trying new things in an effort to find home. You need to enjoy Christ and serve Christ where you are now.

Do you ever think, "I will serve Christ when…"? It doesn't matter what comes next. Something is wrong. You're restless for home, when all the time you're home in Christ.

> Make sure that the home that really matters to you is the home you have in Christ.

If you're a nester, then by all means harness your love of home to make your physical home a place of welcome for Christ. Open your home to your church, to your neighbours, to the needy. But make sure your home helps your service rather than hindering it. Don't make your house a sacred place, a castle with a drawbridge. Make sure Christ comes first, and that your door is open. Don't be so concerned for cleanliness and tidiness that people feel uncomfortable. Don't be so concerned for a cosy little family that your family is not open to others. Don't be carting your children from activity to activity so you have no time for community and mission. Make sure the home that really matters to you is the home you have in Christ.

We need to remember the architecture of the tabernacle, because it points us to our true home and it reminds us of the great privilege of being able to come home to the presence of God. The light is on. There is bread on the table. Let's enjoy our home, and enjoy heading home.

"Therefore, brothers and sisters, since we have confidence to enter the Most Holy Place by the blood of Jesus, by a new and living way opened for us through the curtain, that is, his body ... let us draw near to God with a sincere heart and with the full assurance that faith brings." (Hebrews 10:19-22)

Questions for reflection

1. What difference would it make to you if you were more assured of, and more excited about, your eternal home?

2. Which aspect of the tabernacle's design, and what it points to, particularly resonates with you today?

3. Imagine someone said to you, "What is the point of thinking about the tabernacle? It was where God lived among his ancient people, and that's all we need to know." What would you say?

12. THE PRIESTLY WARDROBE

I was once in a small group meeting when an elderly member said, "Seventy years ago today I was baptised". She was baptised at 14 and now she was 84. She had been a Christian for seventy years—*seventy years!* That's a long time to have faithfully followed Jesus. I found it very moving, just as in the same way I find it moving to hear of Christians who have continued to love God through difficult circumstances.

What's the secret to surviving as a Christian? The world around us often scorns our faith. The world is full of temptations and distractions. And we are full of flaws and failings. So what's the secret?

In Exodus 25 – 27, God gave instructions for the construction of the tabernacle and its furniture. The tabernacle was full of echoes of Eden, so it created a kind of map to show us the way home to God. In chapters 28 – 30, the focus turns to the priests who serve in the tabernacle (**28:1**). The priest is the person who will lead us home.

Sacred garments

Chapter 28 is taken up with describing the clothes or robes the high priest is to wear. "Make sacred garments for your brother Aaron to give him dignity and honour" (**v 2**, see also **v 3-5**). These garments are a kind of uniform. Imagine you are going about your daily business one day, when someone tells you, "Stop!" It makes a great difference to your response if you see that they are wearing a police uniform. It's a sign that they're acting with the authority of the state. In a similar way, the priest's robes give them "dignity and honour". They are a sign that the priest is acting with the authority of God.

But there's more going on than that. These robes are rich with symbolism. The first item of clothing that's described is an ephod (**v 6-8**). An ephod appears to be a kind of tabard—a bit like the training bibs worn by sports players (sports pinnies in the US), but more elaborate. The Israelites are to inscribe the names of the twelve tribes of Israel on two stones, six on each, and place them on the shoulders of the ephod (**v 9-14**). This is the main point of the ephod; it allows the priest "to bear the names [of God's people] on his shoulders as a memorial before the LORD" (**v 12**).

Then there is the breastpiece (**v 15-16**), which is tied to the front of the priest over the ephod (**v 22-28**). Sown into it are twelve precious stones in four rows (**v 17-20**). Again, the twelve stones represent the twelve "sons [or tribes] of Israel" (**v 21**). As a result, "Whenever Aaron enters the Holy Place, he will bear the names of the sons of Israel over his heart on the breastpiece of decision as a continuing memorial before the LORD" (**v 29**).

"The breastpiece of decision" is literally "the breastpiece of judgment". It's probably a reference to the Urim and Thummim, which were kept in a pocket in the breastpiece. We don't really know what these were except that they were used for making decisions. They probably involved different coloured stones which were selected at random to determine God's will—a bit like drawing a raffle ticket, but with complete confidence that God would use the draw to reveal his will. The British commentator Alec Motyer suggests an intriguing alternative: that "the breastpiece of decision" could mean that...

It's as if the priest carries the people into God's presence.

"the high-priestly garments displayed what the LORD thought of his people—his 'decision' about them, that they are his jewels, his precious ones." (*The Message of Exodus*, page 257)

The names of God's people are both on the shoulders and over the heart of the priest. So the priest represents the people. It's as if he carries the people into God's presence.

We need to see this (as the Israelites literally did "see" this) because, by this point in the story of Exodus, we know that it's deadly dangerous for sinful people to come into God's presence. God might "break out against them" (19:22, 24). It's as if God is nuclear, and to enter his presence is to be radiated by his holiness. Or, to use the language of Scripture, God is a consuming fire which burns anything that is impure (Hebrews 12:29). Yet the priest comes into God's presence on the people's behalf.

The next few items of priestly clothing are all designed to reinforce this idea. Exodus **28:31-35** describes the robe the priest must wear, which is hemmed with pomegranates. It is another echo of Eden. When the temple replaced the tabernacle centuries later, it had 400 decorative pomegranates (1 Kings 7:18-20, 42).

The robe is also hemmed with bells. "Aaron must wear it when he ministers. The sound of the bells will be heard when he enters the Holy Place before the LORD and when he comes out, so that he will not die" (Exodus **28:35**). The priest needs the bells "so that he will not die". What's going on?! The bells let God know that it is the priest and not someone else. If it's someone else, then God will break out against them. Of course, this is symbolic—God's doesn't need bells to distinguish between people. In truth, the bells are for the people, not the LORD—an audible reminder that sinners cannot come before God without a mediator.

The next item of clothing is a turban with a plaque saying, "HOLY TO THE LORD" (**v 36-38**). Even our gifts, even the best things we do, are tainted by sin. So our gifts must be brought to God through a priest. Only through the mediation of a priest can our gifts be "HOLY TO THE LORD."

Then a tunic, sash and caps are described; these, again, are to give "dignity and honour" to the priests (**v 39-41**). Lastly, the underwear is described (**v 42**). The priests must wear underwear (from the waist to the thigh) "so that they will not incur guilt and die" (**v 43**). There were similar instructions in 20:24-26—the Israelites were to make altars without steps because going up steps in priestly robes meant "your private parts may be exposed" (20:26).

At this point, you might be suppressing a snigger. And you might be imagining the embarrassment of being a priest whose private parts were exposed. Actually, that's the point. Nudity is embarrassing. Back in the Garden of Eden "Adam and his wife were both naked, and they felt no shame" (Genesis 2:25). But the very first thing that happens when they reject God is they realise they're naked, and try to cover themselves (3:7). Our sniggers and embarrassment are a sign that we still feel that shame. It's a sign that deep down we know we're guilty. So we need a priest to come before God on our behalf.

Washing the priests

But by now you might have spotted a problem with all of this—namely, that the priest is guilty too! All the way through Exodus 28, God speaks not of what some theoretical "priest" will wear, but what "Aaron" or "Aaron and his sons" will wear (Exodus **28:2, 3, 4, 12, 29, 30, 35, 38, 40, 41, 43**). They're going to be the first priests. But they are all too human, and so they, too, are all sinners. Indeed Aaron's eldest sons, Nadab and Abihu, will be killed by God in the tabernacle because they don't approach him in the right way, possibly because they're drunk at the time (Leviticus 10:1-3). Priests are sinful human beings too.

So in Exodus 29, God describes how Moses is to "consecrate" the priests through ceremonial washing and sacrifice (**29:1-3**). In **verse 4**, the priests are to be washed, and **30:17-21** describes the basin required for this. In **29:7**, the priests are to be anointed, and **30:22-25** describes the oil required for this (see 2 Corinthians 1:21-22; 1 John 2:20, 27).

The priests symbolically transfer their sin onto an animal who dies in their place. The word "consecrate" means "to make holy" or "set apart". They're to be washed as a symbolic act of cleansing from sin (Exodus **29:4**). They are to be dressed in their priestly robes and anointed with oil as a sign that they act not in their own right, but consecrated as priests (**v 5-9**).

Then they are to sacrifice a bull and two rams (**v 10-28**). In each case, Aaron and his sons are to lay their hands on the animal (**v 10, 15, 19**). It's a symbolic transference of their sin. It's as if their sin passes to the animal and then the animals dies, bearing the penalty of their sin. In **verses 20-21**, blood from one of the offerings is placed on their ears, fingers and toes, and "then he and his sons and their garments will be consecrated" (**v 21**). Before the priest can represent the people and atone for the people's sin, his own sin must be atoned for.

And all this is not only for Aaron. Israel will always need priests, long after Aaron has gone. So his sacred garments and all they represent "will belong to his descendants", who will "be anointed … ordained [and] minister" in them (**v 29-30**). The high priesthood will outlive the first high priest.

At the end of this process, the priests eat some of the sacrifice. It's a sign that, as we've seen all along, they are accepted into God's presence. They eat a meal in the presence of God (**v 31-33**): "They are to eat these offerings by which atonement was made for their ordination and consecration" (**v 33**). In other words, atonement for their sin must be made before they can be ordained as priests. Indeed, it's not just the priests who are consecrated. The altar is also consecrated (**v 20, 35-37**). The priests are cleansed by blood in chapter 29 and water in chapter 30; and both are pictures of the cleansing that all God's people now enjoy through Jesus (see, for example, 1 John 1:7 and Ephesians 5:25-26).

Contagious holiness

Notice the flow, or movement, in these chapters. The people's guilt is transferred to the priests (Exodus **28:38**). The priest's guilt is transferred to the animals. The animals die. The sin, as it were, reaches a dead end, and the end is death. But then **29:37** says, "For seven days make atonement for the altar and consecrate it. Then the altar will be most holy, and whatever touches it will be holy." Sin is dealt with and now holiness flows back in the other direction.

The Holy Place, inner tabernacle and altar for burnt offerings are anointed with holy oil and therefore communicate holiness to anything that touches them. We could call this "contagious holiness". This makes them dangerous for non-consecrated people, so only priests may have contact with them. All the consecrated meat and bread must be destroyed "because it is sacred" (**v 34**).

Only once the priests are consecrated can the regular business of the tabernacle begin (**v 39-41**). Only then can they "offer on the altar regularly each day: two lambs a year old. Offer one in the morning and the other at twilight." Only now that the priests and altar are consecrated can sacrifices be offered on behalf of the people. Leviticus 1 – 7 will give us much more detail on these regular sacrifices, but the focus of Exodus is on the need for a priest to come before God on our behalf. We can't get home to God on our own. We need a guide. We need a road-maker and a bridge builder.

The robe of the priests is made from the same fabric as the tabernacle itself (Exodus 26:31; **28:6, 31**). And their preparation takes seven days; an echo of the original creation, which the construction of the tabernacle echoes (**29:35**). It's as if the priests are the tabernacle in miniature. The tabernacle is the place in which Israel meet God, and the priest is the person in whom they meet God and through whom they can come to meet God.

With a priest, they can come before God. And so Exodus 29 ends with a lovely description of God relating to his people through this system of tent of meeting, altar and priesthood.

- ■ God eats with his people through "a food offering presented to the Lord" (**v 41**).

- ■ God speaks with his people (**v 42**).

- ■ God meets with his people (**v 42-43**).

- ■ God dwells with his people (**v 45-46**).

Then **30:11-16** lays out instructions about how each Israelite "must pay the LORD a ransom for his life" (**v 12**). It's described as "atonement money" (**v 16**). This involved people queuing up to enrol in a census. The theologian Bernard Ramm says this is…

> "the way in which the covenant was made personal … each Israelite … willing to be counted."
>
> (Cited in Alec Motyer, *The Message of Exodus*, pages 259-260)

And what is the purpose of all this? "Then I will dwell among the Israelites and be their God. They will know that I am the LORD their God, who brought them out of Egypt so that I might dwell among them. I am the LORD their God" (**29:45-46**).

God rescued his people "that" he might dwell among them. But the repetition of "I am the LORD" also suggests that that in turn will be an act of revelation. There is a missional intent. Israel is to expand the boundaries of Eden-tabernacle (just as God intended Adam to expand the border of the Eden-temple) so that the glory of the LORD fills the earth and the nations come to know God.

> God lights up our lives so that we might light up the world.

Month by month, God eats with us as we take communion. He speaks to us as we read the Bible and hear it preached. He meets with us as we come to him in prayer. And he dwells in us by his Spirit. In his grace, he does all this for us. But he also does it for the world. He lights up our lives so that we might light up the world. So "let your light shine before others, that they may see your good deeds and glorify your Father in heaven" (Matthew 5:16).

Questions for reflection

1. How has reading this increased your understanding of what it means for Jesus to be our high priest?

2. "We need a guide ... a roadmaker and a bridge builder." How does Jesus fulfil each of these needs for you?

3. How are you going to be engaged in lighting up the world today?

PART TWO

The cloud-making machine

To understand the significance for us of Exodus 28 – 31, we need to understand the significance of what happens next. Chapter 30 begins with the description of "an altar ... for burning incense" (**30:1**). It's not used for anything other than incense, and though **verses 2-5** give detailed instructions for its design, we're not told what it symbolises. Some people think it represents the prayers of God's people because, in Revelation 5:8 and 8:3-4, prayers are described as incense rising to God. There may be an echo of Exodus in the prayers of Revelation, but there's no mention of prayer in Exodus 30.

What *is* emphasised is the location of the altar of incense. **Verse 6** commands Moses to "Put the altar in front of the curtain that shields the ark of the covenant law—before the atonement cover that is over the tablets of the covenant law—where I will meet with you."

Think about what an altar of incense does. It creates a cloud of smoke. This is to be its exclusive and perpetual purpose (**v 7-10**). It's a cloud-making machine, and it's placed right in front of the Most Holy Place. So it envelopes the Most Holy Place—the place where God meets with Moses—in a cloud of incense.

Where have we seen this before in the story?

"On the morning of the third day there was thunder and lightning, with a thick cloud over the mountain ... Mount Sinai was covered with smoke, because the Lord descended on it in fire. The smoke billowed up from it like smoke from a furnace ... The Lord descended to the top of Mount Sinai and called Moses to the top of the mountain." (19:16-20)

The altar of incense is there because the tabernacle is replicating the experience of Mount Sinai. What happened at Mount Sinai is going to happen routinely in the tabernacle—albeit in symbolic form. A reproduction of the experience of Sinai is built into the routines of the tabernacle.

The reproduction of Sinai is also built into the architecture of the tabernacle. The tabernacle curtains have gold hooks at the top and silver bases (26:6, 18-25). The courtyard has silver hooks at the top and bronze bases (27:9-11). Everything in the tabernacle is made of gold. The altar and basin in the courtyard are made of bronze.

So the metallic journey is from gold to silver and from silver to bronze. Think of these as colour-coded fittings for a self-assembly structure. The gold is on top of the silver which is on top of the bronze. Inevitably, the tabernacle plan is in two dimensions on a flat plane. But it's actually a three-dimensional model. The bronze, silver and gold represent three storeys—the courtyard, the Holy Place and the Most Holy Place.

The courtyard is the plain at the foot of Mount Sinai where the Israelites camped. The Holy Place is the mountain where only the elders went. The Most Holy Place is the top of the mountain to which God descended. (It is interesting that the one item of priestly clothing that is not mentioned is footwear. It may be that the priests were barefoot because they were treading on holy ground, just as Moses had to remove his sandals when he met God on Mount Sinai in Exodus 3:5.)

Like the tabernacle, Mount Sinai had three zones of increasing holiness. Only Moses was permitted to ascend to the top. Aaron and the seventy elders could only go on the slopes (19:22, 24). The third zone was the border of the mountain. Transgressing these boundaries led to death. The glory of the LORD descended on Mount Sinai, and it would do so on the tabernacle (19:9, 16; 24:15-16, 18; 40:34-35).

So the altar of incense is creating a cloud of smoke as a picture of the cloud on Mount Sinai. This is the cloud into which God descended and through which Moses ascended to come before God.

The tabernacle replicates and perpetuates the experience of Mount Sinai. God says, "See that you make them according to the pattern shown you on the mountain" (25:40), and something similar is said in 25:9; 26:30 and 27:8. The tabernacle is patterned on the mountain.

Except that this is not the whole story. These verses don't say, *See that you make them according to the pattern of the mountain*. They speak of "the pattern shown you on the mountain". That's because Mount Sinai is itself only a picture.

The best commentary on this is Hebrews 9. The writer summarises the tabernacle's architecture and furniture in verses 1-5. Then he says that the fact the priests had to keep on making sacrifices shows this was not the real thing (v 6-10). So the question is: What is—and *where* is—the real thing?

A picture of heaven

Hebrews 9:11 says, "When Christ came as high priest ... he went through the greater and more perfect tabernacle that is not made with human hands, that is to say, not a part of this creation". Then verse 24 clarifies that "Christ did not enter a sanctuary made with human hands that was only a copy of the true one; he entered heaven itself, now to appear for us in God's presence."

The tabernacle is a picture of Mount Sinai, and Mount Sinai in turn is a picture of heaven. So the tabernacle courtyard is a picture of this earth, inhabited by humanity. The Holy Place is a picture of the heavenly realms, inhabited by spiritual beings like the cherubim; and the Most Holy Place is a picture of the throne room of heaven, inhabited by God, with the ark representing the footstool of God's heavenly throne. The tabernacle is made of blue cloth embroidered with cherubim (Exodus 26:1)—so stepping into the tabernacle was like stepping into the heavens with angels flying around you.

A picture of Jesus entering heaven

Next, the writer to the Hebrews summarises Exodus 29: "[Moses] sprinkled with the blood both the tabernacle and everything used in its ceremonies. In fact, the law requires that nearly everything be cleansed with blood, and without the shedding of blood there is no forgiveness" (Hebrews 9:21-22).

But, as Hebrews has already shown, Jesus has now come has our great High Priest (4:14 – 7:28). In fact, he is unlike any high priest before him, because, "[Christ] did not enter [the tabernacle of heaven] by means of the blood of goats and calves; but he entered the Most Holy Place once for all by his own blood, so obtaining eternal redemption" (9:12).

Jesus offered a sacrifice, and that sacrifice was himself. "[Christ] has appeared once for all at the culmination of the ages to do away with sin by the sacrifice of himself" (v 26). And through that sacrifice he comes before God in heaven.

> Is Christ the tabernacle or the priest or the sacrifice?! The answer is: all three.

Don't try to think of this as one single image. In Exodus 25 – 27 we saw that Christ is the tabernacle. Now he's the priest in the tabernacle. *And* now he's the sacrifice offered by the priest. Is he the tabernacle or the priest or the sacrifice?! The answer is: all three, and many more things besides. Already in Exodus we've seen that Christ is the Passover Lamb, the manna from heaven, the water of life, the Rock that bears our punishment, the mediator and the embodiment of God's will. Picture after picture in the events and the people and the rituals of the Old Testament are all concentrated into one person: Jesus. All of them are required to express fully his person and work. It is in them and through them that we see the riches of God's grace in Christ. They are piled on top of each other. No one image expresses the fulness of Christ and his work. That's why the Bible has been described as being "the treasury of Christ". In it, we find jewel after jewel, each a beautiful picture of Christ. Each one is to be held up to the light to be appreciated and enjoyed.

It is not that clever humans realised that the tabernacle, and the sacrifices made there, were a useful way of interpreting the cross. God himself provided them as a framework. In history, the Levitical sacrifices came before Calvary—but in the formulation of God's plan, the sacrifice of Christ came first. He was the Lamb ordained before the foundation of the world (1 Peter 1:19-20; Revelation 13:8). Just as Jesus was "the Root of David" (Revelation 5:5) as well as being born into the line of David as a descendant of David, so he was the root of the Passover, the sin offering and the scapegoat, as well as coming as the final, greatest, ultimate Passover Lamb, sin offering and scapegoat. As the Scottish pastor and author Donald MacLeod puts it:

"All of these were divinely configured to prefigure him. The understanding of Jesus' death as a sacrifice is not a human convention, but a divine revelation."

(*Christ Crucified: Understanding the Atonement,* page 65)

My name is written on his heart

Let's put all this together. Jesus is our High Priest, and he offers himself as the sacrifice. Through his shed blood he enters heaven itself. He comes into the ultimate Most Holy Place for he comes into the presence of God.

That's precisely what happened after Jesus died. He rose again and ascended into heaven through the clouds. He ascended through the clouds into the presence of God, just as Moses ascended through the cloud on Mount Sinai into God's presence, and just as the high priest went through the cloud of incense into the Most Holy Place. At his ascension, Jesus entered the heavenly tabernacle through his shed blood to come before God.

And now we come to the point. As Jesus passes through the cloud into heaven, whose name is written over his heart? "Whenever Aaron enters the Holy Place, he will bear the names of the sons of Israel over his heart on the breastpiece of decision as a continuing memorial before the Lᴏʀᴅ" (Exodus **28:29**). And Aaron was only ever a shadow of Jesus.

As long as Jesus is in heaven, he will bear the names of the sons and daughters of God over his heart as a continuing memorial before God. If you've turned to Jesus in faith, he bears your name. Your name is written over his heart. My name may not literally be written on Christ's clothing—but it is as good as literally there. When God looks on Christ, he sees me in Christ. He sees my name, my self, my identity, borne by and wrapped up in Christ.

If you're a Christian, then your name is in heaven. And it's not on some database or in a filing cabinet. It is tied to a person, to Jesus. Jesus ascended to heaven for your salvation. He is the memorial before God guaranteeing your security in heaven.

When you doubt your salvation or when you feel the weight of your sin or when you let God down in a spectacular way, you can look up to heaven and see your High Priest there, with your name written over his heart. You can see Jesus standing there as a memorial before God that you are his child.

And it's even better than that. Look ahead over the remaining years of your life, however long that might be. You don't know what problems you may face—financial hardship, mental illness, loneliness, bereavement, sickness. Can you be sure that you'll stand firm throughout those trials? How might you doubt? How will you sin? How will you cope? You cannot know the answers to these questions. You cannot know how you will respond.

But this you can know. Right now, and for ever, Jesus is in heaven and he bears your name. The hymn *A debtor to mercy alone* by Augustus Toplady ends with this verse, which captures beautifully the confidence a Christian can enjoy:

My name from the palms of your hands,
eternity will not erase;
impressed on your heart it remains
in marks of indelible grace.

Yes, I to the end will endure,
as sure as the promise is given:
more happy, but not more secure,
are glorified spirits in heaven.

Christians who have already died are more happy than us because they're already with Jesus in heaven. But they are not more secure than us. Their future is secure because Jesus is in heaven—and our future is secure because Jesus is in heaven. What's the secret of surviving for seventy years as a Christian? The answer is Jesus. If you're a Christian, when Jesus passed through the cloud into heaven, your name was written over his heart. You're as good as there already. And the only way God can exclude you from heaven is if he excludes his Son.

"Therefore, since we have a great high priest who has ascended into heaven, Jesus the Son of God, let us hold firmly to the faith we profess." (Hebrews 4:14)

Questions for reflection

1. How does the way in which the priesthood and sacrifices point you to Jesus cause you to be more in love with him, and more in awe of him?

2. What concerns you about your future? Meditate on the words of *A debtor to mercy alone*. How might this transform your concerns?

3. How does having "a great high priest who has ascended into heaven" make you determined to "hold firmly to the faith"?

13. THE GOLDEN CALF AND THE GOD OF MERCY

Chapters 25 – 31 describe the instructions given to Moses for the construction and establishment of the tabernacle; chapters 35 – 40 detail the implementation of those instructions; and it all comes to a climax when the glory of God descends on the tabernacle in 40:34-38. But in chapters 32 – 34, this narrative is rudely interrupted. We have been with Moses on the mountain, with God; now we find out what is going on down below with the people.

The agenda for the second half of Exodus is set in 25:8: "Then let them make a sanctuary for me, and I will dwell among them". The goal is the presence of God. The tragic irony of the golden calf is that it is intended to solve the perceived problem of God's absence (**32:1**). It is an attempt to solve a problem that does not exist. But it also highlights the problem of God's presence, summed up in 33:3: "I will not go with you, because you are a stiff-necked people and I might destroy you on the way". In other words,can a holy God live among sinful people, and can a sinful people cope with having a holy God living among them?

The events of chapter 32 are a tragedy and an offence—a "great sin" (**32:31**). The way in which the narrative unfolds shows why.

Israel's fall

In many ways, this event is Israel's "fall", their version of Genesis 3. Israel has been brought out of slavery. They have escaped death through the Passover. They have been birthed anew through the Red Sea. They have been constituted at Sinai as God's covenant people. Israel is a new humanity.

But tragically, the old humanity lurks in the heart of the new humanity. And so here, Israel behaves like humanity in Adam. They reject God. Even as Moses is receiving instructions for the true worship of God in Exodus 25 – 31, Israel sets up an alternative worship—using their gold (**32:2-3**) to make an idol (**v 4**). It is, in a way, Israel's original sin; it sets the culture of Israel, and sets the pattern for their subsequent rebellions against the LORD.

The parallels continue in **verses 21-24**, where Aaron responds like the first Adam. He blames the people, just as Adam blamed Eve. In **verse 24**, rather preposterously, he says that he threw gold into the fire and, as if by magic, "out came this calf". But **verse 4** could not be clearer. Not only did he take the people's gold and make it "into an idol cast in the shape of a calf", but he did so by "fashioning it with a tool". This emphasis on a tool anticipates the critique of Isaiah 44. There, the very act of making an idol exposes its folly, because the idol is so clearly dependent for its existence on a human craftsman. This calf can do nothing for the people. It is a folly to depend on something that depends on them for its very being.

God introduced the Ten Commandments by reminding the people that he had rescued them from slavery in Egypt (Exodus 20:2). Now Aaron uses the same language—but about the golden calf (**32:4**). The people want gods "who will go before us" (**v 1**)—but this is exactly what the LORD had done (14:19; 23:23). The people are robbing God of his glory, exchanging it for a lifeless lump of shiny metal. That very morning they would have collected manna—a sign of God's provision. Yet here they are, exchanging him for a mute, created calf that cost them their gold and can give them nothing. The sixteenth-century Reformer John Calvin commented:

"In this narrative we perceive the detestable impiety of the people, their worse than base ingratitude, and their monstrous madness, mixed with stupidity … Could they not see the pillar of fire and the cloud? Was not God's paternal solicitude abundantly conspicuous every day in the manna? Was he not near them in ways innumerable?"   (*Commentary on Exodus 32:1*)

It is utterly stupid—but this stupidity is the stupidity to which we all succumb whenever we sin. All sin involves a crazy loss of perspective. We lose sight of God's generous provision, and we grasp or envy. Reflecting on this episode, Psalm 106:20 says, "They exchanged their glorious God for an image of a bull".

Then the psalmist adds (just in case you've missed the point), "… which eats grass". It is stupid.

> All sin involves a crazy loss of perspective, so that we grasp or envy.

Paul seems to have this in mind when he says that humanity "exchanged the truth about God for a lie, and worshipped and served created things rather than the Creator" (Romans 1:25). Paul is describing the idolatry of all humanity; and in Exodus 32, Israel's idolatry is a paradigm of all idolatry. The term "sacred cow" comes from this story—your sacred cow is whatever you cannot give up because you believe your security, identity, approval, fulfilment or satisfaction depends on it. Your sacred cow is your idol. The **Heidelberg Catechism** says:

"Idolatry is having or inventing something in which to put our trust instead of, or in addition to, the only true God, who has revealed himself in his Word."

We might assume this story has nothing to say to modern Western people who have left crude idol worship behind. But of course, there are still things we spend all we have on, because we think they will lead us through life and bring us into fulfilment and satisfaction. We may not worship calf-statues, but we are not immune from idolatry. Our desire for created things eclipses our desire for God. It might be people whose approval or love or desire we crave, or objects we must have, or experiences or status we must enjoy. There was a time when each Sunday, as our family walked to church, we would pass our neighbour on his knees washing the wheels of his car with a tooth-brush. He was kneeling in homage to his god. It might be anything. But there will be something. Our idols need not be physical objects. They might be personal freedom or success or wealth or popularity or acceptance or love. These things can become the idols we serve in the sense that they determine our actions. They rule our lives: "People are slaves to whatever has mastered them" (2 Peter 2:19).

Exodus 32 begins, "When the people saw that Moses was so long in coming down from the mountain, they gathered round Aaron and said, 'Come, make us gods who will go before us'" (Exodus **32:1**). *So long.* In fact, it was only forty days (24:18). In just forty days, the people abandoned their declarations of allegiance to the LORD (19:8; 24:3); that is how "quick [they were] to turn away from what [he] commanded them" (**32:8**). The "quick" in this verse contrasts with the "so long" in **verse 1**. The wheels of idolatry turn fast.

What idolatry is

Idolatry is an act of adultery. In Exodus 24, the people had entered into a covenant with God. God had become their husband. They had made covenant vows that were not unlike wedding vows: "When Moses went and told the people all the LORD's words and laws, they responded with one voice, 'Everything the LORD has said we will do'" (24:3). Now, in chapter 32, it is as if a husband has found his wife in bed with another man while they still on their honeymoon.

Our idolatry is no different. Through baptism, we enter into a cov-enant with God. Every time you take communion, you reinforce those covenant commitments. And every time you sin and give your alle-giance to someone or something else, you are a covenant-breaker. When James describes his Christian readers as "you adulterous peo-ple" (James 4:4), he is describing us. When you sin, you are commit-ting adultery.

It's not clear in Exodus 32 whether the people want the calf to replace God (breaking the first commandment) or to represent God (breaking the second commandment). Maybe it's a bit of both. Their declaration in **32:4** refers to "gods" (plural), suggesting that the calf is a partner with the LORD.

It may well be that in **verse 1** they are proposing replacements for God ("make us gods"), and that Aaron is responding with a compromise in which the calf represents God (**verse 4** could read, "This is your god", see NIV footnote). That would make sense of the people's attitude towards Aaron, which is initially antagonistic (the phrase "they gathered round" Aaron in **verse 1** is the phrase translated in Numbers 16:3 as "they came as a group to oppose"). Perhaps this compromise is Aaron's way out. He sets up an altar "in front of the calf" and announces "a festival to the LORD" (Exodus **32:5**). He is using the name that God revealed in Exodus 3 at the burning bush. Aaron is attempting a compromise: a blend of pagan religion and the worship of the LORD. To put it another way, he is breaking the second commandment so that the people might not break the first commandment. So, the next day, the people offer their burnt offerings as good worshippers of the LORD. But then they "indulge in revelry" (Exodus **32:6**). The word implies an orgy.

Idols have no morality, and so idolatry has no morality. A calf is silent. It can't convey moral principles. So idolatry leads to moral breakdown. In 24:11 we are told that the representatives of Israel "saw God, and they ate and drank". Now in **32:6**, the people "sat down to eat and drink and got up to indulge in revelry". This has become a dark parody of true religion. They see god in the image of a bull. They eat and drink, supposedly in his presence, but this time follow it with an orgy.

Why a golden *calf?*

The choice of the idol-shape is not arbitrary. The word translated "calf" need not mean a young cow, and Psalm 106 describes it as a bull. A bull was a common symbol of strength and fertility in surrounding nations. It still is. We talk about a "bull market" to describe a rising market; English national pride is sometimes personified as "John Bull". Israel is co-opting the images of the surrounding cultures to re-imagine God. The people are happy to worship God, but they want to worship him on their terms. They are happy to worship God, but they want to combine this with worldliness and indulgence. They let the nations set the agenda. They want a god who is visible and manageable. Even if they are not replacing God, they are reducing him.

It is the same today. Some people want the benefits of being part of the church, but they do not want to relate to God on his terms. Or they want the blessings of God along with the pleasures of indulgence. They want forgiveness from God, but they do not want to obey his will. Some people want to pick and choose which bits of the Bible they accept. Naturally, we all remould God in our image or our culture's image, rather than remembering that we are made in his image.

And as Christians, we worry that if we do not compromise, then the culture will not respect us. But the world will not respect us any more if we change with every cultural fashion. And if we become no different to the surrounding culture, then we have nothing distinctive or worthwhile to say. If we simply echo the world, then we offer no alternative. The world has plenty of temples to its idols; there is no call or excuse for making God's church into another one.

It is common in our culture for people to think they can decide what God is like. In this way we create our own version of God. We want to think of God as loving, but not holy. We want a god who is merciful, but not a judge. We create a god of our own imagining. It is not so far removed from worshipping an idol we have made. We may not have a metal idol, but we have a mental idol. Beware any sentence, on another's lips or in your own head, that begins, "I like to think of God as..." or "I don't think God would be..."

It is, in Calvin's words, "monstrous madness, mixed with stupidity". Do you really think the eternal God will suddenly change to become what you think he should be? There must be no compromise and there must be no **syncretism**. Treating God on our terms rather than his terms is a dangerous business. God is the LORD, the "I AM WHAT I AM". God sees what the people have done because, in contrast to a blind metal calf, he is the living, ever-present, all-knowing God (Exodus **32:7-8**). And because of his jealousy for his glory (20:4-5; 34:14), his anger burns against the people and he prepares to destroy them (**32:9-10**). That is what God thinks of our idolatry. It is, after all, spiritual adultery.

These words are a particular warning to church leaders. In Exodus 25 – 32, Aaron is the main figure as God speaks to Moses about how Israel will live as his people. Moses is told that Aaron is the one who will lead God's people in worship of the LORD; yet meanwhile, Aaron is leading God's people in compromised idolatrous worship. He is not the initiator of this—but he capitulates to the people and so he is complicit in this. *I will lead you … wherever you want to go,* he says in effect. And that is not leadership; it is cowardice. It is not loving; it is selfish. Leaders must resist the pressures of the culture if they are to lead God's people in true worship of the true God, the only God who can and will "go before us".

Questions for reflection

1. What difference does it make to your view of your sin and yourself when you see sin as idolatry, and idolatry as adultery?

2. In what ways can we replace God in today's culture? In what ways can we reduce him? Which is more attractive, and why?

3. Do you value leadership that leads where you need to go, or where you want to go? Would you appreciate Moses, or Aaron?

PART TWO

The end of the story

When, in Noah's day, "the Lord saw how great the wickedness of the human race had become on the earth, and that every inclination of the thoughts of the human heart was only evil all the time" (Genesis 6:5), he responded by wiping "from the face of the earth the human race [he had] created" (v 7)—the Creator responds to sin by de-creating. Only Noah, who "walked faithfully with God" (v 9), was saved, along with his family. Through them, God would begin to create a new humanity. Likewise, God responded to the builders of the tower at Babel—building in proud opposition to God's purpose for humanity to fill the earth—by confusing and scattering them in judgment (11:1-9), before calling one man, Abram, to become a "great nation" who would be blessed and be a blessing (12:1-3).

There are echoes of this in God's response to Israel's sin in Exodus 32. We have seen that Israel itself was God's new creation, the new humanity. But now the new humanity has proved to be just like the old one (as happened after the flood too—Genesis 9:20-29). And so God responds in the same way. He has, he tells Moses, "seen these people" (Exodus **32:9**). And "they are a stiff-necked people"—they will not bow their heads to the Creator. Humanity's great problem is, in one sense, about the stiffness of our necks—we will not bow them to our rightful ruler. And so the Creator will de-create: "Leave me alone so that my anger may burn against them and that I may destroy them" (**v 10**). Only one man, Moses, who has alone remained faithful, will escape judgment, and God promises that "I will make you into a great nation" (**v 10**).

Israel's story has hardly begun, and yet now it is at an end.

Moses steps in

Then Moses intervenes. He prays on behalf of the people. There perhaps is an implicit invitation from God for Moses to intervene in

verse 10, when he says, "Now leave me alone so that my anger may burn against them and that I may destroy them". The implication is, *When you leave me alone, I will destroy your people, but if you don't leave me alone, then things may turn out very differently.* So Moses pleads for mercy—and his plea is heard. By not leaving God alone, he is not leaving the people alone to face their fate.

What's striking is that Moses prays for mercy on the same basis that God prepares for judgment—the glory of God. In **verses 11-12**, Moses argues that destroying Israel will damage God's reputation. In **verse 13**, he argues that destroying Israel will break God's promises—and therefore damage his reputation for covenant faithfulness. At stake is God's reputation and God's glory. Moses turns "your people" (the people of Moses) in **verse 7** into "your people" (the people of the LORD) in **verse 11**. God's reputation is tied to this group of people.

God hears the prayer of Moses and relents (**v 14**). So this prayer changes the course of history. It makes a difference. It means Israel has a future. There is an element of mystery here—the mystery of God's sovereignty—for elsewhere the Bible is clear that God does not change his mind (Numbers 23:19; 1 Samuel 15:29). Perhaps the best way to look at it is that since God is in charge of all things, he is in charge of our prayers. We freely choose to pray what God has freely

> God intends our prayers to be the means by which he changes the world.

chosen we should, and God freely chooses to respond to the prayers he has ordained we would say. So God intends our prayers to be the means by which he changes the world. He decides to use our prayer to change his decisions!

Moses pursues God's glory through prayer. God invites us to use arguments when we pray (see my books *The Message of Prayer*, chapter 7, and *You Can Pray*, chapter 8). But they are arguments that focus on his promises and his glory. It is possible to argue with God in a way that diminishes his glory, when we argue as though he could be manipulated or managed. But we can argue with God in a way that promotes his glory. We do this by focusing on his promises, his mercy and his reputation. Notice how many times Moses uses the word "you" and "your" in Exodus **32:11-13**. Whether we are praying for ourselves or our church or our world, and whether we are praying about the problems we face or the opportunities of mission, we can use the language of Moses:

> LORD, we are praying for "your people", whom you have saved. Don't let the world say that you have acted with "evil intent". "Do not bring disaster on your people." "Remember your servants ... to whom you swore by your own self." Your reputation is on the line. Remember your promise to have a people "as numerous as the stars in the sky". Fulfil this promise now through the mission of your church—not for the church's sake, or for my sake, but for yours.

Pursuing God's glory in holiness

Perhaps at this point in the story we might be tempted to think that Moses views God as too harsh. But in fact, Moses is passionate for God's glory, just as God is. The text makes this explicit. In **verse 10**, God burns with anger (before showing mercy in **verse 14**). In **verse 19**, Moses burns with anger (after pleading for mercy in **verses 11-13**). Moses shares God's anger at this rejection of his glory.

And both Moses and God bring judgment on those responsible. Moses and the **Levites** hack down 3,000 people (**v 25-28**) and the LORD sends a plague (**v 35**). Having come down the mountain with Joshua and heard the sound of singing coming from the camp (**v 17-18**), Moses sees for himself "the calf and the dancing" (**v 19**) and smashes the tablets of stone (hence the apparent aside of **verses 15-16**). This is not a fit of uncontrolled rage—it is a sign that the covenant is broken (and that it will need to be reaffirmed, which happens in 34:10-28).

So while Moses does not want Israel to be destroyed, he does want them to be holy. He is pleading with God for mercy, but he is not belittling or excusing the sin that deserves judgment and will require mercy if destruction is to be avoided. What is happening must be stopped. The people "were running wild" and were "out of control" (**32:25**). Aaron's attempt at limiting their sin has drastically backfired—as all attempts at compromise with sin will do. We cannot oppose sin by settling for "lesser" sin. It could be that the people are still out of control despite having been made to drink the ground-up calf mixed with water, or it could be that the drinking of **verse 20** and the slaughter of **verse 28** took place simultaneously, even though they are described one after another. What is clear is that Moses wants the people to regain self-control. He intervenes to bring this sin to a halt. Judgment is an act which reveals the true colours of sin. It can be an act of divine discipline designed to produce holiness (Hebrews 12:4-11).

The climax of this section of the story is Exodus **32:29**. Moses says to the Levites who have stood with him, "You have been set apart to the Lord today, for you were against your own sons and brothers, and he has blessed you this day". The word "set apart" is literally "holy". They have proven that they are dedicated—holy—to God. They are blessed for being on God's side (**v 26**), even though that meant choosing against their "own sons and brothers" (**v 29**).

God had declared Israel to be a "holy nation" (19:4-6). They were set aside or dedicated to God so that they would make God known to the nations. But in their revelry they have imitated the nations. What drives Moses is his concern that the people have "become a laughing-stock to their enemies" (**32:25**). Once again, his concern is God's glory. God's reputation requires the holiness of his people—and holiness means being set apart. At heart, to be holy is to make a choice—a choice to follow God rather than follow the world, to side with God rather than the world. The future of God's people as God's people is at stake. If they are not a holy nation set apart for God, then they are just another nation, one among many, waiting to be washed up by the tide of history.

Holiness matters. Moses wants the people to recognise the depth of their sin. This is why he and the Levites kill 3,000 people. They are running wild, and they need to be stopped. It makes this passage uncomfortable reading for us. It seems so brutal. But sin is brutal. This story reveals the deadly seriousness of sin. Temptation presents sin as attractive and harmless. But in reality sin looks like 3,000 rotting corpses. Death is sin made visible.

Holiness matters. This is why Moses makes the people drink the idol in **verse 20**. He literally liquidates it. There is no nice way to say this, but Moses wants the people to see that idols are just excrement. This chapter is meant to shake us out of our complacency. Think about your compromises. Think about those things that are rivals with God for your affections. None of them last. Sooner or later they all decay. Meanwhile, God is the eternal "I AM WHO I AM".

In the middle of the chaos, Moses shouts, "Whoever is for the LORD, come to me" (**v 26**). It is three words in Hebrew: Whoever for-the-LORD to-me. The KJV translated it as, "Who is on the LORD's side? Let him come unto me." And in the chaos of our culture, and in the midst of our own tendency to compromise, the same call comes to us. Whose side are you on?

Pursuing God's glory in mercy

In **verse 10**, God offers Moses the opportunity to be the father of a new nation. But Moses refuses. He is committed to God, but he is also committed to Israel. Then, in **verse 30**, Moses goes a step further. "The next day Moses said to the people, 'You have committed a great sin. But now I will go up to the LORD; perhaps I can make atonement for your sin.'" What Moses has in mind becomes clearer in **verses 31-32**: "So Moses went back to the LORD and said, 'Oh, what a great sin these people have committed! They have made themselves gods of gold. But now, please forgive their sin—but if not, then blot me out of the book you have written.'"

Moses pictures God with a book that contains the names of his people. He is probably drawing on the imagery of ancient kings who listed their subjects, much as modern governments do in a census. This is God's census or register (Psalm 87:6; Isaiah 4:3). Elsewhere, it is called "the book of life" (Psalm 69:28; Philippians 4:3; Revelation 20:12-15; 21:27). Imagine a bouncer standing outside a wonderful party with a list of names on a clipboard so he can check people's right to enter. The Israelites have forfeited their right to be on that list. But Moses offers to be a substitute for them. *If they cannot be forgiven,* says Moses, *then remove my name from your book instead* (a sentiment echoed by Paul in Romans 9:3-4).

But Moses cannot make atonement for God's people. He himself needs atonement. "Whoever has sinned against me I will blot out of my book", says God in reply (Exodus **32:33**). People will be held responsible for their sin. Judgment will fall. It falls in part in **verse 35**, as God sends a plague on the people. But this is only partial judgment. It is a sign of what is to come. Full judgment is postponed.

Because judgment is postponed, God tells Moses to lead the people. God's angel will go before them to give them the land of Canaan (**v 34**). God will bless his people and fulfil his promise. The story began in **verse 1** with the people demanding, "Make us gods who will go before us". Now in **verse 34** it ends with God graciously reiterating the promise that "my angel will go before you".

But judgment is only postponed. It is not cancelled. It cannot be cancelled for God is committed to his glory and holiness. So God continues, "When the time comes for me to punish, I will punish them for their sin" (**v 34**).

It's worth pausing to ask, *If this was the only chapter of the Bible you had ever read, what image of God would it give you?* It appears that God gets into a petulant mood, before being talked out of it by Moses. So the focus is on Moses—and that is the point. This story is intended to show us the need for a mediator. God declares his intention of destroying the people, before implicitly inviting Moses to intercede on their behalf. His plan is to save through the mediation of Moses. This is, after all, not the only chapter of Exodus, let alone the whole Bible—and we have seen in the book of Exodus just how committed God is to keeping his promises, and rescuing and providing for these people, and how as "I AM WHO I AM", he is sufficient within himself, and not swayed this way and that by the behaviour or arguments of others. Sin is adultery—and to respond with judgment is not petulant, but reasonable. But in this chapter, we are meant to look at the mediator. Moses continues as the mediator in **verses 30-35**, but he cannot truly and fully mediate. This chapter sets us up to look for another greater mediator. And that mediator, of course, is Jesus.

Blotted out

In **verse 14**, God shows mercy through the intercession of Moses. But it is Jesus who is our complete and ultimate mediator. Whatever its immediate sources, all divine mercy comes to us ultimately through the mediation of Jesus. Justification, adoption, redemption and forgiveness were ours before the creation of the world in Christ, says Paul in Ephesians 1:3-7.

"When the time comes for me to punish," says God in Exodus **32:34**, "I will punish them for their sin". For God's people, that time came at the cross. On the night before he died, Jesus prayed, "Father, the hour has come. Glorify your Son, that your Son may glorify you" (John 17:1). Throughout John's Gospel, "the time" that has come—the moment of glorification—is the cross (John 12:23-33). The greatest revelation of divine glory is the revelation of divine mercy at the cross. In Exodus 32, Moses pursues glory in mercy. But this is as nothing compared to God's own pursuit of glory in mercy—for God sends his own Son as an atonement for sin.

At Calvary, as Jesus hung in darkness in our place, he was blotted out of God's book. "But now, please forgive their sin—but if not, then blot me out of the book you have written," says Moses in Exodus **32:32**. As

Jesus hung on the cross, he prayed, "Father forgive," and that forgiveness is granted because he was indeed blotted out.

Peter picks up the language of being blotted out in his sermon to the Jerusalem crowds in Acts 3. His hearers, he says, "disowned the Holy and Righteous One" and "killed the author of life" (Acts 3:14-15). "But what God foretold by the mouth of all the prophets, that his Christ would suffer, he thus fulfilled. Repent therefore, and turn again, that your sins may be blotted out" (v 18-19, ESV). Instead of our names being blotted out of the book God has written, our sins are blotted out through the death foretold by the prophets, and foreshadowed by Moses in Exodus 32.

> We tend to settle somewhere in the gap between the standards of the gospel and the standards of this world.

As a result, the risen Jesus says to the Christians in the city of Sardis, "The one who is victorious will ... be dressed in white. I will never blot out the name of that person from the book of life, but will acknowledge that name before my Father and his angels" (Revelation 3:5). Jesus is, as it were, the bouncer on the door of heaven with the list of names. And our names can never be removed from his list. Jesus will acknowledge us before his Father. He will acknowledge us when we come to God in prayer and he will acknowledge us when we come to God in heaven. He will acknowledge us even when we have committed "a great sin" (Exodus **32:31**). He will acknowledge us because he was blotted out for us, instead of us.

We live at a time when the church is full of compromises. Godly religion is being polluted by the values of our culture. The world is setting the agenda for the church. But we, too, in our personal lives face temptations to compromise. We tend to try to settle down somewhere in the gap between the standards of the gospel and the standards of this world. Exodus 32 is a call and a warning and an encouragement to rid ourselves of compromise.

The future of the gospel is no longer tied to the physical descendants of ethnic Israel. So we do not strap a sword to our sides as the Levites did in **verse 27**. But we do take up a sword—the sword of God's word. "Do not conform to the pattern of this world, but be transformed by the renewing of your mind. Then you will be able to test and approve what God's will is—his good, pleasing and perfect will" (Romans 12:2). We wield God's word to discern God's will, and we wield God's word to expose and confront compromise.

But we do this without fear, for we stand safe in the mercy of God. Jesus says to us, *God will never blot out your name, because he blotted out mine*. We do not attack compromise to become God's holy people or to make our place with God safe. We are already God's holy people and our place with God is already safe. The mercy of God to us in Christ means there is a lightness and freedom to our lives. But we still oppose compromise. Through Christ we have been set apart or dedicated for God. And so we live as dedicated people. Whenever we must take sides, we stand on the LORD's side with his word in our hands.

Questions for reflection

1. What goes wrong in our lives and faith if we either forget God's mercy or downplay his holiness?

2. What compromises in obedience do you make yourself, or excuse in others? What about your church?

3. "Jesus says to us, *God will never blot out your name, because he blotted out mine*." How does knowing this motivate you to do something about the compromises you identified in answer to the previous question?

14. SHOW ME YOUR GLORY

Do you ever feel that you can't go on as a Christian? You just can't sustain it. You can't live with God and for God. It's too hard. The demands are too high.

And yet you can't live without God. You love him too much. Or you need him too much. To face life without God is scary. To face the next life without him is terrifying.

The dialogues between God and Moses in these chapters address the problem raised by the golden calf in chapter 32. While Moses is on Mount Sinai hearing from God, the people make a golden calf and worship it. Moses' intervention means that the people are not wiped out, and judgment is suspended. Yet they are now faced with this problem: they can't live with God and they can't live without him.

We can't live with God

In **33:1-3** God says he will keep his promise to Abraham by giving the Israelites the land of Canaan: "But I will not go with you, because you are a stiff-necked people and I might destroy you on the way" (**v 3**). God will not live among his people.

It's important to observe where the story of the golden calf fits in the book of Exodus. God has just given Moses detailed instructions on the construction of the tabernacle. Those instructions are introduced in 25:8: "Then let them make a sanctuary for me, and I will dwell among them". We then have seven chapters on how the sanctuary is to be built, all preparing for the day when God will dwell among his people. But chapter 32 suddenly shows us that *while this is happening,* the people are worshipping the golden calf. And so now God says, *I will not go with them. I will not dwell among them.* The tabernacle project is cancelled.

Why will God not go with them? Because "I might destroy you on the way ... If I were to go with you even for a moment, I might destroy you" (**33:3, 5**). We met this idea when the people first gathered at the foot of Mount Sinai and were warned not to approach "or the Lord will break out against them" (19:20, 24).

God is holy. He is like the sun. If you or I went anywhere near the sun, we would be instantly burnt up. Anything impure that comes into God's holy presence is destroyed. God is a consuming fire.

We can't live without God

If we can't live with God, then **33:1-3** looks like a good deal. God will give his people the promised land, but without the threat of his presence. All the blessings of God, but without God himself. Would you take that deal?

Often, we live as though we would. Here's how it looks. You want God to bless you: to forgive you, to rescue you from hell, to protect you, to provide a spouse or a job or good health. But you don't really want God himself. You don't want the demands his presence makes. You don't want to make the changes his presence demands. You don't want holiness. So this looks like a good deal.

But it is, in fact, "distressing" (**v 4**). The people begin to mourn—they wear no ornaments, and God says they are right not to do so (**v 5**). It does not sound like a good deal to them. **Verses 7-11** look back to the meetings of God and Moses. One reason why these verses are included at this point is to give a sense of what's being lost. God meets with his people (**v 7-8**), his presence symbolised by the pillar of cloud (**v 9**). When the people see the pillar of cloud, they worship God because they know he's present among them (**v 10**). "The Lord would speak to Moses face to face, as one speaks to a friend" (**v 11**). God has been among his people as a friend. But now God says he would be among them as an enemy who might destroy them (**v 3, 5**). This is what's distressing—God withdrawing his presence because the golden calf means he is now no longer a friend, but an enemy.

In **verses 12-13**, Moses is saying, *You've told me to lead this people. But I can't do it on my own. I need to know who's coming with me.* It is a plea for God's presence.

So in **verse 14** God assures Moses that "my Presence will go with you, and I will give you rest". But the word "you" in this statement is singular, not plural. God is assuring Moses that he will be with him, Moses—but not with the people, Israel. And this is not enough for Moses. Moses is pleading for God to be present among his people. Without God's presence, there's no point in going to the promised land (**v 15**). So we could paraphrase this exchange as follows:

Moses: *Who will go with us? (**v 12-13**).*

God: *I, the LORD, will go with you (singular), with you alone, Moses (**v 14**).*

Moses: *With me on my own is not enough. Please go with us, with me and your people. It's your presence with your people that makes the difference (**v 15-16**).*

I think that this is one of the most remarkable moments in the Bible story. For all his faults, this is what makes Moses one of the great men of history. He turns down God's blessing if it comes without God himself. He turns down God's presence if it's for him alone.

He comes before the God who has just said, "I might destroy you", and negotiates with him. And his bottom line, his only aim, is the presence of God among the people of God.

God has already offered to start again with Moses (32:10). But Moses prays for "me and your people" (**33:16**). He asks God to "remember that this nation is your people" (**v 13**; see 19:4-6). He points out to God that it is his presence among them that "will distinguish me and your people from all the other people on the face of the earth" (**33:16**). He is saying: *God, it is your presence that makes us your people.*

It is God's presence that makes us his people. So there are strong parallels with Pentecost, when the coming of the Spirit transformed a rag-bag of flawed, timid men and women into a bold, proclaiming community of Jesus (Acts 2:1-4). We are nothing without God's presence. We have nothing without God's presence. The greatest judgment of God is his absence instead of his presence—that's what hell is.

> The greatest judgment of God is his absence.

God offers Moses all the blessings of the promised land without having to worry about the consuming presence of God (Exodus **33:2-3**). And Moses turns it down (**v 15**) because he knows that the promised land without the God who promised it is not worth having. All the blessings of being part of the church without knowing God are not worth having.

We each need to feel the challenge of that. Imagine a woman who married a man for his house, his car or his money. Hear her saying, "I prefer it when he's away on business". Don't treat God like that. And don't avoid it just out of some obligation. Pursue God because knowing God is the blessing. Look forward to eternity because it will be with God, and that is the blessing.

The American pastor Mike McKinley writes:

"It's worth asking ourselves: if heaven gave me everything—the job, the girl or guy, the car, the health, the wealth—but Jesus wasn't there, would I be content there? Or if heaven gave me nothing except Jesus, would I be satisfied? Deep down, I think I often answer 'yes' and 'no'. That's because I love other things too much, and I love the Lord Jesus far, far too little."

(Passion: How Christ's Final Day Changes Your Every Day, page 119)

Moses loves God. That is why he says, in effect, *You can give us the promised land, flowing with milk and honey, but without you—what will it matter? What will we have?* The land is their inheritance, but even more, God is their inheritance.

We are promised something more precious than heaven—we are promised God himself. Without his presence, all else is nothing. We are nothing.

So, why are you a Christian? Is it because you get forgiveness or hope or blessing or community? That's great. God's blessings in the gospel are bountiful beyond measure. But be like Moses. Pursue God for God's own sake. If you only love God's blessings, then your faith may falter when life is hard. If you only love what God gives, then what will happen if he ever withholds it?

Some people are happy to relate to the church. They want the benefits the church brings. They want a place to hang out, or they want a group of people who will help them out, or they want the forgiveness that Christians talk about. But they do not really want God. They do not want God the Holy One, the consuming fire, the glorious presence, the One who calls sin adultery, is angered by compromise, and insists on holiness.

The tension

After all, as Moses says to God, God's people cannot be God's people if God is not with them! "How will anyone know that you are pleased with me and with your people unless you go with us? What else will distinguish me and your people from all the other people on the face of the earth?" (**v 16**). It's another reference to God's reputation. The only other time the word translated "people" in **verse 13** (*gôy*) is used in Exodus is in 19:5-6, where it refers to the missional identity of God's people. Moses, it seems, echoes this to remind God of his missional purposes. If God abandons Israel, then God abandons his mission to the world.

In response to this plea, God relents: "I will do the very thing you have asked" (**33:17**). God is sovereign. He is the "I AM WHO I AM". It was always God's intention to do this very thing—but he chose to do it through the courageous intervention of Moses, in order to highlight the problem that we can't live with God and we can't live without him.

In **verse 17**, the LORD repeats the words of Moses from **verse 12**: he will do what Moses pleads for "because I am pleased with you and I know you by name". This dialogue highlights the mediatorial role of Moses (see also **34:9**). And so it sheds light on the role of Jesus. Moses turned down God's presence if it would be for him alone—Jesus left God's presence so that we could know God's presence. Jesus would die rather than leave God's people without God. Jesus experienced God's absence—he was "forsaken" (Mark 15:34)—so that we might enjoy and experience his welcome.

You can't live with God and you can't live without him. In these chapters, it's almost as if God and Moses negotiate a deal, a way forward, a *modus operandi* following the fiasco of the golden calf. God can't dwell among his people, but without him they're not his people. How will this tension be resolved?

Mercy through God's name

Moses goes a step further. "Now show me your glory," he asks in Exodus **33:18**. What does God promise to do in response? Two things.

First, "I will cause all my goodness to pass in front of you" (**v 19**). The LORD arranges to put Moses in a cleft in the rock (**v 21-22**) so that he can pass by and Moses is able to see the afterglow of his glory (**v 22-23**). But Moses cannot see God's glory directly. "You cannot see my face, for no one may see me and live" (**v 20**).

Second, "I will proclaim my name, the LORD, in your presence" (**v 19**). We get an intimation of that "name"—character—here: "I will have mercy on whom I will have mercy, and I will have compassion on whom I will have compassion". Moses asks God to show him his glory.

He wants to see God. He wants a visual image. He wants to know what God looks like—that's what Moses means by "glory". But instead, God declares his name. Instead of a description of the way the God looks, we get a description of the way God is. God is not known through a visual image. He cannot be pictured. That's why you cannot make an idol and say, "This is what God is like".

Moses is told to chisel out replacement tablets—the sin of God's people has broken the law, but they still need to know and be governed by it (**34:1**)—and go up Mount Sinai the following morning (**v 2-4**). "Then the LORD came down in the cloud and stood there with him and proclaimed his name, the LORD. And he passed in front of Moses" (**v 5-6**). And this is the name God proclaims—this is the glory of God:

> "The LORD, the LORD, the compassionate and gracious God, slow to anger, abounding in love and faithfulness, maintaining love to thousands, and forgiving wickedness, rebellion and sin. Yet he does not leave the guilty unpunished; he punishes the children and their children for the sin of the parents to the third and fourth generation." (**v 6-7**)

How can a holy God live among sinful people? Because God is compassionate and gracious; because God is abounding in love and faithfulness; because God forgives wickedness, rebellion and sin. There's hope in God's name, for his name is full of mercy.

As we've already seen, in the Bible a person's name represents them and their character. And here we see God's character: merciful and compassionate, full of grace and truth. What is God like? He's the God who burns with anger, but he's also the God who is slow to anger. He's the God who does not ignore sin, but he's also the God who forgives sin. Terence Fretheim says that **verses 6-7**…

> "may be said to be a statement about God toward which the entire Exodus narrative is driving." (*Exodus*, page 7)

Moses responds with prayer. In the second commandment, God told the people not to worship any representations of God, "for I, the LORD your God, am a jealous God, punishing the children for the sin of the parents to the third and fourth generation of those who hate me, but showing love to a thousand generations of those who love me and keep my commandments" (20:5-6). This language is echoed in the declaration of God's name. Of course, this is particularly appropriate, because the problem is that the people have just worshipped an image of God. And so Moses prays to the God of mercy for mercy. To the God who has just declared that his name—his character—involves him "forgiving wickedness ... and sin" (**34:7**), Moses worships (**v 8**) and prays, "Forgive our wickedness and our sin" (**v 9**).

This is our great hope—the merciful name of God. But there's still an unresolved tension. For God is also just. "He does not leave the guilty unpunished" (**v 7**). This is our great problem—the holy judgment of God.

The solution

This tension is left unresolved throughout the Bible story. God forgives sin and God punishes sin. We can't live without God, but we cannot live with him. The tension is left unresolved until "the Word became flesh and made his dwelling among us. We have seen his glory, the glory of the one and only Son, who came from the Father, full of grace and truth" (John 1:14). Moses could not see God. All he encountered was the word of God. But now the Word has become flesh. And not only that; the Word has made his dwelling among us—literally, he has "pitched his tent" or "tabernacled" among us. Here is God's presence ,in the person of God's Son, dwelling among God's people. And, says John, "we have seen his glory". God tells Moses, "You cannot see my face, for no one may see me and live" (Exodus **33:20**). But now John has looked into the face of God and seen his glory. In the Son, we see God's glory, and we live.

There's a hint of this in the strange apparent contradiction in Exodus 33. **33:19** says that no one may see God's face and live—and when God spoke to Moses in 3:6, "Moses hid his face, because he was afraid to look at God". But **33:11** says the LORD routinely spoke to Moses "face to face, as one speaks to a friend". How can Moses both not be able to see God's face, and speak face to face with God? How is this possible? It suggests there is some differentiation within God. It is only a hint at this stage in the story. But with the coming of Jesus, it becomes clear that God is three Persons. And from the beginning Jesus is the revelation and mediator of God.

But still a question remains: How can you and I see God and live? How can a holy God live among his people? John explains: "The law was given through Moses; grace and truth came through Jesus Christ" (John 1:17). How is it that God can "[forgive] wickedness, rebellion and sin" and, at the same time, "not leave the guilty unpunished" (Exodus 34:7)? The answer is Jesus. Forgiveness and punishment, mercy and justice, grace and truth meet in Jesus. When he died, your guilt was punished so that you could be forgiven. Your judgment was taken so you could enjoy mercy. The truth of your sin was recognised and accounted for, so that you could know the joy and peace and life of God's grace.

> We cannot live without God—through Christ, we don't have to.

We can't live without God—and, through Christ, we don't have to. God has dwelt among us in Jesus. It is only with the coming of Jesus that God's "name" in Exodus 34 truly makes sense! Guilt has been punished in the person of Jesus so that forgiveness flows to his people. "If I were to go with you even for a moment, I might destroy you," says God in **33:5**. But now God has destroyed his people in the person of his Son. So there is no penalty left to pay, and we can live with God with confidence now, and enter his promised land and the full glory of his presence in the future. We cannot live without God—and we need never know what it is like to be without him.

Questions for reflection

1. Have you ever considered the truth that, outside Christ, the holiness of God ought to terrify you?

2. Are you in danger of wanting God's blessings, but not wanting God himself?

3. In what sense are you, as a follower of Christ, in a more privileged position than Moses was? How does this make you feel?

PART TWO

We've seen the main answer to the question of how God can live among his people: because of mercy through God's name, won by God's Son. But there are two other answers that these chapters give us.

Identity through God's covenant

At the beginning of chapter 34, Moses takes two new tablets of stone up the mountain with him, because God is going to reaffirm his covenant (**34:10**). (The first two tablets had been smashed in response to the people's idolatry in 32:19). And then we get a selected list of laws in **34:10-28**, which might seem to be a strange interruption to the story. They can feel like a rather downbeat interlude in the drama of the narrative.

But the covenant outlined in chapters 20 – 24, which is summarised in these verses, is part of the solution to the problem of God's presence. How can God live among his people? Because the covenant shapes their identity.

So the rationale for this selection of laws is that they shape identity. God begins by reminding his people that his salvation marks them out as a distinctive people (**34:10**). "I will do wonders never before done in any nation in all the world." Every culture has its stories that shape its identity. But nothing can match the story of God's salvation.

Laws that protect identity

God reminds his people of laws that protect their identity by forbidding any mixing with surrounding nations. They are not to:

- join in political treaties with other nations (**v 11-12**)
- join in religious practices with other nations (**v 13-15**)
- join in marital relationships with other nations (**v 16**)

The summary is, "Do not make any idols" (**v 17**)—which is, of course, precisely what Israel had done in chapter 32! So at the heart of this call to be separate and distinctive is another declaration of God's name: "Do not worship any other god, for the LORD, whose name is Jealous, is a jealous God" (**34:14**). Again, this echoes the second commandment—the commandment the people have just broken, where God had warned them that he would react jealously to spiritual adultery (20:4-6).

This is why God is jealous—he is jealous for his people's affection and commitment (Zechariah 8:2-3; Joel 2:18; Psalm 79:5; Zephaniah 3:8; Nahum 1:2; Isaiah 63:15). We often think jealousy is a bad thing, and often it is—but not always. If I wasn't jealous for my wife's affection, there'd be something seriously wrong with our relationship.

This revelation of God's name becomes important in the rest of the Bible story (Numbers 14:18; Nehemiah 9:17; Psalms 103:8, 17; 145:8; Jeremiah 32:18-19; Nahum 1:3; see also Deuteronomy 5:9-10; 1 Kings 3:6; Lamentations 3:32; Daniel 9:4). Ezekiel, for example, can be seen as a preacher of Exodus. Ezekiel's visions of God in Ezekiel 1 echo the **theophany** at Mount Sinai in Exodus 19 – 20. Ezekiel 20 narrates the story of Israel in Egypt as a tale of rebellion. Ezekiel's warnings to the nations climax in an extended prophecy against Egypt. And the book of Ezekiel, like the book of Exodus, ends with a detailed description of a new temple. But most importantly, more than sixty times Ezekiel gives the reason for an event as being that people may "know that I am the LORD"—a key phrase, as we've seen, in Exodus. Ezekiel picks up the theme of jealousy—here are just three examples (but see also 5:5-6, 13; 8:5; 16:36-42):

"I will direct my jealous anger against you, and they will deal with you in fury. They will cut off your noses and your ears, and those of you who are left will fall by the sword." (23:25a)

"Therefore prophesy concerning the land of Israel and say to the mountains and hills, to the ravines and valleys: 'This is what the Sovereign LORD says: I speak in my jealous wrath because you have suffered the scorn of the nations. Therefore this is what the Sovereign LORD says: I swear with uplifted hand that the nations around you will also suffer scorn.'" (36:6-7)

"Therefore this is what the Sovereign LORD says: I will now restore the fortunes of Jacob and will have compassion on all the people of Israel, and I will be zealous for my holy name. They will forget their shame and all the unfaithfulness they showed towards me when they lived in safety in their land with no one to make them afraid. When I have brought them back from the nations and have gathered them from the countries of their enemies, I will be proved holy through them in the sight of many nations." (39:25-27)

Jealousy is the rationale for both judgment and salvation (39:25-27). And Ezekiel 20 in particular echoes God's response to the golden calf in Exodus 32.

It is not just Ezekiel. In John 2:17, Jesus is consumed with zeal or jealousy for God's house, the temple. This comes just before he identifies his resurrection body as the new temple. And Paul says to the Corinthian church, "I am jealous for you with a godly jealousy" (2 Corinthians 11:2).

The image of marriage is not coincidental. God's relationship with his people is a marriage-like covenant. Our spiritual unfaithfulness is likened to adultery. This is why the covenant is so

> We're not in a dating relationship with God, where our commitment can correlate to our feelings.

important. We're not simply in a dating relationship with God in which our commitment correlates to our feelings. No, we are in a covenantal relationship. Just as in a marriage, we're bound to one another through covenant promises. And, as in a marriage, these promises keep the relationship strong when times are hard. The covenant is God's gift to us. It reassures us of his commitment and it ties down our commitment.

How can God dwell among his people? One answer is that the covenant maintains our distinctive identity. We don't always live faithfully according to this identity, which is why the covenant also makes provision for sin. God binds himself to his gracious promises in covenants to give a double sense of assurance. This is even clearer for us under the new covenant, the covenant made through the blood of Jesus (Luke 22:20). But the covenant is also there to shape our identity and keep us from compromise.

Worship that reinforces identity

Exodus **34:18-24** is a reminder of the key festivals in the Israelite calendar. These are important because they commemorate identity-forming events. They are there to help the people to remember:

- the Passover in the Festival of Unleavened Bread (**v 18**). They are to remember their redemption from Egypt as they redeem their firstborn (**v 19-20**).

- the rest God has given them from oppression as they keep the Sabbath (**v 21**).

- God's provision as they celebrate the Festival of Weeks (**v 22-23, 26**).

Each festival recalls God's salvation and care. They reinforce Israel's identity. The laws about avoiding yeast and not cooking a goat in its mother's milk may also be reminders against mixing with other nations (**v 25-26**).

We, of course, no longer keep these old-covenant festivals. But Christ has given us new identity-forming acts: baptism and the Lord's Supper. They are covenant acts. Baptism replaces circumcision and the Lord's Supper replaces Passover. But they function in a similar way. They remind us of God's salvation and our identity. They remind us of God's covenant commitment to us and our commitment to him.

Moses says God's presence "will distinguish me and your people from all the other people on the face of the earth" (**33:16**). Baptism and the Lord's Supper remind us that we're distinctive people marked by God's presence.

It can be hard to be different in your home, workplace or school. It's tempting to compromise or fit in. But every time we take bread and wine, we're invited to feast on Christ. We're reminded that our reward is God himself. We're reminded of his commitment to us.

In 1 Corinthians 5:6-8, Paul is using the language of Exodus **34:25** to talk about the Lord's Supper, with the purpose of calling on the church to rid itself of immoral behaviour:

"Don't you know that a little yeast leavens the whole batch of dough? Get rid of the old yeast, so that you may be a new un-leavened batch—as you really are. For Christ, our Passover lamb, has been sacrificed. Therefore let us keep the Festival, not with the old bread leavened with malice and wickedness, but with the unleavened bread of sincerity and truth."

Transformation through God's glory

Moses comes down from the mountain. But he has been exposed to the afterglow of God's glory. As a result his face is radiant (Exodus **34:29**)—so radiant that everyone is afraid to come near to him (**v 30**). So Moses wears a veil whenever he speaks to the people (**v 31-35**), which he takes off when he speaks with God.

God's glory is transforming. It makes us radiant. In Exodus, only one person experiences God's glory, and so only one person is transformed by that glory. But "we have seen his glory" (John 1:14), because God's glory has been revealed to us in the person of his Son. So Paul reflects on this story in 2 Corinthians 3:13 – 4:6 to describe how God's glory transforms every Christian.

Paul says that, in a sense, the veil remains to this day (2 Corinthians 3:13-15; 4:3). People do not recognise the glory of God because they do not recognise Christ. Their hearts shrink in fear from the glory of God. But "whenever anyone turns to the Lord," says Paul, "the veil is taken away" (3:16). When Moses was in the tabernacle before God, he could take the veil off because he was turned towards God and not towards the people (Exodus **34:34**). It's the same when we turn to God in repentance—the veil that hides God's glory is taken away, and our eyes are opened to see in Christ the glory of God.

Moses coming down the mountain after meeting God is a picture of what humanity should have been. Moses radiated God's glory so that his face shone. In a similar way, we were made to reflect God's glory. And that's how it can be again. We can be people who radiate with divine glory.

My wife was commenting how someone we had just met is always smiling. His face is full of joy. Yet he has known tragedy in his life, including the loss of a child—this is not some superficial happiness. His face radiates with a sense of glory. Your face may not be naturally smiley, but your life can radiate with divine glory. You can be "transformed into his image with ever-increasing glory" (2 Corinthians 3:18).

> We become what we were created to be by looking at God's glory.

What you look at determines who you are (Matthew 6:22-23). The focus of your attention will shape your attitudes and priorities. If your focus is adverts, media or peers, then you will be conformed to the pattern of this world (Romans 12:2). But when we turn to Jesus, says Paul, we see "God's glory displayed in the face of Christ" (2 Corinthians 4:6). And when we see the glory of God, our lives shine with that glory. It transforms us, so that we bring light to the world and praise to God.

What you look at matters. In Exodus 32:5, Aaron "saw" the Israelites worshipping the calf, and then organised a festival which included an idolatrous orgy (v 6). In **33:18**, Moses asks to "see" the glory of the

LORD—and as a result, he "radiates" God's glory. We become what we were created to be by looking at God's glory.

But how do we see the glory of God? Where's the glow? There's a big surprise in Exodus 34. Exodus 34 does not say that Moses was radiant because he "saw" God's glory, but "because he had spoken with the LORD" (**34:29**). Moses was radiant because he had heard God speak his name: "The LORD, the LORD, the compassionate and gracious God, slow to anger, abounding in love and faithfulness" (v 6). At the time he heard that, he couldn't see anything except a rock face!

And this is how you can encounter God's glory. In 2 Corinthians 4:4 Paul speaks of "the light of the gospel that displays the glory of Christ". We see Christ's glory in the gospel message. "God, who said, 'Let light shine out of darkness,' made his light shine in our hearts to give us the light of the knowledge of God's glory displayed in the face of Christ" (v 6). At creation, God spoke and brought light from darkness; and this creative power is unleashed again when God's word is spoken today. Through God's word, we see "the light of the knowledge of God's glory displayed in the face of Christ".

To sum it up: we see the glory of Christ as we hear the story of Christ. Day by day, week by week, read your Bible, hear the word preached, sing the word, encourage others with the gospel and be encouraged. Do it all with a sense of expectant looking—looking to hear the glory of Christ in the story of Christ.

Moral effort, fear of judgment and sets of rules cannot bring lasting change. But amazing things happen when we "turn to the Lord" (2 Corinthians 3:16). "We ... are being transformed into his image." As we see the glory of Christ in the gospel, so we become more like him—people who are full of grace and truth. We are changed "with ever-increasing glory", "from one degree of glory to another" (v 18, ESV).

How can God live among us? By transforming us into his likeness through a vision of his glory. "We know that when Christ appears, we shall be like him, for we shall see him as he is" (1 John 3:2). Seeing

Christ will transform us so that we are more like him, until we are just like him, and live with him for ever. That transformation begins and continues through the vision of Christ in the gospel.

God told Moses, "You cannot see my face, for no one may see me and live" (Exodus **33:20**). That's the message of the law. But in the gospel, we see "the glory of God in the face of Christ" (2 Corinthians 4:6, ESV). In the face of Christ we see "the compassionate and gracious God, slow to anger, abounding in love and faithfulness" (Exodus **34:6**). In the cross of Christ, we see our guilt punished so God can "[forgive] wickedness, rebellion and sin" (**34:6-7**). Can you see it? It's a transforming vision.

Questions for reflection

1. How can you ensure that you tell yourself the story of God's salvation each day?

2. We look at the glory of God in the face of Christ by hearing the story of Christ. Does this truth need to change your feelings about Bible-reading and/or your method of Bible-reading?

3. "What you look at matters." Do you need to change anything? What do you need to stop looking at? What do you need to start looking at?

15. A TASTE OF GOD'S GLORY

We noticed when we were looking at Exodus 25 – 31 that the tabernacle echoes the Garden of Eden, and the construction of the tabernacle echoes the creation of that garden. And, as we've seen all the way through Exodus, it's not just the tabernacle—the whole story of this book is a story of re-creation, from Israel's creation-like fruitfulness in chapter 1 to God's de-creation and re-creation through the plagues and the parting of the Red Sea. There are two more echoes of creation in Exodus 31.

First echo: the Spirit

The account of creation begins with the Spirit or the wind of God "hovering over the waters" (Genesis 1:2). It's the Spirit of God, or breath of God, who gives life to the clay figure of the first man (Genesis 2:7). "By the word of the Lord were the heavens made, their starry host by the breath of his mouth" (Psalm 33:6). The word of God came on the breath of God—and Psalm 104:27-30 says the Spirit continues to animate creation.

If the construction of the tabernacle as a place for God to dwell among his people echoes the creation of the earth as a place for God to dwell among his people, then we would expect to find the Spirit of God animating the creative process. And that's exactly what we see in Exodus 31: "Then the Lord said to Moses, 'See I have chosen Bezalel son of Uri, the son of Hur, of the tribe of Judah, and I have filled him with the Spirit of God, with wisdom, with understanding, with knowledge and with all kinds of skills'" (Exodus **31:1-3**). The Spirit empowers Bezalel, giving him the ability to work in metal, stone, wood and "all kinds of crafts" (**v 4-5**). God also appoints Oholiab to assist Bezalel and says, "I have given ability to all the skilled workers to make everything I have commanded you" (**v 6**). The same emphasis is found when Bezalel and Oholiab are commissioned; Moses says, "The Lord has chosen Bezalel … and he has filled him with the Spirit of God" (**35:30-31**). And the other workers are repeatedly described as those to whom "the Lord has given skill and ability" (**v 34-35; 36:1-2**). The tabernacle and its furniture are made by human beings (**35:32-33**), but those humans are empowered and equipped through the animating work of the Spirit, and their work is funded by a freed people freely contributing what they can (**36:3**—see page 90).

Second echo: the Sabbath

As we have noted, seven times in the account of creation we read, "God said" (Genesis 1:3, 6, 9, 14, 20, 24, 26). And seven times in the tabernacle instructions we read, "The Lord said to Moses" (Exodus 25:1; 30:11, 17, 22, 34; **31:1, 12**). Both accounts end with a description of the Sabbath (Genesis 2:1-3; Exodus **31:12-18**). Indeed, God specifically links the Sabbath to creation in **verse 17**, when he says, "It will be a sign between me and the Israelites for ever, for in six days the Lord made the heavens and the earth, and on the seventh day he rested and was refreshed"—and so Israel must "observe the Sabbath, because it is holy to you" (**v 14-15**). This is a day which is dedicated to God by being set apart for God. It is a time in which his people can meet with him. The tabernacle is a holy place and the Sabbath is a holy time. Both are set apart so that God can meet with his people.

Exodus 31 says the Sabbath is a sign of the covenant that God makes with Israel through Moses (**v 13, 17**). Just as the tabernacle as a holy place is replaced by Jesus, so Sabbath as a holy time is replaced by Jesus. Jesus is the one in whom we meet God and the one in whom we find rest. The Sabbath day points to the eternal Sabbath that we share with God through Jesus. That is why **verse 13** says, "You must observe my Sabbaths" (plural). What is in mind is not just one day in seven, but the seventh year of rest for the land and the jubilee year of restoration.

Sabbath is a sign of the covenant with Israel because Israel is (or is meant to be) a model of the new creation: the people through whom God will undo the work of Adam. They are the new humanity with a new Sabbath creating a new home where they can meet God.

The reintroduction of "I am the LORD" in the midst of the Sabbath instruction suggests that the Sabbath is missional. The Sabbath reminds Israel that they are a **sanctified** people, who reveal God's holy character.

The plan and promise of a new creation

What is the point of all these echoes back to creation? The answer is that the construction of the tabernacle is a pointer forward to a new creation. What God did at creation is symbolically repeated in the tabernacle as a sign that God will recreate the world as a place in which he dwells with his people. The tabernacle is the plan and the promise of the new creation.

The story of the exodus is, as we have seen, a blueprint of the means of salvation. We are redeemed from slavery and death through the blood of sacrifice. But the book of Exodus also contains a blueprint of the content of salvation. The tabernacle doesn't just happen to be like the new creation—it's deliberately designed to be a picture of the new creation. The tabernacle is the architect's model, a visual representation of the promise that God will dwell among his people.

Chapters 25 – 31 emphasise that the tabernacle is to be built according to the pattern on the mountain (25:9, 40; 26:30 and 27:8). Now in the account of its construction in chapters 35 – 39, this is paralleled with an emphasis on the tabernacle being built just as God commanded (**31:11**).

The instructions for its construction in chapters 25 – 31 worked from the centre outwards for they were presented in a theological order. The description of the construction in chapters 35 – 39 repeats much of this material. But the order is different. It is presented in chronological order—materials are gathered, builders are appointed, the tabernacle itself is built, and then it is filled with furniture and priestly garments.

It's not enough for the writer to give the instructions and then add that this is what the people did. He repeats the instructions with a parallel level of detail, but this time as a description of what was built. The table opposite shows just one example of how the description of the construction matches the instructions. (I've not selected the best example I could find. I've simply picked the first item described in the instructions.) You'll see how they are exactly parallel, except for the change from commands to description. The only exceptions are instructions about how it is to be used rather than how it is to be made.

We find the same close parallelism throughout this section:

Instruction	Completion
25:10-20	37:1-9
25:23-39	37:10-24
26:1-33, 36-37	36:8-38
27:1-8	38:1-7
27:9-19	38:9-20
28:1-43	39:1-31
30:1-6	37:25-29

The point is clear: the construction exactly matches the instructions. This becomes explicit in the making of priestly garments in chapter 39, in which we're told *ten times* that everything is being done "as the LORD commanded Moses" (**39:1, 5, 7, 21, 26, 29, 31, 32, 42, 43**). And, as if that were not enough, the account ends with an inspection:

Exodus 25:10-20	Exodus 37:1-9
Have them make an ark of acacia wood—	Bezalel made the ark of acacia wood—
two and a half cubits long,	two and a half cubits long,
a cubit and a half wide,	a cubit and a half wide,
and a cubit and a half high.	and a cubit and a half high.
¹¹ Overlay it with pure gold,	² He overlaid it with pure gold,
both inside and out,	both inside and out,
and make a gold moulding around it.	and made a gold moulding around it.
¹² Cast four gold rings for it	³ He cast four gold rings for it
and fasten them to its four feet,	and fastened them to its four feet,
with two rings on one side	with two rings on one side
and two rings on the other.	and two rings on the other.
¹³ Then make poles of acacia wood	⁴ Then he made poles of acacia wood
and overlay them with gold.	and overlaid them with gold.
¹⁴ Insert the poles into the rings	⁵ And he inserted the poles into the rings
on the sides of the ark to carry it.	on the sides of the ark to carry it.
¹⁵ The poles are to remain in the rings of this ark; they are not to be removed.	
¹⁶ Then put in the ark the tablets of the covenant law,	
which I will give you.	
¹⁷ Make an atonement cover	⁶ He made the atonement cover
of pure gold—	of pure gold—
two and a half cubits long	two and a half cubits long
and a cubit and a half wide.	and a cubit and a half wide.
¹⁸ And make two cherubim	⁷ Then he made two cherubim
out of hammered gold	out of hammered gold
at the ends of the cover.	at the ends of the cover.
¹⁹ Make one cherub on one end	⁸ He made one cherub on one end
and the second cherub on the other;	and the second cherub on the other;
make the cherubim of one piece with the cover, at the two ends.	at the two ends he made them of one piece with the cover.
²⁰ The cherubim are to have their wings spread upwards,	⁹ The cherubim had their wings spread upwards,
overshadowing the cover with them.	overshadowing the cover with them.
The cherubim are to face each other,	The cherubim faced each other,
looking towards the cover.	looking towards the cover.

"All the work on the tabernacle, the tent of meeting, was completed. The Israelites did everything just as the LORD commanded Moses" **(v 32)**. Everything is brought to Moses for inspection. And to ensure that we know that everything is inspected, it is all listed **(v 33-41)**. What is the outcome? "The Israelites had done all the work just as the LORD had commanded Moses. Moses inspected the work and saw that they had done it just as the LORD had commanded. So Moses blessed them" **(v 42-43)**.

A model of the new creation

The point of all of this is to emphasise that the tabernacle really is built as God commanded. This means it is built according to the pattern on the mountain. And that in turn means it is an accurate model of the new creation (a symbolic one, as we'll see).

The links to creation continue. **Verses 32** says, "So all the work on the tabernacle, the tent of meeting, was completed"—and **40:33** says, "And so Moses finished the work". The words "completed" and "finished" are the same word in Hebrew. And it's the word used to describe the completion of creation in Genesis 2:1-2: "Thus the heavens and the earth were *completed* in all their vast array. By the seventh day God had *finished* the work he had been doing" (my emphasis). Moreover the words "saw" in Genesis 1:31 and "inspected" in Exodus **39:43** are the same word in Hebrew, as are the words "made" and "done". So we could translate them, "God inspected all that he had made, and it was very good" and "Moses inspected the work and saw that they had made it just as the LORD had commanded". Just as God inspects creation, so Moses inspects this model of re-creation; and both give their blessing to the finished work.

So far we've seen the links between the tabernacle and Eden, Sinai, Jesus and heaven! These links are not random. They're not the product of creative **exegesis**. These links exist because the tabernacle is part of the bigger story of God dwelling with his people. Here's the story in summary. The God of heaven dwelt with humanity in Eden. But, when humanity rebelled against God, God's holy presence became dangerous. But God did not give up on his plan to dwell among his people. He rescued Israel and met with them at Mount Sinai. He had the tabernacle built as a plan and promise of his intent to dwell among his people. In time this was replaced by the temple, which was built with the same proportions, only double the size (1 Kings 6:17, 20). That plan was fulfilled in the coming of Christ as God-in-flesh dwelt among us. That plan is anticipated in the church. And then finally that plan will be realised in the new creation, when the voice from the throne will say, "Look! God's dwelling place is now among the people, and he will dwell with them" (Revelation 21:3).

We can summarise it like this:

- God is present in heaven.

- God is present in Eden.

- God is present at Mount Sinai.

- God is present in the tabernacle and in the temple.

- God is present in Jesus.

- God is present in the church and in Christians.

- God is present in the new creation.

When put like this, it becomes unsurprising that we find parallels backwards and forwards from the tabernacle to all the other occasions and locations of God's presence. These connections exist because God designed them into the story. The tabernacle is his plan and promise to dwell among his people—a plan in which he recreates the earth as his dwelling place with a recreated humanity in a recreated time. Israel is that recreated humanity in microcosm. The tabernacle is that new creation or heaven-on-earth in microcosm. The Sabbath is that recreated time in microcosm. The tabernacle is a divine statement of cosmological intent (Exodus 25:8-9, 40; 26:30; 27:8; **31:11; 39:32, 42-43**).

It's a symbolic plan. For example, it's not that the new creation will literally be a tent! Instead the tabernacle is full of symbols—like the ark, the bread and the lamp. Each is telling us what the new creation is like:

- The ark shows us that the new creation is a place where God reigns.

- The table shows us that the new creation is a place where God eats with his people.

- The lampstand shows us that the new creation is a place where we walk in God's light.

- The lampstand also shows us that the new creation is a place where we receive life from God.

- The law shows us that the new creation is a place in which creation is re-ordered.

- The priest shows us the new creation is a place where we can come into God's holy presence.

So when we get to the end of the story in John's vision of the new Jerusalem in Revelation 21 – 22, right at the end of the Bible, we find that it has all sorts of echoes of the tabernacle. There are plenty of other things going on as well, because John's vision is gathering up other anticipations from the Bible story (not least of which is Ezekiel's vision of a new temple in Ezekiel 40 – 48). But the echoes of the tabernacle are clear enough.

Like the Most Holy Place, the city that John sees is a perfect cube (Revelation 21:16-17). This means there is no longer a special sacred space. Now the whole city is a Most Holy Place. We no longer visit God in his tabernacle. We inhabit the tabernacle. The whole earth is God's house, in which we dwell with him. John says, "I did not see a temple in the city, because the Lord God Almighty and the Lamb are its temple" (Revelation 21:22). There's no one place that is the tabernacle or temple. Everywhere is the temple because God is present everywhere.

Like the tabernacle, its furniture and the priestly garments (Exodus 25:3-7, 11, 24, 31; 28:17-20; **35:5-9, 22, 27; 38:24**), the city is made of jewels and gold (Revelation 21:18-21).

Like the lamp in the tabernacle (Exodus 25:31-40; 27:20-21), the city has a lamp. But now "the Lamb is its lamp" and the nations walk by its light (Revelation 21:23-24; 22:5). Like the tree-like lamp in the tabernacle that echoes the tree of life (Exodus 25:31-40), the city has the tree of life. And just as the lamp in the tabernacle is in bud, blossom and fruit simultaneously, so the tree of life yields fruit every month (Revelation 22:2). The tree of life stands on either side of the river that flows from the throne of God and the Lamb (Revelation 22:1-2). It represents the life that constantly and eternally flows from the sacrifice of Christ.

> The tabernacle was designed to make it feel as if you'd stepped into heaven.

Like the tabernacle, the new creation is heaven-on-earth. We've seen that the blue of the tabernacle and the embroidered cherubim were designed to make it feel as if you'd stepped into heaven. But the new creation really is heaven-on-earth. In his vision John sees the Holy City "coming down out of heaven from God" (Revelation 21:2, 10). It's not that we get zapped up to heaven. Heaven comes down so that heaven and earth are united.

So here are three ways of thinking about the future:

1. *Heaven without earth.* Christians who believe heaven replaces earth tend to treat this earth with little concern. They believe the earth will be junked at the end of history and treat it accordingly or view it as intrinsically evil.

2. *Earth without heaven.* Many people around us don't believe in heaven or life after death. They simply live for present pleasure (1 Corinthians 15:32). And as Christians, it's all too easy for us

to focus on this present age rather than the as-yet-unseen age to come.

3. *Heaven-on-earth.* This is the future to which the tabernacle points us. This vision liberates us to receive this world as a gift from God even while we lament its brokenness, and to look forward to its transformation. And these attitudes translate into practical actions. Receiving this world as a gift translates into a celebration of creativity. A lament of its brokenness translates into a concern for the poor and the care of creation. And looking forward to heaven-on-earth translates into the proclamation of the gospel.

Questions for reflection

1. How can you ensure that you tell yourself the story of God's salvation each day?

2. What impact does it have on someone's view of success, failure and frailty if they believe in heaven without earth, or earth without heaven?

3. How does the building of the tabernacle excite you about the new creation that it pointed to, and that God's people are heading to?

PART TWO

Glory

The tabernacle is a glimpse of the new creation because it is patterned on the new creation. And there's more. In Exodus 40, the work has been done and inspected. So God tells Moses to set everything up and anoint it all (Exodus **40:1-11**), and then to wash and anoint the priests (**v 12-15**). As in chapters 36 – 39, where the instructions of chapters 25 – 30 are all but repeated to emphasise the obedience of the people, so here in chapter 40, **verses 17-33** echo **verses 1-15**. The message is clear: everything is done by Moses "as the LORD commanded him" (**v 16, 19, 23, 25, 27, 29, 32**). Seven times we're told he worked "as the LORD commanded him", and then we are told his work was finished (**v 33**—another echo of creation). And then…

> "the cloud covered the tent of meeting, and the glory of the LORD
> filled the tabernacle. Moses could not enter the tent of meeting
> because the cloud had settled on it, and the glory of the LORD
> filled the tabernacle." (**v 34-35**)

Twice we're told "the glory of the LORD filled the tabernacle"—so much so that even Moses was forced to evacuate. What's more, even though the glory of God settled down, as it were, so that the work of the tabernacle could begin, it didn't go away (at least, not until Ezekiel 10, centuries later). The presence of God continued with his people wherever they went, symbolised by the pillars of cloud and fire (Exodus **40:36-38**). Something very similar happened in 1 Kings 8:10-13 after the people had settled in the land, when the tabernacle was replaced by a permanent temple.

Of course, a tabernacle and temple full of his glory but without any people is not the scenario God is after. The good news is that Exodus is not the end of the story. Indeed, our Bibles create an artificial conclusion, because we tend to stop reading at the end of the book of Exodus and see the next book, Leviticus, as not linked to what immediately precedes it. But in fact, the very next words in the Bible are an invitation to approach God through sacrifice (Leviticus 1:1-2). Through sacrifice, we can experience the glory of God.

This glory is the climax of the construction of the tabernacle; and it's the climax of the story of the exodus. God has rescued his people from slavery and death so that they can enjoy his presence and see his glory. Everything so far has been leading up to this moment. Of all the blessings God gives (and there are many), this is the greatest: God himself, in his glory. And this is the promise given to us in the gospel of the tabernacle: one day in a new creation we will eternally enjoy God in his glory.

The tabernacle was a taste of God's glory. The new creation will be its eternal fulfilment. In the end and at the end, what we get from God is God.

But en route there are two big anticipations of God dwelling with his people and showing them his glory.

First anticipation: Jesus

We've already quoted John 1:14: "The Word became flesh and made his dwelling among us". We've seen that "made his dwelling" is literally "pitched his tent" or "tabernacled". Jesus is the true tabernacle—the place where God meets with humanity. In Matthew 12:6, Jesus says, "I tell you that something greater than the temple is here" (see also John 2:19-21.)

But John 1:14 continues, "The Word became flesh and made his dwelling among us. We have seen his glory, the glory of the one and only Son, who came from the Father, full of grace and truth." That's an extraordinary claim! After all, no one had to evacuate the room whenever Jesus entered. In one sense, his glory was hidden. But we see the perfections of God in the person of Jesus. We see it in his "grace and truth". We see it as he reveals God's glory in his love, holiness, beauty, justice and so on. Jesus is the anticipation of and the clearest glimpse of the new creation. He is the One in whom and through whom God dwells among us.

Nevertheless, we have not seen the full, glorious brightness of his splendour—with one significant exception. There was a moment when his full glory was revealed. On one occasion Jesus took Peter, James and John up a mountain to pray, and, "as he was praying, the appearance of his face changed, and his clothes became as bright as a flash of lightning. Two men, Moses and Elijah, appeared in glorious splendour, talking with Jesus" (Luke 9:29-30). It's striking that one of the men is Moses; and, Luke tells us, they discussed Jesus' imminent "departure"—which is literally his "exodus" (v 31). Peter suggests they build three "shelters" for Jesus, Moses and Elijah (v 33). Literally, it's three "tabernacles". But Peter has missed the point. It makes no sense to build a tabernacle, because Jesus, the true tabernacle, is with them.

> Jesus longs for you to be with him and see his glory. If that doesn't change you, nothing will.

Instead, "while he was speaking, a cloud appeared and covered them, and they were afraid as they entered the cloud" (v 34). Here is a cloud on a mountain. This is Mount Sinai again. This is the moment the altar of incense was designed to replicate. This is the climax of the exodus story as the cloud of God's glory descends on the tabernacle. And, just as he did at Sinai, God speaks from the cloud: "This is my Son, whom I have chosen; listen to him" (v 35). The message from the cloud is: *Jesus.*

And this is the glory Jesus longs to share with us. Jesus prayed, "Father, I want those you have given me to be with me where I am, and to see my glory, the glory you have given me because you loved me before the creation of the world" (John 17:24). Jesus longs for you to be with him and see his glory. If that doesn't change your perspective on life, nothing will.

I don't know what the future will bring your way. There may be triumphs. There may be problems. There will be highs and lows, and most of it will probably be fairly mundane. But Jesus longs for you to be with him, and to see his glory.

Second anticipation: the church

Ephesians 2:21-22 says, "In [Christ] the whole building is joined together and rises to become a holy temple in the Lord. And in him you too are being built together to become a dwelling in which God lives by his Spirit" (see also 1 Corinthians 3:16-17). Paul is talking about the church, where Jew and Gentile are united in Christ. And he is saying that the place where people can meet God is no longer the tabernacle, nor the temple that replaced it. *Your church* is now the place where people meet God as you proclaim and live the gospel. People need to update their address book. God's address is no longer "The tabernacle, Sinai wilderness, nr Egypt" or "The temple, Jerusalem, Israel". Now God's address is "Your church, Your town".

If the tabernacle was once the architect's model, and we are now the tabernacle, then that means that we are the prototype of the new creation:

- Like the ark, we are the place where God reigns.

- Like the table, we are the place where God eats with his people in the communion meal.

- Like the lampstand, we are the place from which the light of the gospel shines.

- Like the lampstand, we are the place where people can find life in Christ.

- Like the law, we are the place where creation is being re-ordered.

- Like the priest, we can enter God's holy presence.

Unbelievers will come to our meetings and say, "God is really among you!" (1 Corinthians 14:25).

Paul goes further in 1 Corinthians 6:19-20, because he says there that individual Christians—you and I—are the temple of the Holy Spirit:

"Do you not know that your bodies are temples of the Holy Spirit, who is in you, whom you have received from God? You are not your own; you were bought at a price. Therefore honour God with your bodies."

Paul is inviting us to think about what we would deem appropriate and inappropriate behaviour in the temple. You might want to think about a cathedral. Whatever you think about cathedrals, they tend to make people behave with a certain reverence. The principle seems to be, *If you wouldn't do it in the temple, then you shouldn't do it at all—because now you are the temple.*

The tabernacle, too, has a revelatory or missional purpose. Explaining its construction, God says, "Then I will dwell among the Israelites and be their God. They will know that I am the LORD their God, who brought them out of Egypt so that I might dwell among them. I am the LORD their God" (Exodus 29:45-46). God rescued his people "that" he might dwell among them. But the repetition of "I am the LORD" also suggests that this in turn will be an act of revelation; that there is a missional intent. Israel is to expand the boundaries of Eden-tabernacle as Adam was intended to so that the glory of the LORD fills the earth and the nations comes to know God. The task of the church is the same—to extend the boundaries of the Eden-tabernacle through the proclamation of the gospel.

The people of God's glory

Who are the people among whom God is present and to whom God reveals his glory? In Exodus 40, they were the people whose previous act was to build an idol. They were the people who had just chosen an inanimate calf over the living God. They were sinners steeped in sin—they were people like you and me. God revealing himself to Moses is all well and good, but what about those of us who can't be like

Moses? The glorious good news of the story of the exodus is that God is present among sinners like you and me.

Chapters 25 – 31 describe the construction of the tabernacle as a sevenfold act of re-creation climaxing in the Sabbath. God tells Moses to remind the people to keep the Sabbath (**31:13**). Then the narrative is rudely interrupted by the story of the golden calf in chapters 32 – 34. But Exodus 35 begins where Exodus 31 left off—with a reminder of the Sabbath laws (**35:1-3**). Indeed, if you read **31:18** followed by **35:1**, you probably wouldn't notice a break. After the sin of the golden calf and the mediation of Moses, we're back on track.

And we're back on track with a freewill offering. The materials (**v 4-9**) and skills (**v 10-19**) required for the construction of the tabernacle are willingly given by the people as an offering to God (**v 20-29**). Many of these materials were probably part of the plunder that the people took from Egypt (12:35-36). Since the plunder of a battle belonged to the victor, there is a sense in which this plunder belonged to God. But the willingness of the people is emphasised in the narrative (**35:5, 20, 21, 22, 26**; plus, "skilled" in **v 10, 25** means "wise of heart"). Indeed, the people have to be told to stop giving because they've already given "more than enough" (**36:4-7**). The book of Exodus began with the Israelites "slaving" on the building projects of Pharaoh. It ends in chapters 35 – 40 with them working on another building project: the building of God's tabernacle. As we've noted, the word for "slaving" and "worshipping" is the same. The people are still slaving, but the service of God brings freedom, joy and generosity.

> One sign that we are servants of God is the generosity of our giving.

So it is with us. We used to spend our money pursuing selfish ends. We were slaves to our selfish desires. We worked on what our enslaving idols demanded. But God has liberated us. We're still slaves—but now we're slaves to righteousness (Romans 6:19). And one sign of that is the generosity of our giving.

Among us

How can God live among sinful people? It is because this is God's name: "The LORD, the LORD, the compassionate and gracious God, slow to anger, abounding in love and faithfulness, maintaining love to thousands, and forgiving wickedness, rebellion and sin" (Exodus 34:6-7). This is the name he revealed to Moses after the golden calf.

But it is not just among his people that God comes in glory. The tabernacle, as we have seen, is a symbolic re-creation of Eden and thereby also a prototype of the new creation. It is this "space" which is filled with God's glory. As such, the filling of the tabernacle with the glory of God is an anticipation and promise of the day when the whole "earth will be filled with the knowledge of the glory of the LORD as the waters cover the sea" (Habakkuk 2:14). It will be a day when we will see Jesus face to face. We will see in full what Moses only glimpsed. We will gaze upon the Lamb who was slain and we shall cry, "Worthy!" (Revelation 5:9).

But right now, today, we live in a world into which God has entered, in human form. We live in a world in which God walked and ate and spoke—a world in which Jesus lived and died and rose again. And we live in a world in which Jesus continues to be present among us, through his Spirit.

So we end the book of Exodus with this expectation: the living God is among us and will be at work among us. The God who appeared to Moses, who sent the plagues, who rescued his people, who parted the waters, who provided in the desert, who spoke his law, who designed the tabernacle, who passed by Moses... that God is among us, and will be at work among us. Expect God to speak to you through his word. Expect God to comfort you through his people. Expect God to work as you proclaim the name of Christ. Expect God to change lives through the gospel. And together, we will see the glory of God in the face of Christ.

Questions for reflection

1. "In the end and at the end, what we get from God is God." How does looking at who God is and what God does in the book of Exodus make that statement infinitely, eternally exciting?

2. How can you play your part in ensuring that your local church is a suitable place for God to list as his address on earth?

3. As you have enjoyed Exodus, what has changed in your view:

   - of God?

   - of yourself?

   - of your purpose in life?

GLOSSARY

Adoption: the truth that Christians have been adopted as God's children and heirs (see Romans 8:14-17).

Agrarian economy: a society in which the majority of individuals' livelihoods are based on growing crops.

Anarchy: where there is no government or authority, leading to chaos.

Atoning: providing a way of coming back into friendship with someone.

Autonomy: the ability to make our own decisions without being directed by anyone or anything else; to be self-governing.

Blasphemous: when God is disrespected or mocked, or conduct or speech that will cause God to be disrespected or mocked.

Cain and Abel: Adam and Eve's first two sons. When God accepted Abel's offering and not Cain's, Cain killed his brother (see Genesis 4:1-16).

Calvary: the place near Jerusalem where Jesus was crucified.

Canaan: an area on the eastern Mediterranean coast, to the north of Egypt and the south of Syria (in modern-day terms). When referring to the land God had promised to give his Old Testament people (see Genesis 12:6-9), it is often known as the "promised land".

Cherubim: a type of angel—God's warrior-messengers.

Circumcision: God told the men among his people in the Old Testament to be circumcised as a way to show physically that they knew and trusted him, and belonged to the people of God (see Genesis 17).

Conversion: the moment when someone first acknowledges Jesus as God's Son and their Lord, and turns to him as their Saviour.

Covenant: a binding agreement between two parties.

Deism: belief in a Creator God who made the world, but who does not intervene in or interact with his creation.

Divine revelation: where God communicates directly with someone.

Elijah, Elisha: two Old Testament prophets who announced God's judgment for his people's idolatry.

Esther: a Jewish woman who married the Persian King Xerxes during the time when most Jews were living in exile, under his power. One of the king's chief administrators, Haman, attempted to organise the wholesale massacre of the Jews, but Esther prevented it.

Ethical: an action that is right, according to a set of moral principles.

Euphemism: an indirect way of saying something else.

Exegesis: interpreting and explaining the Bible.

Fall: the moment when Eve and Adam disobeyed God and ate from the tree of the knowledge of good and evil (see Genesis 3).

Functional: actual; real.

Generic: general; not specific.

Gentiles: either refers to everyone who is not a Jew (i.e. part of Israel); or to everyone who is not a member of God's people (so in the New Testament, it sometimes refers to non-Christians).

Grace: undeserved, overflowing generosity.

Hades: the realm of the dead in Greek mythology.

Heidelberg Catechism: catechisms explain what Christians believe in the form of questions and answers. The Heidelberg Catechism was written in Germany in 1563.

Hyssop: a type of wild shrub.

Incarnate: the incarnation was the coming of the divine Son of God as a human, in the person of Jesus Christ.

Isaac: one of the **patriarchs**.

Jacob: one of the **patriarchs**.

Levites: one of the twelve tribes of Israel; the descendants of Jacob's son Levi. Levites served as priests in Israel.

Mandate: order or command.

Martyr: someone who dies for their faith.

Metaphors: images which are used to explain something, but that are not to be taken literally (e.g. "The news was a dagger to his heart").

Midian: an area on the northwest Arabian Peninsula, east of Egypt.

Moral, ceremonial and civic aspects: Some theologians have divided the Law of Moses into three categories: moral—laws defining what is right or wrong, applicable in any culture (e.g. "Do not kill"); ceremonial—laws describing how the Israelites were to worship God, especially in the tabernacle; and civic—laws which laid out how Israel was to be run as a nation.

Mount Zion: the mountain on the side of which Jerusalem was built; also refers to the "new Jerusalem"—the eternal home of Christians.

Mysticism: trying to commune with God and experience him through practices such as meditation.

Nepotism: where those in power show special favour to friends or relatives.

New Moon celebration: a monthly burnt offering.

Objective: a truth which is based on facts, not feelings, e.g. "I am married to this woman".

Pagans: a word used in the Bible to refer to non-Christians.

Paradigm: a model or pattern.

Patriarchs: the "first fathers" of Israel, to whom God gave his promises—Abraham, Isaac and Jacob.

Pentecost: a Jewish feast celebrating God giving his people his law on Mount Sinai (Exodus 19 – 31). On the day of this feast, fifty days after Jesus' resurrection, the Holy Spirit came to the first Christians (Acts 2), and so "Pentecost" is how Christians tend to refer to this event.

Pilgrims: people on a long journey.

Popish: relating to the Pope, the leader of the Roman Catholic church.

Postmodern: the mindset that is typical in today's Western societies; a general scepticism, particularly about power and authority, and a belief that there are no absolute truths, only relative ones, so that it is each individual's right to decide what is true for them.

Pronoun: words such as *I, you, he, she, it,* etc.

Prototype: model.

Providence: The protective care and power of God, who directs everything for the good of his people.

Puritan: a member of a sixteenth- and seventeenth-century movement in Great Britain which was committed to the Bible as God's word, to simpler worship services, to greater commitment and devotion to following Christ, and increasingly to resisting the institutional church's hierarchical structures. Many emigrated to what would become the US, and were a strong influence on the church in most of the early colonies.

Rebirth: the idea that we must be "born again" to new life, in a spiritual sense (see John 3).

Redemption: the act of freeing or releasing someone; buying someone back for a price.

Reformer: one of the first two generations of people in the fifteenth and early-sixteenth centuries who, as "Protestants", preached the gospel of justification by faith, and opposed the Pope and the Roman church.

Sanctified: pure.

Scapegoat: a goat which would symbolically have the sins of the people transferred onto it, before being released into the wilderness, taking the "sins" away.

Seed: descendant or offspring.

Sojourner: a person who stays somewhere temporarily; a traveller.

Sovereign: royal; all-powerful.

Subject (of this verb): a verb is a "doing" or "action" word. The "subject" of the verb is the person or thing who is doing the action.

Subjective: something which is based on feelings and opinions, e.g. "She is the most beautiful woman in the world".

Sufism: a strand of Islam that emphasises seeking to commune with God through mystical experience.

Syncretism: incorporating aspects of different religions into your beliefs; seeking to combine religions into one system of belief.

Tabernacle: a large, tented area where the Israelites worshipped God, and where his presence symbolically dwelled (see Exodus 26; 40).

Theological / Theologian: theology is the study of what is true about God. A theologian is someone who makes these studies.

Theophany: when God appears visibly to a human (or humans).

Wet-nurse: a woman employed to breastfeed another woman's child.

Yoke: a piece of wood fastened over the necks of animals and attached to the plough or cart that they are to pull.

APPENDIX:
MAP OF THE EXODUS

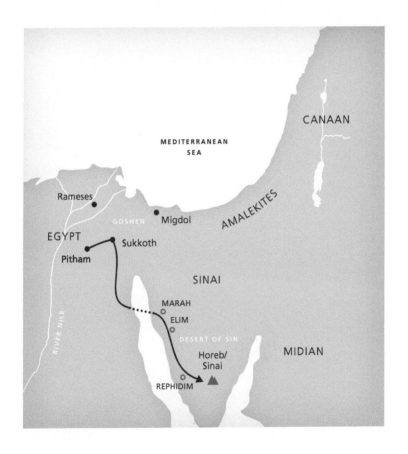

BIBLIOGRAPHY

Commentaries on the book of Exodus

- John Calvin, *Commentaries* (available online at www.ccel.org)
- Peter Enns, *Exodus* in the NIV Application Commentary series (Zondervan, 2000)
- T.E. Fretheim, *Exodus* in the Interpretation Commentary series (Westminster John Knox Press, 1991)
- John L. Mackay, *Exodus* (Mentor, 2001)
- Alec Motyer, *The Message of Exodus* in the Bible Speaks Today series (IVP, 2005)
- Philip Graham Ryken, *Exodus: Saved for God's Glory* in the Preaching the Word series (Crossway, 2005)

Books on the book of Exodus

- W. Ross Blackburn, *The God who Makes Himself Known: The Missionary Heart of the Book of Exodus* (Apollos, 2012)
- Tremper Longman III, *How To Read Exodus* (IVP Academic, 2009)
- Ed. Brian S. Rosner and Paul R. Williamson, *Exploring Exodus: Literary, Theological and Contemporary Approaches* (Apollos, 2008)

Books on the tabernacle and Israel's worship

- Tremper Longman III, *Immanuel In Our Place: Seeing Christ in Israel's Worship* (P&R, 2001)
- Vern Poythress, *The Shadow of Christ in the Law of Moses* (Wolgemuth & Hyatt, 1991)
- Frank H. White, *Christ in the Tabernacle* (Partridge & Co, 1871)

Other perspectives

- G.K. Beale and Mitchell Kim, *God Dwells Among Us* (IVP, 2014): a look at how the theme of God's presence unfolds through the Bible story.

- John Coffey, *Exodus and Liberation: Deliverance Politics from John Calvin to Martin Luther King Jr.* (Oxford University Press, 2014): a historical exploration of how the exodus story has influenced Western politics.

- Mike Wilkerson, *Redemption: Freed By Jesus from the Idols We Worship and the Wounds We Carry* (Crossway, 2011): a guide to personal change based on the book of Exodus.

Other works quoted in *Exodus For You*

- Augustine, *Sermons*

- Donald Bridge, *Signs and Wonders Today* (IVP, 1985)

- Tim Chester, *The Message of Prayer* in the Bible Speaks Today series (IVP, 2003)

- Tim Chester, *You Can Pray: Finding Grace to Pray Every Day* (P&R, 2014)

- Christopher Hitchens, *God Is Not Great: How Religion Poisons Everything* (Atlantic Books, 2007)

- Martin Luther, *Large Catechism* (available online at www.ccel.org)

- Martin Luther, *Luther's Works* (available online at www.ccel.org)

- Donald MacLeod, *Christ Crucified: Understanding the Atonement* (IVP Academic, 2014)

- William McEwen, *Grace and Truth or, The Glory and Fulness of the Redeemer Displayed* (John Gray and Gavin Alston, 1763)

- Michael McKinley, *Passion: How Christ's Final Day Changes Your Every Day* (The Good Book Company, 2013)

- John Owen, *Of Communion with God with Father, Son and Holy Ghost* (available online at www.ccel.org)
- J.I. Packer, *Knowing God* (Hodder & Stoughton, 1998)

Exodus for...
Bible-study Groups

Tim Chester's **Good Book Guide** to Exodus is the companion to this resource, helping groups of Christians to explore, discuss and apply the book together. Eight studies, each including investigation, apply, getting personal, pray and explore more sections, take you through the whole book. Includes a concise Leader's Guide at the back.

Find out more at:
www.thegoodbook.com/goodbookguides

Daily Devotionals

Explore daily devotional helps you open up the Scriptures and will encourage and equip you in your walk with God. Published as a quarterly booklet, *Explore* is also available as an app, where you can download Tim's notes on Exodus, alongside contributions from trusted Bible teachers including Timothy Keller, Mark Dever, Juan Sanchez, Mike McKinley and Sam Allberry.

Find out more at:
www.thegoodbook.com/explore

More For You

1 Samuel For You

"As we read this gripping part of Israel's history, we see
Jesus Christ with fresh colour and texture. And we see
what it means for his people to follow him as King in an
age that worships personal freedom."

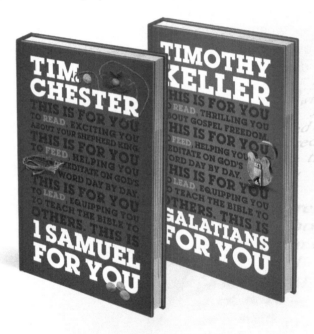

Galatians For You

"The book of Galatians is dynamite. It is an explosion of joy
and freedom which leaves us enjoying a deep significance,
security and satisfaction. Why? Because it brings us face
to face with the gospel—the A to Z of the Christian life."

Coming Soon...

Exodus For You is the eleventh in the *God's Word For You series.* Other titles are:

- **Judges For You** *Timothy Keller*
- **1 Samuel For You** *Tim Chester*
- **Daniel 1 - 7 For You** *David Helm*
- **Romans 1 - 7 For You** *Timothy Keller*
- **Romans 8 - 16 For You** *Timothy Keller*
- **Galatians For You** *Timothy Keller*
- **Ephesians For You** *Richard Coekin*
- **Titus For You** *Tim Chester*
- **James For You** *Sam Allberry*
- **1 Peter For You** *Juan Sanchez*

Forthcoming titles include:

- **Micah For You** *Stephen Um*
- **John For You (two volumes)** *Josh Moody*
- **Acts For You (two volumes)** *Al Mohler*
- **Philippians For You** *Steven Lawson*

Find out more about these resources at:
www.thegoodbook.com/for-you

Good Book Guides
for groups and individuals

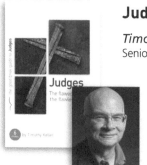

Judges: The flawed and the flawless

Timothy Keller
Senior Pastor, Redeemer Presbyterian Church, Manhattan

Welcome to a time when God's people were deeply flawed, often failing, and struggling to live in a world which worshipped other gods. Our world is not so different—we need Judges to equip us to live for God in our day, and remind us that he is a God of patience and mercy.
Also by Tim Keller: Romans 1–7; Romans 8–16; Galatians

Daniel: Staying strong in a hostile world

David Helm
Lead Pastor, Holy Trinity Church, Chicago

The first half of Daniel is well known and much loved. The second is little read and less understood! David Helm leads groups through the whole book, showing how the truths about God in the second half enabled Daniel and his friends—and will inspire us—to live faithful, courageous lives.

Esther: Royal rescue

Jane McNabb
Chair of the London Women's Convention

The experience of God's people in Esther's day helps us in those moments when we question God's sovereignty, his love, or his faithfulness. Their story reveals that despite appearances, God is in control, and he answers his people's prayers—often in most unexpected ways.

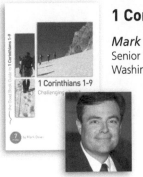

1 Corinthians 1–9: Challenging church

Mark Dever
Senior Pastor of Capitol Hill Baptist Church in
Washington DC and President of 9Marks Ministries

The church in Corinth was full of life, and just as
full of problems. As you read how Paul challenges
these Christians, you'll see how you can
contribute to your own church becoming truly
shaped by the gospel.
Also by Mark Dever: 1 Corinthians 10–16

James: Genuine faith

Sam Allberry
Associate Minister, St Mary's Maidenhead, UK

Many Christians long for a deeper, more whole-
hearted Christian life. But what does that look like?
This deeply practical letter was written to show us,
and will reveal how to experience joy in hardships,
patience in suffering and whole-heartedness in how
you speak, act and pray.
Also by Sam Allberry: Man of God; Biblical Manhood

1 Peter: Living well on the way home

Juan Sanchez
Preaching Pastor, High Pointe Baptist Church, Austin, Texas

The Christian life, lived well, is not easy—because
we don't belong in this world. Learn from Peter
how to journey on rather than retreat, and to do
so with joy and hope, rather than gritted teeth.